CONTRARY NEIGHBORS

Contrary Neighbors

SOUTHERN PLAINS AND REMOVED INDIANS IN INDIAN TERRITORY

BY
DAVID LA VERE

UNIVERSITY OF OKLAHOMA PRESS : NORMAN

Also by David La Vere

The Caddo Chiefdoms: Caddo Politics and Economics, 700 A.D. to 1835
(Lincoln, 1998)
Life among the Texas Indians: The WPA Narratives (College Station,
Texas, 1998)

This book is published with the generous assistance of the Wallace C.
Thompson Endowment Fund, University of Oklahoma Foundation.

Library of Congress Cataloging-in-Publication Data

La Vere, David.
    Contrary neighbors : Southern Plains and removed Indians in Indian
territory / by David La Vere.
        p.   cm. — (The civilization of the American Indian series ; v. 237)
    ISBN 0–8061–3251–5 (alk. paper)
    1. Indians of North America—Southern States—History.   2. Indians
of North America—Relocation—Indian Territory.   3. Indians of North
America—Indian Territory—History.   Indians of North America—
Cultural assimilation—Indian Territory.   5. Culture conflict—Indian
Territory—History.   6. Hunting and gathering societies—Indian Territory—History.   I. Title.   II. Series.
E78.S65 L3 2000
975'.00497—dc21   00–023051

Contrary Neighbors: Southern Plains and Removed Indians in Indian Territory
is Volume 237 in The Civilization of the American Indian Series.

1 2 3 4 5 6 7 8 9 10

To Gary Clayton Anderson,
mentor and friend

CONTENTS

ILLUSTRATIONS

PHOTOGRAPHS

following page 126

Peter Pitchlynn, principal chief of the
   Choctaw Nation
George W. Grayson, principal chief of the
   Creek Nation
Members of the Choctaw Light Horse in 1893
Students and faculty at Bloomfield Academy, 1870
Cherokee and Delaware leaders in 1866
Kiowa, Apache, Comanche, and Wichita delegates
   with P. B. Hunt in Washington, D.C., early 1870s
Comanche women and child in front of a
   buffalo tepee, early 1870s
Wichita village on reservation, ca. 1900
Caddo Indians killing beef on reservation
Indian scouts of Troop L, 7th Cavalry

MAPS

ACKNOWLEDGMENTS

I very much enjoyed researching and writing this book, but as with any work like this, I could not have done it without the assistance of a whole army of friends and colleagues. I am especially indebted to John R. Lovett and the staff of the Western History Collections at the University of Oklahoma in Norman; Bill Welge and Phyllis Adams and the entire staff of the Oklahoma Historical Society Indian Archives in Oklahoma City; Dan Littlefield, head of the Native American Press Archives at the University of Arkansas at Little Rock; Linda Pine, John Jackson, and Kris Dudoich at the University of Arkansas at Little Rock archives; Tom Dillard, who was then the archivist at the University of Central Arkansas; and Madeleine Bombeld and Mary Corcoran, the interlibrary loan administrators at the University of North Carolina at Wilmington. I am very thankful to UNC-Wilmington for a Cahill Award, which partially funded my research, but especially to my colleagues in UNC-Wilmington's Department of History who enthusiastically supported my endeavor, even providing me with a Mosely Award to help out.

Indian friends in Oklahoma and elsewhere who made their history come alive for me include Terri Baker, Choctaw; Vernon Hunter, chairman of the Caddo tribe; Cecile Carter, Caddo; Mike

Meeks, Kiowa; Stuart Owings, Wichita; Phil Newkumet, Caddo; Ernest Toppah, Kiowa; Randlett Edmonds, Caddo; Richard Welch, of the Eastern Band of Cherokees; Roscoe Shememe, Caddo; Buntin Williams, Caddo; and Linda Oxendine, Lumbee.

Friends throughout the country and the profession gave tremendous moral and intellectual support for this work. They include Loretta Price, University of Arkansas at Pine Bluff; Clyde Ellis, Elon College; Brian Hosmer, University of Wyoming; Mike Green and Theda Perdue, University of North Carolina, Chapel Hill; Gary Anderson, University of Oklahoma; Andrew Clark, University of North Carolina at Wilmington; Andrea Kalas at Discovery Channel; and Buddy Ebron and Danny Ryan of Wilmington, North Carolina. As always, special gratitude goes to my mother, Ann La Vere, and my sisters, Rhonda and Tracy La Vere.

CONTRARY NEIGHBORS

CHAPTER ONE

INTRODUCTION

Then one sort of men began to settle down, and another sort became more distinctly nomadic. . . . The two ways of life specialized in opposite directions. . . . It was inevitable that nomad folk and the settled folk should clash, that the nomad should seem hard barbarians to the settled peoples, and the settled peoples soft and effeminate and very good plunder to the nomad peoples.

H. G. WELLS
The Outline of History

While I was working on my book *The Caddo Chiefdoms*, I came to grasp the sheer magnitude of the diaspora of Native American peoples from the eastern part of the United States onto the southern prairie-plains that took place between 1780 and 1840. It was a tremendous migration in which thousands upon thousands of people straggled along in dribs and drabs on their own personal trail of tears. It is truly difficult to convey the enormity of this movement of peoples across the American South. The forests and fields between Appalachia and the Southern Plains were choked with migrating Indian people. A Southerner could not travel far without seeing a Choctaw family or a Cherokee village on the move. Stop along any crossroads and it would not have been strange to see small parties of Chickasaws, Seminoles, and Creeks, even Shawnees and Delawares, pass by. Stand there long enough and you would have seen entire nations of Indians trudging along the roads of the South, moving west, always moving west.

If it was a diaspora for eastern Indians, it was an invasion to those people who lived on the southern prairie-plains. Within just a few years, Caddos, Wichitas, and Osages, even Comanches and Kiowas, found their lands overrun by these eastern Indians, Indians who were culturally very different. Like any peoples whose lands are invaded, these Indians of the southern prairie-plains now fought to repel this incursion. For me, it conjured up images of Goths, Vandals, and Huns crashing against the walls of the Roman Empire.

As I pondered the consequences of this Indian invasion, certain things happened to me personally that made me look at my information in a new light. In 1996 I attended a powwow at Tahlequah, Oklahoma, with a good friend of mine, Terri Baker, a Choctaw woman who teaches English there at Northeastern State University. Tahlequah is the capital of the Cherokee Nation, and since Northeastern State University attracts Indian students from throughout Oklahoma, the powwow was full of dancers, drummers, and onlookers from a variety of Indian nations. Terri is a warm, generous person with a dry wit and that Indian gift for seeing the humor in often ironic situations. As we watched the dancers, Terri leaned over and began telling of an incident she had witnessed at an earlier powwow. It seems that during the middle of the powwow she heard an argument break out behind her, and it rapidly escalated into a noisy confrontation. Two young Indian students— one a Cherokee, the other an Osage—were just about ready to come to blows. The face-off was broken up before someone threw a punch, and everyone gathered around and asked them what had caused such a row. The Osage student stood there glowering, then, with his voice quivering with rage, he thrust his finger toward the Cherokee and sputtered, "His people killed my people at Claremore Mounds!" Terri grinned at me and said, "And you know, the Osage student was correct. Cherokees did kill about thirty-eight Osages at Claremore Mounds . . . in 1817!" The story stuck with me. I was surprised that after all this time these ancient hurts still boiled to the surface. It started me thinking about how Indian people might view each other.

As I traveled through Oklahoma and spent time with Indian friends, I began to see an even greater difference among Indian peoples, particularly between those who were considered Southeastern Indians and those who were Plains Indians. In eastern Oklahoma my Cherokee, Choctaw, Creek, Seminole, and Chickasaw friends would make good-natured, albeit cutting, remarks about Comanches and Kiowas, saying things such as, "They think they're the only real Indians." In western Oklahoma, among my Comanche, Kiowa, and Wichita friends, I would hear similar remarks made about the Cherokees and Choctaws, such as, "They think they're so superior," or, "They're not real Indians." Let me say, though, this does not mean these peoples did not actually see each other as Indians or that they did not have problems in common. They often agreed when it came to comparing problems they had with the federal or state government. It also did not mean that personal friendships could not develop between the two; Terri's best friend is a Kiowa woman. Still, there often seemed to be an underlying edginess when Southeastern and Plains Indians got together. That, even at the turn of the millennium, these Indian peoples could see the world and their past in such different ways intrigued me.

So I began to mull over my ideas about the eastern invasion of the prairie-plains and the continuing differences between these peoples. As I researched, I came to realize that early on, both groups—Southern Plains Indians and Southeastern Indians—possessed wholly different images of each other.

Let me provide an example. Peter Pitchlynn, principal chief of the Choctaws during the middle years of the nineteenth century, was known for his devout Christianity. Originally a Presbyterian, he later became a Lutheran, and as he grew older he became even more pious. Now Pitchlynn was chief of an Indian people who had until about 1800, just a few years before he himself was born, deified the sun, the moon, the earth, and even corn and deer. In fact, many of his own people still did. But Pitchlynn was a "progressive" Choctaw who had adopted an American culture, and like many progressive Choctaws, Chickasaws, Cherokees, Creeks, and Seminoles, Pitchlynn equated Christianity with "civilization" and progress. One day, in trying to explain why he thought the Choctaws were so advanced, Pitchlynn stated, "If it were not for the Bible, we would be savages, worse than the Comanches."[1]

Though an Indian himself, Pitchlynn divided native peoples into two great categories: those who were "civilized" and those who were "savages." During the nineteenth century, "civilization" was equated with contemporary American culture, and for Indians to be "civilized," they "must dress, think, act, speak, work, and worship the way rural United States citizens ideally did."[2] So to Pitchlynn, Choctaws and the other eastern Indian peoples who farmed, professed Christianity, and lived by codified laws were "civilized." Plains Indians, such as the Comanches and Kiowas, who were hunter-gatherers, were non-Christians, and lived by the law of blood, were "savages." All was not lost though, as "savages" could become "civilized" by adopting the trappings of rural American culture, which would also be proof of their "civilization."

Unfortunately for Pitchlynn, the Southern Plains Indians had their own opinion of him and his "civilized" eastern Indians. The Comanches and Kiowas had no such exalted impression of "civilization" and often viewed the Choctaws and the other Southeastern Indians as something less than true Indians—more as inferior, artificial Indians. Happy with their own culture, the Southern Plains Indians ignored "civilization" and the Southeastern

Indians' efforts to "civilize" them. Instead, they tended to view the Southeastern Indians as invaders rather than bearers of anything worthwhile, save the guns and other manufactured goods the Plains Indians might acquire through raids or trade.

Herein lies the heart of my argument. The Southern Plains Indians and Southeastern Indians existed as two wholly different peoples. They had completely different cultures, had different ways of life, and looked at the world in very different ways, despite being grouped together into one "Indian" racial category by white Americans. Once they were forced to become neighbors in Indian Territory during the nineteenth century, instead of creating a middle ground of cooperation and unity, they remained different, suspicious, and separate. Their interactions and relations in Indian Territory, always complex, ranged from raids and counterraids to diplomatic councils and trade connections but did little to bring about any melding of these two types of peoples. If anything, their differences became only deeper and wider, more exacerbated, and the turn of the twentieth century saw them no closer than at the turn of the nineteenth century. And in many ways their traditional culture and their history keep them separate at the turn of the twenty-first century.

Unfortunately, Americans like to see cohesion rather than contrariety. But the sheer diversity and complexity of Indian peoples and their cultures are among the hardest things for non-Indians to grasp. For most people, the term *Indian* or *Native American* conjures up a certain stereotypical image. It is usually that of a Comanche or Lakota warrior galloping across the plains, his eagle-feather headdress whipping in the wind, an arrow nocked in his bow, ready to take down a running buffalo, or his Winchester cocked and leveled, ready to kill an unsuspecting settler. It makes no difference whether an Indian is a Southeastern Choctaw, a Northeastern Pequot, a Plains Comanche, a Northwest Coast Tsimshian, a California Chumash, or a Southwestern Pueblo; for many non-Indians, an Indian is an Indian.

Naturally, this is not so, as Indians definitely saw themselves as individual peoples and certainly different from those "others" around them. It did not take long for a Comanche child to realize he or she was Comanche, a member of a particular people specially chosen and blessed by the Creator and different from the Kiowas or Choctaws. And Kiowas and Choctaws felt the same way. Similarly, Cherokees and Chickasaws, despite both being Southeastern Indian peoples, knew they were different from each other, as did Caddos and Wichitas, Shawnees and Delawares, Kiowas and Apaches, all of them unique, different, and in their hearts and minds superior to any other people on the face of the earth.

Regardless of their uniqueness, before the early nineteenth century it is possible to divide Indian peoples into two general categories based on their mode of production, meaning how they produced whatever it was that allowed them to live, survive, and prosper. On one hand there were agricultural peoples, and on the other, hunter-gatherers.

Mode of production is the most important, and most basic, element to any society, because how a people sustain themselves gives rise to their religion, their laws, and their life ways and contributes to their identity as a people. About A.D. 700, as maize agriculture flourished in the southeastern part of what became the United States, the ancestors of the Cherokees, Choctaws, Chickasaws, Creeks, Seminoles, Caddos, and other peoples in that area began developing similar beliefs and social systems geared to the yearly cycle of the crops. In this Southern Agrarian Tradition, the Sun, the Moon, and the Corn Mother became important deities. The Cherokees venerated the mythical Selu, who gave her life to provide maize to her people. Indian peoples celebrated the Green Corn Ceremony, or Busk, which honored the corn and was considered a ritual of renewal. This agricultural religion reached its zenith among the Southeastern peoples during the Mississippian cultural tradition, which lasted from about A.D. 700 to about 1700 and which was characterized by extensive maize agriculture, large towns, priest-chiefs, ranked societies, clan membership, matrilineal descent, and the construction of platform mounds.

In contrast, people with a hunting-gathering mode of production developed beliefs and social systems, which anthropologists call the Northern Hunting Tradition, that were geared toward animals. Adapting to the cycles of the animals they hunted, these peoples were semisedentary, if not nomadic, and lived in small, family-oriented bands. Their religion ensured a supply of game. While the Sun was still an important object of veneration, the Northern Hunting Tradition placed emphasis on animal deities, such as the Lakotas' White Buffalo Woman. And hunting-gathering peoples felt a kinship with certain animals, as the Tonkawas did with wolves. Shamans, instead of priests, performed the necessary rituals. Men who were the most successful hunters and warriors rose to leadership positions.

This is not to say these characteristics were mutually exclusive, as at one time thousands of years ago all peoples of North America had been hunter-gatherers. But as time went on and their cultures adapted to their environments, hunter-gatherers and agriculturalists came to be two wholly different peoples who viewed the universe in totally different ways.

By the late 1700s, and certainly before, these agriculturalists and hunter-gatherers in North America could also be grouped geographically according to shared traits. Draw a diagonal line across the continent from about San Diego in the southwest to Maine in the northeast, and with a few exceptions, such as the Southern Plains, the Mississippi River valley, and a few others, hunter-gatherers tended to be north of the line and agriculturalists south of it. Of interest to this study are the southern prairie-plains, which lie south of the Arkansas River and extend from western Arkansas and eastern Texas to the Rocky Mountains. It is this area into which most of Indian Territory fell. Before the coming of Europeans, the Southern Great Plains had been home to small bands of hunting-gathering peoples who lived along its rivers and streams. These early Jumanos, Coahuiltecans, and Caddoans hunted and gathered on foot, using dogs as work animals; planted a smattering of crops along the riverbeds; and made exchange relations with the Puebloan peoples to the southwest. About 1400, Athapaskan peoples from Canada began moving down the front range of the Rocky Mountains and onto the Southern Plains. These hunting-gathering ancestors of the Apache and Navajo peoples took over this Pueblo-Plains trade and developed complex interdependent relations with the maize-growing Pueblo peoples of the Southwest in which the Apaches exchanged buffalo meat and hides for Pueblo corn and bread. At the same time, the Apaches also began to overpower, incorporate, or drive off these early Plains hunter-gatherers.

The world of the Southern Plains Indians changed during the sixteenth and seventeenth centuries as Spaniards moved into the Southwest and brought horses with them. It was not long before Spanish and Pueblo horse herds became the targets of raids by the Apaches, who saw their potential as work animals and mounts. Those who possessed them could become better hunters and warriors, gaining wealth and status. Some of these horses escaped to the grassy Southern Plains, became feral, multiplied rapidly, and created a wild horse population that by the middle of the eighteenth century may have numbered in the millions. As horses made their way into the Indian exchange networks, they dispersed throughout the plains and prairies. By the early 1680s the Caddo and Wichita Indians on the eastern margins of the Southern Plains were trading them to the Indians of Illinois. The 1684 Pueblo uprising against the Spanish in New Mexico sent even more horses out to the plains and beyond.

So by 1700 horses began to multiply on the Great Plains, and over the next century such Indian peoples as the Shoshones, Comanches, Lakotas, Cheyennes, Crows, Kiowas, and Arapahos acquired them. Here dawned the famous Plains Indian "horse culture." With horses making it easier to hunt buffalo and therefore easier to provide food for their families, these peoples began to

move back out to the plains. During the 1700s, even such horti-
culturists as the Cheyennes and Lakotas abandoned this settled
way of life and went back to being nomadic hunter-gatherers,
because hunting buffalo from horses proved easier and more lucrative than farming. But as all these people flowed out to the great
buffalo herds, they began to crowd each other. During the late
1600s, one of the Shoshonean groups from Montana, Wyoming,
and Colorado, the Comanches, began migrating south to escape
the crowding on the Northern Plains and put themselves closer to
the sources from which horses seem to have come.[3] On the Southern
Plains, the Comanches battled the Apaches for territorial and
economic supremacy while making close military and economic
alliances with the Wichitas and Caddos of eastern Texas.

During the middle of the eighteenth century, the Kiowas, a
plains hunting-gathering people from around the headwaters of
the Yellowstone River and closely associated with the Crows, also
began to move onto the Southern Plains. The Kiowas had been
close friends and allies of the Canadian Athapaskan peoples. One
group of these northern Apaches, though they spoke a different
language, attached themselves to the Kiowas and became a distinct
part of the Kiowa people known as the Kiowa-Apaches. As the
Kiowas and Kiowa-Apaches moved onto the Southern Plains, they
collided with the Comanches. Though both the Comanches and
Kiowas contested the area between the Brazos and Arkansas
Rivers, in 1790 the two peoples made a peace that has lasted to this
day. They became strong allies and closely associated with each
other. On the Southern Plains, the Comanches and Kiowas formed
a barrier against other Indian peoples moving west, just as the
Lakotas, Cheyennes, and Arapahos did on the Northern and
Central Plains.[4]

If anything, horses only strengthened these Plains Indians'
hunting-gathering mode of production. These Indians continued
to live in small nomadic bands and chased the buffalo herds on
which they came to depend. Warfare and raiding became para-

mount enterprises and ways for any man to gain status, wealth, and power. Their religion remained centered on animals and the sun. The Sun Dance, for most Plains peoples, became one of the most important ceremonies of their society.

As the horse culture arose on the Southern Plains, it affected those agricultural peoples to the east, such as the Osages, Wichitas, and Caddos, living on the prairies and in the woodlands bordering the plains. Long before Europeans arrived in North America, the Caddoan-speaking Wichitas had lived among the river valleys on the prairies and eastern plains of present-day Kansas and northern Oklahoma. Originally hunter-gatherers who hunted buffalo on foot, during the Mississippian cultural tradition they came under the influence of the Caddoan Spiro chiefdom in eastern Oklahoma and so developed a smattering of horticulture, growing small plots of corn, beans, and squash. The Wichitas were some of the earliest peoples on the eastern edge of the Great Plains to acquire horses, which increased their capacity for hunting buffalo. Before they could establish themselves as full-fledged mounted hunter-gatherers, as the Cheyennes and Lakotas had, the Wichitas found themselves pushed south by the powerful Lakotas. By the early decades of the eighteenth century the Wichitas had been driven out of the Arkansas River valley to the Red, Brazos, and Trinity River valleys of eastern Texas. They now found their access to the Southern Plains blocked, at first by the Apaches but later by the Comanches and Kiowas. While they might make periodic buffalo hunts on the plains, they remained tied to their semipermanent, settled villages on the eastern prairies. For most of the eighteenth and early nineteenth centuries, the Wichitas existed as a people "in between," essentially a people with a hunting-gathering mentality but forced by circumstances to adopt much of an agricultural way of life.[5]

The Osages were also a prairie people, covering a territory that included much of western Missouri, western Arkansas, eastern Oklahoma, and eastern Kansas. During the early 1700s, once the French founded Saint Louis and Saint Genevieve along the Mississippi River, the Osages found an economic outlet for surplus horses and hides. These exchange relations, along with the guns and other manufactured goods they received from the French, fueled a tremendous Osage expansion. Throughout the eighteenth century mounted Osage warriors struck south and west, raiding Wichita and Caddo villages with impunity. The Osages had always combined horticulture with hunting and gathering, as most agricultural peoples did, but now with horses they increased their trips to the plains to hunt buffalo.[6] Wanting to expand onto the Southern Plains, they found themselves hemmed in to the west by the Comanche and Kiowa barrier and facing a serious threat coming from the east.

The Caddos, consisting of the Kadohadachos, or Caddos proper, who lived along the Red River in Louisiana, and the Hasinais, who lived along the river valleys of eastern Texas, were the westernmost of those peoples sharing Southeastern Indian cultural traits. Like the Southeastern Indians, they no longer built great temple mounds, but they still grew large crops of corn, beans, and squash. Their acquisition of horses loosened their ancient agricultural ties to the Southeast and increasingly sent them onto the plains for buffalo and into closer relations with the Comanches and Wichitas. Still, their position as a gateway between the plains and prairies to the west and the woodlands to the east, between Spanish Texas and French Louisiana, allowed them to control much of the trade on the Southern Plains and thereby exert a considerable amount of power. The Caddos made close economic and military alliances with the Comanches and Wichitas and often assisted them in their battles with the Plains Apaches. The wealth of Caddo villages made them attractive targets to the expanding Osages, and for much of the late eighteenth century Caddo villages suffered almost constant attacks from Osage raiders. These raids dwindled in the early nineteenth century as both the Osages and the Caddos faced a veritable invasion of Indians from the Southeast.[7]

Long before the coming of Europeans to North America and before the Plains horse culture developed, the Indian peoples of the Southeast were also developing shared cultural traits. Stretching from the Carolinas to eastern Texas, the descendants of the Mississippian cultural tradition, such as the Choctaws, Cherokees, Chickasaws, Creeks, Caddos, and others, carried on their ancient agricultural mode of production. Though men hunted, it was the women's corn fields and their gathering techniques that provided the lion's share of their subsistence needs. So Southeastern Indians remained matrilineal, lived in large settled communities, raised huge crops of corn, and followed an agriculture-oriented religion.

Cultural similarities did not mean all thought alike, and the Southeastern Indian societies often waged war against each other. During the Mississippian cultural tradition, the great mound-building chiefdoms often tried to expand militarily in order to bring additional communities under their control and so acquire large quantities of tribute to help shore up the chief's position. After the establishment of European colonies in the Southeast during the seventeenth century, warfare only increased. European colonies went out of their way to acquire Indian allies, and the Indian peoples, because these European colonies usually provided valuable manufactured goods of firearms, ammunition, and other manufactured commodities, often tied themselves diplomatically and militarily to one European nation or another. Caddos attacked the Natchez at the behest of the French. Yamasees raided weaker Indian nations to acquire slaves for the English. Timucuas of Florida helped the Spanish repel French coastal invaders. During the eighteenth century, with the great wars for empire under way, French-allied Choctaws attacked English-allied Chickasaws, while English-backed Cherokees devastated Spain's Apalachee and Timucua allies.

This early association with Europeans dramatically affected the Southeastern Indian societies. Besides warfare, much of the initial contact with Europeans came through the deer hide trade. Because of this, Southeastern Indians soon found French, English, Scottish, and Scotch-Irish traders visiting their villages on a regular basis.

Like it or not, Euroamerican culture, with all its attractions, opportunities, and vices, now entered their homes. Some Southeastern
Indians responded positively to this unfamiliar culture, and some
negatively, but heightening its influence was that many of these
European traders either married or made sexual relationships with
Indian women, and from these unions came children. Southeastern
Indian societies being matrilineal, these children of Indian women
and European men were immediately considered "Indian" and
automatically members of their mother's clan. On the other hand,
European fathers often wanted to educate their children along
European lines, so many traders sent their children to schools in
the colonies or Europe. Many, but not all, of these educated Indian
children, having been immersed in Euroamerican culture, now saw
the "advantages" of "civilization" and aggressively tried to move
their Indian societies into adopting the trappings of Euroamerican
culture.

As Southeastern Indians and European society increasingly
collided, these "progressive" Indians, living with one foot in the
Indian world and the other in the Euroamerican, found themselves
thrust into political leadership positions. The Indians needed
someone who could speak English and who understood the Euroamericans. The Euroamericans needed someone who was not too
alien whom they could deal with, who was already amenable to
Euroamerican culture, and who could clearly articulate their desires
and demands to the Indians. Because of this, progressives steadily
increased their influence within their respective nations. The progressives' growing power, and their willingness to adopt Euroamerican culture, by the late eighteenth century created a schism
in many Southeastern Indian societies. Progressives advocated
adopting more Euroamerican cultural traits. In reaction to this,
traditionalists found nothing wrong with the old ways and
demanded their society's adherence to them.

This schism between progressives and traditionalists was only
exacerbated by the new United States government. Leaders steeped

in Enlightenment philosophy, such as George Washington, Henry Knox, Thomas Jefferson, and others, though they generally viewed all Indians as "savages," believed that Indians could "progress" up the social ladder to "civilization" and eventually assimilate into mainstream American society. Surely, they reasoned, all Indians eagerly wanted to become civilized and reap civilization's benefits. But to become civilized, the Indians would have to give up all aspects of their own culture and model their societies on the capitalistic agrarian society then predominant in the United States. Essentially, Indians would have to become Christian, learn to speak English, adopt whites modes of dress and deportment, and settle down into a Euroamerican farming life-style. This last was possibly the most important to white leaders, for it would mean that Indians would give up tribal lands held in common and individual Indian families would settle on privately owned tracts of land. There the men would work the fields and tend herds of hogs, cattle, or horses while the women would move into the house and perform the chores white women did, such as taking care of children; carding, spinning, and weaving cotton or wool; and tending small gardens. Surplus crops or animals would be sold on the market for profit. Profits would be reinvested in their farming operations, allowing the more industrious Indians to purchase slaves or additional lands and expand their farms into full-fledged plantations. Eventually, through education and intermarriage, the Indian culture would die out, with Indians no longer viewing themselves as Indians but totally assimilated into the larger American population.[8]

It was a one-size-fits-all policy and ignored the differences between agricultural and hunting-gathering peoples and the limitations of the geographical area in which they lived. Nevertheless, the government demanded that all Indians accept this vision. So assimilation became the goal of United States Indian policy for the next two hundred years. Certainly government officials believed it would yield specific benefits. First, it would open up more land for white settlers moving west. As Indians took up private ownership of plots of land for farming, surplus tribal lands could then be purchased from the Indians and sold to the burgeoning, ever westward-moving white farming population. Second, it would eliminate Indian wars, or at least lessen the expense of them. One of the biggest sources of friction between Indians and Americans was white settlers' squatting on lands claimed by the Indians. Raids and murders committed by both sides often escalated into war as whites demanded that the government send troops to protect them and punish the Indians. Now, as Indians peacefully gave up surplus lands, began farming their own private plots of land, and adopted white culture, Euroamerican leaders reckoned there would be no more Indian wars. Finally, the new policy would save the Indians from extinction. The idea of exterminating the Indians was seen as un-Christian and did not sit well with "enlightened" Americans. Still, these same Americans admitted that times were changing, and Indians, for their own survival, would have to acculturate and assimilate.[9]

With these benefits in mind, during the late eighteenth and early nineteenth centuries the federal government enacted a variety of laws and programs to "civilize" the Indians while using treaties to wrest land away from them. A series of Trade and Intercourse Acts attempted to regulate the interaction between white traders and the Indians. Government-backed trading posts were built among various Indian peoples where they could trade their hides for manufactured goods but also incur debts that could only be extinguished by a land cession. Missionaries, often partially financed by the federal government, set up churches and schools among the major Southeastern Indian nations. While Indians were slow to accept them, missionaries experienced much more success after the end of the War of 1812. The government also sent out Indian agents who acted not only as the government's representatives but also as teachers and advocates of American "civilization." Benjamin Hawkins, agent to the Creeks in Georgia and Alabama, created a model farm, set up spinning and weaving classes for Creek women, supplied farm and home implements, and constantly preached the gospel of capitalist agriculture. It mattered little that the South-eastern Indians had long been successful agriculturalists; in the government's eyes they were still "savages" because they did not farm the "correct" way, as women still controlled the fields and farming. Though the government's civilization program might appear benevolent, there was always a violent edge to it. Officials and settlers insisted that the Indians obey state and federal govern-ment laws, that Indian lawbreakers be punished according to American law, and that severe punishment then be exacted if the Indians did not behave accordingly.[10]

The government's program struck at the very foundations of Southeastern Indian society by essentially trying to move a community-based society to one based on individual rights. The tenets of capitalistic agriculture went against Indian concepts of kinship and reciprocity. In Southeastern Indian societies, land was owned by the people as a whole, and crop surpluses were shared by the community. Obligations of reciprocity and hospitality demanded that guests be fed and food shared. Even Southeastern Indian law was community-based, not recorded but understood by all, with the disapproval of the people usually enough to pre-vent crime. When crimes such as murder took place, a law of blood, or clan revenge, was essential to restore harmony. So the govern-ment's attempts to "civilize" the Southeastern Indians required vast changes in the minds, hearts, and traditions of these Indians.

Despite this, the government's program found favor with many Southeastern Indian progressives. Now they aggressively advocated changes to their societies, if only to be better able to deal with the Americans on an equal basis and withstand the constant demands by settlers and officials for their lands. As Protestant missionaries flocked to the Indian nations, more and more Indians accepted Christianity and sent their children to the missions to be educated in Euroamerican ways. Capitalistic agriculture gained ground, with some Indians modeling themselves on Southern planters and using gangs of African-American slaves to grow huge amounts of cotton for the market economy. Soon, Indian-operated plantations, taverns, general stores, and ferries sprang up throughout the Southeast. Even on smaller farms run by more traditional families, the "civilization" program had an impact. Since the Southeastern Indians considered farming to be woman's work, but something advocated by the Americans, many men made an appearance of working the fields. In reality they concentrated on raising large herds of cattle and hogs, which was not too much of a departure from the traditional man's role as hunter. Women still did most of the field work, as well as the spinning and weaving.[11]

To protect this newly gained private property, many Southeastern Indians, under the leadership of the progressives, began codifying their laws and creating national governments. In 1808 the Cherokees established a national police force to stop horse theft and protect property. Other laws soon appeared banning clan-based blood revenge, giving only the National Council the authority to sell land, and allowing men to pass their property on to their wives and children rather than to their sister's children, as matrilineal descent demanded. In 1827 the Cherokees wrote a constitution, complete with a chief executive, bicameral legislature, and court system. Sequoyah had created the Cherokee syllabary, which made it possible to write the Cherokee language, and in the 1820s the Cherokees began publishing the *Cherokee Phoenix*, a weekly newspaper written in both Cherokee and English.[12]

While the progressives articulated their peoples' "official" stance on acculturation, traditionalist Cherokees, Creeks, Choctaws, Chickasaws, and Seminoles, who normally lived in the backwaters of the Southeast, probably paid the progressives little mind. Few spoke English, and most possessed little, if any, American-style education and neither liked nor accepted the direction their societies were taking. They felt the progressives did not possess the authority to speak for them. In most instances the traditionalists remained committed to the ancient ways and ignored, if at all possible, the demands, laws, and deals made by the progressives with the United States.

When pressure by the progressives or the United States became too intense, traditionalists often found ways around it. During the 1790s the government of Spanish Louisiana had granted the petitions of several large bands of Choctaws and Cherokees to settle west of the Mississippi River on Caddo and Osage land, respectively. These immigrant bands were the most conservative of their people and felt the best way to preserve their old ways was to move west so they could live as they wanted. In 1810, traditionalist Cherokee chiefs Duwali, Saulowee, and Talontuskee moved their people to the Saint Francis River in Arkansas and became known as the Western Cherokees. In 1813, young men of the very conservative Upper Creek towns, upset at the changes besetting Creek society and angered at what they felt was the betrayal of ancient ways by some progressive Creeks, began attacking Lower Creek towns, where most of the progressives lived. And so began the Creek Civil War. The Red Sticks, as the traditionalist warriors called themselves, were finally defeated the next year at the Battle of Horseshoe Bend on the Tallapoosa River by the combined forces of White Stick Creeks, Cherokees, and the United States Army led by Andrew Jackson. In 1827, Chief White Path, a traditionalist Cherokee, vigorously opposed the creation of the Cherokee constitution, and though he could not prevent its adoption, he continually worked to stem the Cherokees' move toward American acculturation.[13]

While the Five Tribes underwent these divisions, some Southeastern Indians such as the Caddos, being farthest away from the Americans, were little affected by the "civilization" program. They remained committed to their ancient ways and were not divided into progressive and traditionalist factions. John Fowler, head of the government's Indian trading post on Sulphur Fork Creek in northwestern Louisiana, constantly complained that the Caddos refused to acculturate. "Considering the length of time this tribe has had constant intercourse with the whites, they are singularly savage and far inferior to any Indians" that visited the post.[14]

The Caddos notwithstanding, after the end of the War of 1812 the progressives of the Southeastern Indian societies took control of most of the leadership positions created by their newly drafted constitutions. Progressive families extended their influence through their ability to deal with the United States government. The progressive Creek McIntosh family, led by William McIntosh, vigorously preached American acculturation and became important Creek leaders as well as advisors to the Cherokees. The Cherokees elected the progressive John Ross as their principal chief in 1828. Progressives such as Greenwood LeFlore and the Pitchlynn family became leaders in the Choctaw nation, while the Colbert family became men of authority among the Chickasaws. This upper echelon of Southeastern Indian leaders remained unified and committed to the belief that the only way their peoples could survive as distinct Indian nations was to acculturate, and so they quickly led their peoples down the path toward American "civilization."

By the 1820s and '30s, progressives could look with pride at the changes in their societies. Even many whites expressed amazement at how "civilized" the Southeastern nations had become. They soon began referring to the Cherokees, Creeks, Choctaws, Chickasaws, and Seminoles as the Five Civilized Tribes. Nowadays, the term *Five Civilized Tribes* has fallen out of favor. We tend to call them the Five Major Tribes or just the Five Tribes, as we question what exactly "civilization" means. After all, the Southeastern Indians were an ancient civilization in their own right. And was Euroamerican civilization any better than Indian civilization? But "Civilized Tribes" was a name these Southeastern progressives adopted for their own nations. They actually saw themselves "civilized" as white Americans defined it, and they were proud of the direction their societies were taking. So in calling themselves the Five Civilized Tribes they showed they stood in polar opposition to the "wild" and "savage" Plains Indians, who were increasingly becoming a fixture on America's expanding horizon. In this book I often use the term to designate these acculturated Indian nations.

If anything, being "civilized" gave the progressives a sense of controlling their own destiny, as they could be both "civilized" and "Indian." Southeastern Indian leadership, at least at first, hoped to keep their nations' lands intact, and in the face of the burgeoning white population streaming west they displayed numerous treaties signed with the British, French, and Americans that recognized them as independent nations and guaranteed them their lands. They pointed to their peoples' progress toward "civilization" as proof the Americans had nothing to fear from them. Still, guarantees meant little once land-hungry American settlers reached the domains of the Southeastern Indians. Settlers insisted that these Indian "savages" were standing in the way of their economic advancement. Not accepting Indian claims, white settlers squatted on Indian land, then demanded that the state and federal governments remove the Indians from it.[15]

This caused a problem among American leaders. While they could congratulate the Southeastern Indians on their civilization, they were disappointed that the Indians refused to give up their lands and assimilate. Sensitive to the settler vote, national and state leaders realized something had to be done. Exterminating the Indians was not an option, because it was un-Christian. Instead, government officials now decided upon removing the Indians west of the Mississippi River, to some location beyond the reach of white settlers—on to lands whites would never want. There they could live until they were ready to assimilate into white society. By the mid-1820s, Indian removal became a new tactic of the government's assimilationist policy. Needing a place to remove them, the government created Indian Territory in 1825. It originally stretched from the Red River in the south, just north of Mexican Texas, to the Great Bend of the Missouri River in Nebraska and west from the western borders of Arkansas and Missouri to the hundredth meridian.

At first, removal for the Southeastern Indians was to be voluntary. It was hoped that they would see the benefit of removing to Indian Territory and willingly exchange their lands in the east for lands in the west. To achieve this, during the 1820s the government sponsored several exploring expeditions by Southeastern Indians to Indian Territory. Groups of Choctaws, Chickasaws, and Cherokees were to inspect the area, choose the lands on which their people would settle, then return home and convince their people to sign a removal treaty. Though several Indian groups explored the area, they came away less than impressed, with one of their biggest concerns being the proximity of the Plains Indians, who they feared might attack them. Much to the chagrin of the government, none of the Southeastern Indian nations volunteered to remove.[16]

The proponents of Indian removal received a tremendous boost with the election in 1828 of Andrew Jackson, who firmly believed the Southeastern Indians should move west. In 1830, Congress passed the Indian Removal Act, which stipulated that the Indians should exchange their lands east of the Mississippi River for lands in Indian Territory. This land, the government explained, would be theirs forever. The Indians would also receive aid in their removal to the west. In theory, removal would still be voluntary, as the Indians had a choice: they could remove or remain in the east as individual residents within the states and under the laws of those states. In reality, this meant they would probably be recognized as Free People of Color. If they wished to remain an Indian nation, then they would have to move west. With this policy in mind, the government now sent treaty negotiators out to the various Southeastern nations. To speed up the process, most Southern states passed obnoxious laws targeting the Indians and went out of their way to make life so miserable for them that removal would be a relief. With these state laws intact and Jackson's refusal to support the Indians, the government pressured the Indians to sign removal treaties.[17]

North of the Ohio River, the government experienced almost immediate success. Many of the Indian nations of the north had been shattered by centuries of warfare. Unlike the Southeastern Indians, whose lands possessed well-defined boundaries, the Indians of the Old Northwest, such as the Shawnees, Kickapoos, Delawares, Potawatomis, Sacs and Foxes, and a host of others, tended to live in small, scattered bands, with often overlapping land claims. The Shawnees, Delawares, and Kickapoos, who came to play a significant role on the Southern Plains, already had a long history of migration and movement. The Shawnees, under their great leader Tecumseh, had been militarily defeated by the United States in 1811, and a Kickapoo leader, Mecina, in 1819 had destroyed property in the Northwest to prevent his people from losing their lands. But by the late 1820s these as well as other Old Northwest Indians had already lost much of their lands by treaties made with the United States government. By the early 1830s the Shawnees, Delawares, and Kickapoos occupied lands near Cape Girardeau, Missouri, and in 1832 they signed a removal treaty that extinguished their title to those lands and moved them west to Indian Territory in what is present-day Kansas.[18]

In the Southeast, removal went slower, because the government had to extinguish Indian title to lands it had long recognized as legally belonging to those Indians. Though many Cherokees and Choctaws had already migrated west, most Southeastern Indians, both progressives and traditionalists, did not want to leave their ancestral lands. The topic of Indian removal has been thoroughly covered by many fine historians, so it is enough to say that between 1825 and 1840, just about all the Indians in the Southeast signed removal treaties and were marched along their "trail of tears" to Indian Territory. Some smaller nations, such as the Caddos, merely had their land claims in the east extinguished for a promise of cash and goods but received no guarantee of lands. As the Caddos did, these groups often moved into Mexican Texas. The Cherokees, Choctaws, Chickasaws, Creeks, and Seminoles got a better deal.

In their removal treaties they received lands in Indian Territory with a promise from the government to protect them from the Plains Indians. By 1840, except for a few small pockets left on marginal lands, most eastern Indians lived in Indian Territory.[19]

In Indian Territory, the Cherokees, Choctaws, Chickasaws, Creeks, and Seminoles reestablished their nations and societies. Without the stresses of removal, and away from encroaching white settlers, the Five Major Tribes actually flourished. Though the nations were still divided between progressives and traditionalists, the progressives were firmly entrenched in positions of political leadership. As they had in the east, they continued to push their nations aggressively toward an American acculturation. Churches, schools, national capitols, wood-frame houses, newspapers, and printing presses all sprang up. Progressives again participated in capitalistic agriculture, acquiring large numbers of black slaves in order to produce quantities of cotton and corn, as well as mules and horses, for the market economy. This is not to say that all ancient traditions passed away. There were still a large number of traditionalists who refused to recognize the authority of the progressives or participate in the market economy but remained subsistence farmers and committed to the ancient ways as best they could. Stomp dances were just has heavily attended as church services, and stickball games remained a popular participatory and spectator sport. Still, progressive Cherokees, Choctaws, Creeks, Chickasaws, and Seminoles boasted they were just as "civilized" as whites.[20]

After their removal to Indian Territory and before the Civil War, the biggest threat the Five Major Tribes faced came from the Plains Indians to their west. The Five Tribes' reestablishment of their nations during the 1830s and '40s coincided with a mental change that was beginning to take place among many white Americans as to what constituted an Indian. Before this, when Americans thought of Indians, in their minds they saw James Fenimore Cooper's Chingachgook, a buckskin-clad, long rifle–toting Iroquois stalking the trails of the eastern woodlands. But as Americans moved steadily toward the plains, this image of what a "real" Indian should be was replaced by that of fierce, horseback-riding, buffalo-hunting Comanches and Lakotas. In some ways the Southeastern Indians, particularly the progressives, bought into this image. While Southeastern Indians insisted upon their own "Indianness," they acknowledged that the Plains peoples were also Indians, but of a different type. If the peoples of the Five Tribes saw themselves as "civilized," they saw the Plains Indians as "savage" and often referred to them as the "wild Indians."[21]

Forced by circumstances to become neighbors, as these two different Indians peoples met on the prairie-plains, they developed a cultural class consciousness. According to British historian E. P. Thompson, "Class happens when some men, as a result of common experiences (inherited or shared), feel and articulate the identity of their interests as between themselves, and as against other men whose interests are different from (and usually opposed to theirs). . . . Class-consciousness is the way in which these experiences are handled in cultural terms: embodied in traditions, value-systems, ideas, and institutional forms."[22]

Certainly the progressive leaders of the Five Tribes felt they shared a certain cultural class consciousness that set them apart from the Plains Indians. Their Southern Agrarian Tradition gave them common inherited traits, while they all shared the experience of forced removal from the Southeast. Most of these progressives were of the same ilk, possessing some American-style education, sometimes attending a Christian church, speaking English, wearing fine American-style clothes, and running successful farms, plantations, or businesses, which made them participants in the market economy. Their acculturation to American standards of "civilization" gave them common values, ideas, and institutional forms, which by the 1830s and 1840s made them firmly believe their way of life was superior to that of the Plains Indians. They saw themselves as the achieved goal of what all Indians should strive to become: peaceful, settled, acculturated Christian farmers. On the other hand, from where they sat in eastern Indian Territory, they saw the Plains Indians as the antithesis of this: violent, nomadic, savage, heathen, hunters—Indians who must be "civilized" just as the Southeastern tribes had been "civilized."

With the Five Tribes already convinced their Plains neighbors were "savages," it did not take long for them to find proof of this. As white settlers later would, these resettled farming Indians came to fear their new neighbors and dreaded the nights when the Comanche Moon rose high and Plains raiders swooped down on their farms. And like white settlers later would, these removed Southeastern Indians constantly insisted that the government live up to its treaty promise to protect them. These uneasy relations posed a dilemma for the Five Tribes. They could not demand the extermination of the Comanches, because they were Indians themselves and so could not insist that Indians were subhuman or devils or use any of the cant that whites often mouthed. Nor did they want to. Instead, taking a page from the government's "civilization" book, often with a paternalistic attitude and certain in the rightness of their own ways, the Five Tribes undertook their own program to "civilize" the Indians of the Southern Plains. Through diplomatic measures, economic activities, missionary efforts, and often outright violent retaliation, the Five Tribes tried to halt the Southern Plains Indians' raids and persuade them to settle down and accept "civilization."

Unfortunately for the efforts of the Five Tribes, the Southern Plains Indians were no slouches in developing their own cultural class consciousness. The Comanches and Kiowas saw no need to acculturate. Unlike the Southeastern Indians, few of their children were the products of American men and Southern Plains women— children who would be sent to school, discover the benefits of American "civilization," and then lead their people down this road. In fact, the opposite was true. Most children of mixed ancestry among the Southern Plains peoples were the products of Indian men and American or Mexican women captives. A good example of such was Comanche chief Quanah Parker, who was the son of Texas captive Cynthia Ann Parker and Kwahadi Comanche chief Peta Nocona. These children rapidly assimilated into Southern Plains societies, meaning there was no division between progressives and traditionalists, at least not until the Southern Plains Indians had been militarily defeated in the 1870s. Also, except for a few unsuccessful Spanish missions during the eighteenth century, there had been little attempt to acculturate the Southern Plains Indians.

The feeble efforts of the Five Tribes to "civilize" the Plains Indians during the 1830s and 1840s bore little success, for these decades saw the Southern Plains Indians at their most powerful. And while the Plains peoples recognized the removed Southeastern Indians as "Indians," they did not view them as "red brothers." Rather, the Plains Indians saw the Civilized Tribes as effete, weak Indians, allies of the white man, invaders of their land and therefore targets of opportunity—targets that young men could raid in order to acquire wealth, status, and power. So the Comanches and Kiowas, and even some Osages and Wichitas raided the territories of the Five Major Tribes, where the Chickasaws, who along with the Seminoles were the westernmost of the Five Tribes, bore the brunt of these raids. Only after 1875, when the Comanches and Kiowas had been defeated and settled on reservations, did any number of citizens of the Five Major Tribes venture among the Plains Indians, where they worked as cowboys or in the boarding schools.

Despite these interactions, close relationships between the Five Civilized Tribes and the Plains Indians never developed. Some Prairie Indians, such as the Caddos and Wichitas, after being placed on reservations in the late 1850s and supported with farming implements by the government, gave up their traditional alliance with the Comanches and Kiowas and made relationships with the Five Tribes. This, though, was about as close as the relationship got.

Even after their defeat in 1875, the Comanches and Kiowas in western Oklahoma remained separate and distinct from their Five Civilized Tribe neighbors in eastern Oklahoma. By the 1890s and early years of the twentieth century, the government's land allotment program began to break up the reservations in order to give each individual Indian a plot of land. As this program progressed, the Five Tribes and the Southern Plains Indians found their lands and tribal society under assault. Now they were much more concerned with keeping their own heads above water than helping each other. During most of the twentieth century, poverty continued to keep them apart. A true pan-Indian alliance between them never developed, for the gulf between them was just too wide. Though the Plains Indians and the Southeastern Indians might now have much more in common, the gulf between them can still be seen.

CHAPTER TWO

FIRST ENCOUNTERS

I believe these long, protracted difficulties grew out of encroachments upon the Osage hunting grounds by the Cherokees, who were generally considered the aggressors.

CORNELIA PELHAM
missionary to the Osages, 1820

Like ripples in a pond, events taking place in England's and France's Atlantic colonies sent the first eastern woodland Indian peoples across the Mississippi River and onto the southern prairies and plains. In the early seventeenth century, the Five Nations of the Iroquois League—the Senecas, Cayugas, Oneidas, Onondogas, and Mohawks—fought a series of devastating wars with their Iroquoian and Algonquian neighbors. With a growing dependency on European manufactured goods, the Five Nations needed to acquire ever more beaver pelts to trade with the Dutch at Albany. They also needed to take captives in order to replenish their population, which had been decimated by disease.

To satisfy these needs, the Five Nations expanded west, destroying the Hurons by 1648, the Neutrals by 1651, and the Eries by 1656. As the Iroquois pushed west into the Ohio River valley, they drove Algonquian peoples ahead of them. These twin assaults disrupted the societies of the Dhegihan Siouan societies who lived there. Under pressure from the Iroquois and Algonquians, the Dhegihan Siouan peoples began a slow migration west. As they reached the Mississippi River, they split, with the Omahas, Poncas, and Kansas moving northwest while the Osages moved onto the prairie-plains of western Missouri and the Quapaws into southern Arkansas. The Osages and Quapaws had only recently arrived in the Mississippi River valley when the French first met them in 1673.[1]

This migration into the new country was not a peaceful one. The Quapaws and Osages did not move into a virgin land, but into areas filled with people who had been living there for hundreds, if not thousands, of years. As the Quapaws neared the confluence of the Mississippi and Arkansas Rivers, they fought the Chickasaw, Illinois, and Tunica Indians until they finally displaced the Tunicas and took over their lands. By 1698 the French noted that the Quapaws, numbering between fifteen and twenty thousand, had built several villages on ancient Mississippian temple mound sites. There they cultivated large fields of corn, some over eight square miles in size. Despite their hostilities with the Tunicas, the Quapaws developed fairly peaceful relations with the Caddos further west on Red River, often exchanging pottery, wooden platters, and canoes for salt and bows made of bois d'arc wood, a Caddo specialty.[2]

The Osages proved even more formidable, drawn to the prairie-plains by the immense buffalo herds and the access to horses. The Southern Plains and the prairies on their eastern periphery had long been the home to millions of buffalo, but the area also proved ideal for horses. Bénard de La Harpe, a Frenchman who visited the Caddo and Wichita villages along the Red River about 1720, was impressed with the fertility of the land, believing "the region furnished a quantity of horses that could be fed at little expense."[3] By that time the Southern Plains may well have been the home to several hundred thousand horses, maybe more, and La Harpe noted that the Caddos and Wichitas captured these "very beautiful horses which they esteemed very much, for they could not be without them for hunting or war."[4] The Osages had obtained horses as early as the 1690s and wanted more, but they were blocked from the Spaniards' and Pueblos' corrals in New Mexico and from the herds of wild horses on the Southern Plains by the Wichitas and Caddos. The Caddos and Wichitas took a dim view of the Osages' hunting horses on territory they considered their own. And Osage offers of corn and buffalo meat in exchange for horses fell on deaf ears. The Caddos and Wichitas, being farmers, already grew large quantities of corn and beans, and their location on the edges of the plains gave them easy access to buffalo. Since exchange relations between the two groups did not exist, the necessary kinship bonds that had to be made between exchange partners never materialized. Therefore, conflict broke out. On one side, were the Caddos and Wichitas, who felt they had to defend their land. On the other the Osages, who needed horses and would hunt them when they could, trade for them if possible, but raid for them if need be.[5]

The herds of wild horses attracted other peoples as well. About the same time the Osages appeared on the prairies, the Comanches, also drawn by horse herds, began arriving on the upper reaches of the Southern Plains and contested control of the area with the Apaches. Just as the Osages found the Caddos and Wichitas living in their "new" lands, the Comanches found the Plains Apaches in theirs. The Athapaskan-speaking Apaches were themselves relative newcomers to the Southern Plains, possibly having arrived from Canada as early as the thirteenth century, but definitely having appeared in the area by the sixteenth. Long before the Apaches arrived, the Caddos and Wichitas of the Mississippian cultural tradition possessed exchange relations with the Pueblo villages of the Pecos and Rio Grande Valleys. As the Apaches wedged themselves between the Caddoans on the eastern side of the plains and the Pueblos on the west, they disrupted an age-old

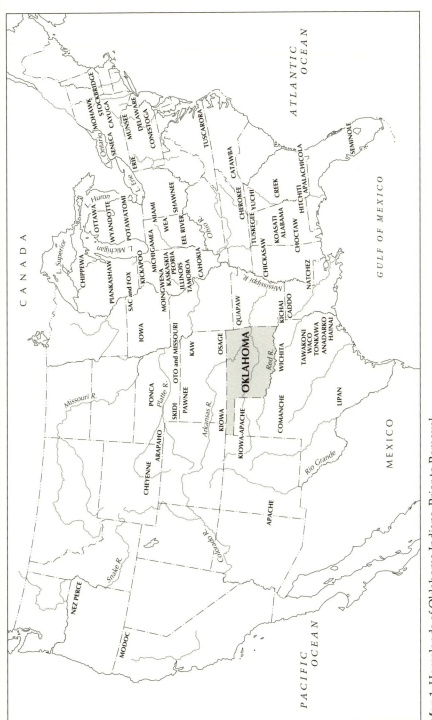

Map 1. Homelands of Oklahoma Indians, Prior to Removal

trade between the two. As with the Osages, because the Wichitas and Caddos were economic rivals with the Apaches, kinship bonds necessary for exchange to take place never developed. The groups remained non-kin, and violence often erupted between them. Not only did the Apaches try to prevent Wichita and Caddo trade with the Pueblos, but they also tried to bar them from the plains horse herds. The Wichitas and Caddos fought back, developing a bitter hatred for the Apaches, which was returned in full measure. The two Indian peoples had few peaceful interactions and no kinship relations to speak of, but raided each other whenever possible. Once the Spanish arrived in New Mexico, they often invited the Apaches to their villages to trade. Apache bands usually arrived bearing Wichita and Caddo captives, which the Spaniards bought to use as slaves. So when the Comanches appeared on the Southern Plains and began battling the Apaches, the Wichitas and Caddos found an ally who hated the Apaches as much as they did—and one powerful enough to have sure access to the large herds of horses on the Southern Plains.[6]

Horses and other items produced by the Indians, such as animal hides, possessed an appeal far beyond their own borders, and not long after the Comanches and Osages arrived on the southern prairie-plains, Europeans also appeared in the area. By the early years of the eighteenth century, the Spanish had erected an arc of missions and presidios stretching from western Louisiana at Los Adaes all the way through San Antonio to the Rio Grande. But more important to the Indians of the southern prairie-plains were the French. The French hoped to seal off the English colonies on the eastern seaboard from any further western expansion by creating their own colony of Louisiana along the Mississippi River while at the same time satisfying the needs of mercantile capitalism by acquiring hides, horses, and slaves from Indian trade partners. To achieve these goals and connect Louisiana with their outposts in Canada, the French established a series of forts and trading posts, several of which would have a direct bearing on the Indians of the

Southern Plains. These included Fort Saint Jean Baptiste des Natchitoches and Fort Saint Louis de Cadodaquiox on the Red River among the Caddos. Near the Osages they built Fort Orleans on the Missouri River, the Arkansas Post near the mouth of the Arkansas River, and Fort de Chartres on the east bank of the Mississippi River in Illinois.

In return for deer hides, horses, and slaves, the French provided a host of manufactured goods to the Indians, including beads, bolts of cloth, shirts, pants, skirts, and tobacco, but even more importantly, they traded metal goods such as kettles, needles, hoes, axes, and, most prized, firearms. The actual killing power of these early flintlock muskets has been greatly overestimated, as Indians mainly received cheap trade muskets, which were highly inaccurate and prone to break, and gunpowder that was usually of inferior quality and suffered in rainy or humid weather. Because these guns were muzzle-loaders, which meant that the gunpowder and ball had to be rammed down the barrel, they were virtually impossible to reload on horseback.

This did not mean that firearms were useless in battle. Unlike arrows, which might be dodged, balls flew unseen, and if by chance one struck its target, it created a horrendous, possibly fatal wound. Even better was the musket's psychological advantage. The flash, the roar, the smoke all had an unnerving effect on one's enemies and gave the gunner a feeling of power, even if the ball did not hit its target. On the eastern prairies and in the woodlands of Arkansas and Louisiana, where dismounted warriors often had the chance to take careful aim and fire, the musket might prove more accurate, but the combatants were still hampered by cheap guns, defective powder, and the elements. On the plains, mounted warriors usually got off an initial volley of gunfire, then joined in close combat. In reality, iron-tipped arrows and metal-edged tomahawks, war clubs, knives, and lances played a much larger role in the actual killing or maiming of opponents during the eighteenth and early nineteenth centuries than did firearms. It would not be until the middle part of the nineteenth century, with the development of metal cartridges, that firearms became lethally dependable.

Few Indians tried to figure out the ratio between rounds fired and enemies killed, and besides, muskets were just accurate enough to be encouraging. Also, firearms proved very effective for hunting deer, when the hunter could take sure aim and fire. With the musket being a point-and-shoot weapon, like the bow and arrow, it did not take long for the Indians to become proficient with it in hunting. Pénicaut, a French carpenter who traveled through Louisiana during the early years of the eighteenth century, reported on Louisiana Indians' hunting techniques and proficiency. "When they go hunting, they go dressed in deer skins with the antlers attached. They make the same motions that a deer makes; and when the deer notices this, he charges them; and when he gets in good musket range, they shoot at him and kill him. With this method they kill a great many deer; and it should be acknowledged that in hunting buffalo as well as bear and deer they are more skillful than the French."[7] With the Indians' hunting ability, and because hides, particularly deer hides, fueled French mercantile capitalism, the French provided quantities of manufactured goods to the Indians in exchange for these hides, but also for horses and Indian slaves.

The introduction of manufactured goods brought tremendous changes to Indian societies throughout the continent. Initially seen as luxuries that alleviated drudgery in Indian life, manufactured goods became greatly desired by Indians, who used them in particularly Indian ways. Cloth clothes were warmer in winter and cooler in summer and soon replaced buckskin clothing. Metal kettles were more versatile and durable than clay jars, and many Indian peoples soon forgot how to make pottery. Even better, when a kettle wore out, it could be broken up and made into arrow points or cut into decorations to be used on personal items or clothes. Ready-made glass beads replaced shell beads, while metal needles allowed Indian women to bead beautifully intricate designs onto clothes and moccasins, something virtually impossible with bone needles. Metal hoes made the growing of crops easier and more productive than had been possible with digging sticks, while metal hatchets proved much more efficient than stone axes. Some items, such as alcohol, had a deleterious effect. Most Indians believed in the importance of dreams and visions, and alcohol seemed to enhance this spiritual quest. This often resulted in drunken brawls or accidents in which people were injured or killed.

Over the years, as manufactured goods replaced Indian-made items, they went from luxuries to necessities as the Indians developed a dependency on them and therefore needed a constant supply of them. Because most Indian societies were based on kinship and its resultant obligations, a person who could control a sure supply of European manufactured goods and then generously share these items with his or her kinspeople gained tremendous prestige and power in their society. This meant that many Indians went out of their way to marry their daughters or nieces to European traders or adopt these traders into their families. Indians expected their new Euroamerican relatives would uphold their kinship obligations by providing gifts of manufactured goods. If marriage was not feasible, a surer way of acquiring manufactured goods was to trade for them with large quantities of hides, horses, or captives.[8]

This demand for European manufactured goods unleashed a lethal cycle in relations among Indian peoples. As manufactured goods became necessities, Indian villages needed a constant supply of replacement kettles, clothes, hoes, and other items they could not create themselves. Firearms became particularly sought after, initiating a weapons race. If one Indian community received firearms, then their neighbors, especially their ancient enemies, felt they needed them, too. Acquisition of firearms then created the constant need for ammunition and gunpowder. In the end, all these goods could only be procured by exchanging hides, horses, or captives to Euroamericans.

Acquiring hides, whether beaver furs or deer hides, was easy, in theory, since Indians had been doing this as part of their way of life for thousands of years. But now, in the Southeast, Indians turned to hunting deer with a vengeance, and it was not long before they had overhunted the animals in their own areas. Forced to range farther afield, hunting parties began to clash in the woods, with the loser's stockpile of hides being the spoils of war. It did not take long before skirmishes in the woods evolved into full-fledged raids on other people's villages. Captives might also be taken and, like hides, exchanged to Europeans who needed them for their plantations.

With this economic impetus, bloody Indian wars broke out in the Southeast. Cherokees fought Creeks and Catawbas. Choctaws fought Chickasaws. Tuscaroras fought Yamasees. And the list could go on and on, with scores of smaller Indian nations in the region also caught up in the cycle of raids and wars.[9]

Horses caused similar things to happen on the prairie-plains. Theoretically, Plains Indians, such as the Apaches and Comanches, could capture wild horses, and many surely did. But capturing horses required different skills than hunting them, and even for these Plains Indians, it sometimes proved easier to raid each other's herds or the corrals of Spanish missions and presidios in Texas and New Mexico. Caddos and Wichitas, who lived on the periphery of the plains and often made hunting trips to the plains, might also capture wild horses but always had to be careful of Apache raiding parties. It would have been easier to raid the Spanish for horses, but the Spanish presence in eastern Texas was weak. A surer way for the Caddos and Wichitas to acquire horses was to arrange an exchange relationship with their Comanche allies. Fortunately, about that same time the French established several outposts on Red River, and French traders willing to exchange manufactured goods for hides, horses, and captives soon appeared in Caddo and Wichita villages. Not only did these goods allow the Caddos and Wichitas to increase production of deer and buffalo hides, but they made for a solid Caddo-Wichita-Comanche alliance and exchange network. Now Caddos and Wichitas provided the Comanches with firearms, metal-edged weapons, and other goods. These made the Comanches more formidable warriors, and they eventually pushed the Apaches into southern Texas and northern Mexico. In return, the Wichitas and Caddos received horses and Apache captives. A portion of these they kept for themselves for use as gifts to increase status among their own people or to exchange with other Indian peoples. The remainder they exchanged with the French for manufactured goods.[10]

For the Osages, the establishment of French outposts in their area also made them better warriors and allowed them to intensify their raids against the Caddos and Wichitas, who blocked their direct access to the horses herds on the plains. These conflicts between the Osages and the Wichitas and Caddos during the eighteenth century can rightly be called the Horse Wars. Now horse-mounted Osage warriors, carrying French firearms and metal-edged weapons, became the scourge of the Wichitas and Caddos, raiding their villages and carrying off quantities of horses, hides, and captives. Most of these they exchanged with French traders on the Arkansas and Missouri Rivers for additional firearms, ammunition, and manufactured goods. More than just raids, these attacks became a contest for control of the southwestern woodlands and southern prairies as the Osages tried to expand their territorial and economic hegemony. The Caddos and Wichitas fought back as best they could, but the raids and counterraids initiated a century of devastating warfare between the Caddos and Wichitas and the Osages.

As early as the 1720s, if not sooner, the Osages seemed to strike fear in the hearts of the Caddos. When La Harpe visited the Caddo and Wichita villages along the Red River in 1719–20, his Caddo guide panicked when he found Osage footprints on the prairie. It took all of La Harpe's persuasiveness to prevent the guide from deserting them and get him to lead on, but when they saw smoke on the horizon, the guide became convinced Osages were in the area, and nothing La Harpe could do could make him continue.[11] Not long after, La Harpe met a party of thirty frightened Caddo buffalo hunters who were hurrying off the plains because they had spotted an Osage campfire. Once again, La Harpe's guide, upon hearing this news, refused to go further.[12]

By the 1730s, warfare between the Osages and Caddos became so fierce that even the French found themselves targets. A large population of unlicensed traders, *gaboteurs*, as the French called them, congregated between the Arkansas and Red Rivers. These outlaws often traded with both the Osages and the Caddos in violation of French laws, which required that only officially licensed traders or post commandants provide goods to the Indians. The gaboteurs on the Arkansas River made kinship relations with the Osages, while those on the Red River made similar relations with the Caddos and Wichitas. Osage raiders killed several luckless French traders near Natchitoches and looted their goods. Caddo warriors did the same near the Arkansas River. For many French-men, it became too dangerous to travel the roads between Natchi-toches and the Illinois posts.[13] The French, and later the Spanish, once they acquired Louisiana, tried to adjudicate a peace between the Osages and Caddos. Little came of it, as the French and Spanish needed both peoples as economic and military allies and so could not make punitive raids, levy sanctions, or cut off the manufac-tured goods to either in order to force them to make a peace.[14] Besides, the gaboteurs easily circumvented colonial laws regarding supplying the Indians with goods. So the Osages and the Caddos and Wichitas found they could turn to their European kinspeople for goods to help fuel their wars against each other.

Even Spain's taking over the administration of Louisiana in 1762 made absolutely no impact on the relations between the Osages and Caddos. Spanish officials in Louisiana and Texas hoped to bring about peace between the Indian peoples in the two provinces as well as stop Comanche and Apaches attacks on Spanish outposts in Texas by limiting the amount of firearms and manufactured goods provided to the Indians. This new policy barely caused a hitch in the number of firearms getting to the Indians, because the gaboteurs, whom the Spanish now called *contrabandistas*, made up the shortage. Even worse, in the eyes of the Spanish, English traders from Canada and the east side of the Mississippi River stepped up their trading activities with the Indians, particularly the Osages.[15] During the 1770s and 1780s, Osage raiding parties swooped down upon Caddo and Wichita villages, scooping up horses, hides, and captives and leaving dead and wounded in their wake while stunned survivors demanded that the Spanish fulfill their promise to stop them. The Spanish proved just as powerless as the French, and the raids became so fierce that by the mid-1780s the Caddos and some of the Wichitas had moved their villages south from the upper Red River in order to escape them. The Osages became the virtual masters of a territory stretching from the Missouri River on the north to the Red River on the South, from the Mississippi River on the east to the prairie-plains on the west. By the late 1780s the Osages prepared to push further west to the Southern Plains and gain direct access to the huge horse herds there, but in late 1789 a force of seven hundred Comanche and Wichita warriors repulsed them. This defeat blocked Osage westward expansion, and so once again they set their sights on the Caddo villages, their raids continuing unabated into the nineteenth century.[16]

Another policy of the Spanish in Louisiana would have much more far-reaching effects not only on the Caddos and Wichitas, but on the Osages as well. With the loss of the French and Indian War, France, in order to keep its territory west of the Mississippi River out of English hands, ceded all of it to Spain, though it was forced to give up all its claims to lands east of the Mississippi to England. Suddenly Spain found itself looking across the Mississippi River at the aggressive English colonies. Fearing that the colonists would next try for Spanish Louisiana, the Spanish hoped to forestall this by building an Indian barrier that would repel any English attack. This meant keeping good relations with the Indians already living in Louisiana and was one of the reasons why the Spanish could never bring themselves to send a punitive military expedition against the Osages or cut off trade to stop them from raiding the Caddos and Wichitas. It also meant allowing any Indians from the British side of the Mississippi to immigrate into Louisiana. Soon, a host of Indians from the British colonies were making their way into Spanish Louisiana. By the mid-1780s, Spanish officials could list their Indian allies living south of the Osages as the Caddos, Rapides, Pacanas, Alabamas, Choctaws, Ochanias, Biloxis, Chickasaws, Appalaches, Pascagoulas, Coushattas, Illinois, and Miamis.[17]

For the Choctaws and Chickasaws, the Spanish invitation in the 1770s to come live in Louisiana was not their first trip across the river. During the first years of the eighteenth century, Chickasaw raiding parties began striking westward. Always allies and economic partners of the English, the Chickasaws hoped to take captives that they could exchange to South Carolina traders for manufactured goods. Spurred by the English demand for slaves, the raids only increased over the next few years until the Chickasaws drove the Quapaws away from the Mississippi River and up the Arkansas. Chickasaw slave raids soon reached as far as the Caddo villages on the Red River.[18] The Indian slave trade began dying out in the 1730s, leaving the deer hide trade as the main economic activity between the Indians and the English and French. As competition for deer hides increased across the Southeast, hunting parties from various Indian nations now began encountering each other in the forests and prairies. Choctaw and Chickasaw parties, as they ventured across the Mississippi River, often clashed with Caddo parties on lands the Caddos had long claimed as their own. Adding to this rivalry was the bitter competition for empire between the English and the French, who used trade as a means to hold on to their own Indian allies and undercut the allies of the other. Both expected their Indian allies to fight for them in the event of war.[19]

The French and Indian War of 1754 to 1763 forced the Indians of the Southeast to choose sides. The Chickasaws remained with England, while smaller nations who had been ravaged by English slave raids sided with the French. The Choctaws divided into hostile factions, one pro-French and the other pro-English. The Cherokees followed their own agenda, and while not exactly French allies, attacked and captured English Fort Loudoun in eastern Tennessee. The Creeks, except for the killing of eleven English traders by the Upper Creeks, remained neutral. When the war ended with an English victory in 1763, many of the smaller nations who had supported the French fled to the west. Some English allies, such as the Chickasaws, continued raiding across the Mississippi. Others in the Southeast, now unable to play the English against the French, found English interference in their lives and nations intolerable. English encroachment on their lands and culture, as well as the insistence that the Indians abide by English laws, made additional Indian peoples and factions decide to move west. Wanting to build this Indian barrier, the Spanish government in Louisiana welcomed these refugees and immigrants. In some cases, such as that of the Choctaws, Spain actively encouraged several factions to settle in Louisiana. Officials hoped those groups would not only become part of the barrier, but also keep the powerful Choctaws split into squabbling factions and so weaken any English alliance. By the late 1760s and early 1770s, at the invitation of the Spanish government, hundreds of Choctaws crossed the Mississippi River and settled along the Ouachita and lower Red Rivers.[20]

The relocation proved disastrous for the Caddos, for the Choctaws became both invaders and trade rivals. Choctaw bands hunted the lands traditionally claimed by Caddo peoples, and parties regularly clashed in the woods between the Ouachita and Sabine Rivers. Like the Osages, Choctaw bands raided Caddo villages, seizing hides, horses, cattle, and crops. When this happened, the

Caddos responded with counterraids and revenge killings. A veritable flood of Indians from the east now swirled around the Spanish post of Natchitoches. According to Commandant Louis de Blanc, the Choctaws and Chickasaws attacked not only the Caddos but many European residents as well.[21]

Pleas from the Caddos and Wichitas and the Natchitoches commandants to no avail, the Spanish had opened a Pandora's box when they had allowed the immigrant Indians into their colony. They could not have stemmed this tide had they wanted to. By the mid-1790s, bands of Choctaws, Chickasaws, and other Indians were petitioning to settle in Spanish Texas. And having learned nothing from the plight of Louisiana, the Texas governor agreed. By 1803, Daniel Clark, while making a trip through the Natchitoches area, commented that the "Cadoquias, called by the abbreviation Caddos, . . . can raise from 3 to 400 warriors, are the friends of the whites and are esteemed the bravest and most generous of all the Nations in this vast country, they are rapidly decreasing, owing to the intemperance and the numbers annually destroyed by the Osages and Choctaws."[22]

By the late eighteenth century, bands of Creeks and Cherokees joined the mix of Choctaws, Chickasaws, and other Indian peoples streaming west of the Mississippi River. Creek factions, such as the Alabamas and Koasatis, or Coushattas, moved into lower Louisiana, while bands of Cherokees crossed into upper Louisiana. As early as the 1770s, bands of Cherokee hunters had crossed into present-day Arkansas, while in 1788, Toquo, a Cherokee headman, asked the Spanish commandant at Saint Louis to allow his people to settle in Louisiana. Spanish governor Esteban Miró approved the relocation of up to six Cherokee villages. Most of these Cherokees settled along the Saint Francis River in present-day Arkansas and Missouri. This region of the Ozark highlands appealed to the Cherokees, as its forests, mountains, and teeming game were similar to their traditional homeland in the southern Appalachians. Even better, the lowlands were good for farming and herding while being far enough away from meddling American settlers.[23]

As the eighteenth century ended, the trickle of Cherokees and other Southeastern Indians moving across the Mississippi River became a rising tide. With the formation of the United States, the federal government increasingly demanded the right to regulate Indian affairs. It also encouraged, if not insisted, that the Indians become "civilized." This meant giving up traditional ways and accepting an Anglo-American culture, which included Christianity, capitalistic agriculture, and proper gender roles in which men farmed and controlled the property while women spun, sewed, and did the housework. These demands were also accompanied by constant pressure on the Indians to continually cede "excess" lands to the federal or state governments, which would then provide those lands to the ever-growing number of white settlers moving west of the Appalachians.

As these settlers moved west, the first major Indian nations they came into contact with were the Cherokees and Creeks. Both of these peoples initially resisted American encroachment on their culture and lands. During the 1780s and early 1790s, Cherokee warriors such as Doublehead, John Watts, The Ridge, who later became known as Major Ridge, and others fought several pitched battles against the Tennessee militia. But Cherokee military action against the United States pretty much ended in 1794 after a series of defeats in which several of their towns were destroyed. Cherokees leaders made peace with the American government and accepted an agent who constantly advocated that they adopt an American "civilization." Not only the Cherokees but also, as the settlers spread throughout the Southeast and as the United States government began to take control of that area, most of the other major Indian nations in the Southeast began to be pressured to adopt American culture and cede their lands.[24]

These peoples were already torn by factionalism, and the demands of the Americans only heightened the schisms. Some

Southeastern Indians, while accepting the cultural demands of the Americans, insisted on national unity, a centralized government, and an end to making any more land cessions to the United States. Others hoped to continue resisting American demands and not only remain true to the old ways but also remain on their traditional lands in the Southeast. Among the Creeks, these traditionalists instigated the Creek Civil War in 1813 and attacked the towns of those Creek progressives who were willing to accept American acculturation. Getting caught up with the then raging War of 1812, the traditionalist Red Stick Creeks were finally defeated by a coalition of American troops, White Stick Creek progressives, and Cherokee auxiliaries, all led by Andrew Jackson, who forced all the Creeks to cede land as an indemnity. Even before the Creek Civil War, a third faction of Southeastern Indian ultratraditionalists placed retaining their traditional culture as a top priority and were willing to cede land and move west in order to keep their ancient ways intact. Because traditional Cherokee politics demanded consensus, those who could not agree with the majority normally removed themselves. Already willing to leave their homeland and now in the minority, many Cherokees, anxious to continue following the old ways and to escape the influence of the Americans, began moving west of the Mississippi River.[25]

As early as 1805, the Lewis and Clark expedition reported two large Cherokee villages on the Saint Francis River in Missouri. Cherokee hunting and trading partners soon fanned out through the area. In 1807, John Sibley, the United States Indian agent at the former French and Spanish outpost of Natchitoches on the Red River, reported being visited not only by such local Indians as the Caddos but also by bands of immigrant Choctaws, Creeks, Apalachees, Pascagoulas, Chickasaws, and Cherokees. The Cherokees arrived from up the Red River with two canoes filled with deer skins they hoped to trade. There was a tense moment, Sibley explained, because about seven years before, the Caddos had accidentally killed a Cherokee man roaming through their country, and the brother of the Cherokee victim was one of those who arrived with the canoes. No problems arose, as the man assured Sibley that the Caddos had satisfied his brother's death, and he held no animosity toward them. During that same summer of 1807, the eastern immigrant Indians probably had their first contact with the Plains Indians when Sibley hosted a large party of Texas Caddos, Wichitas, and Comanches, who visited him in Natchitoches.[26] In that same year, a Pascagoula chief, Pinaye, leading a mixed band of Indians, visited the Spanish Texas outpost of Nacogdoches. Pinaye met with the post's Spanish commandant, Francisco Viana, and explained that he represented his own and also several Cherokee, Chickasaw, and Shawnee villages, and they wanted to settle in Texas. The request passed up the Spanish chain of command to Nemesio Salcedo, commandant of Spain's Internal Provinces, who tentatively approved the entry of these Indians into Texas.[27]

This Cherokee presence west of the Mississippi River continued to grow and soon became officially known as the Cherokee Nation West. Urged to emigrate west by President Thomas Jefferson, by 1809 enough had emigrated to the Arkansas Territory that the president appointed Major Jacob Wolf as their agent. The next year counted over two thousand Cherokees living south of the Arkansas River in Arkansas, with their numbers growing every year. The Cherokees who remained in the east took a dim view of this migration. Trying to keep a united front in the face of encroachment by the United States, the Cherokee National Council called these immigrants traitors. Still, the National Council's disapproval did little to stop the emigration of these people, who valued their ancient lifeways over their ancestral lands. By 1817 almost a third of the entire Cherokee nation lived west of the Mississippi River. Enough lived in Arkansas that the United States government negotiated a treaty with them in which the Cherokee Nation West ceded its rights to land in the East in return for a guarantee of land in Arkansas.[28]

Now it came time for the Osages to feel the lash of invaders as large bands of Choctaws, Chickasaws, and particularly Cherokees

settled on the lands they had wrested from the Caddos and Quapaws. Choctaw and Chickasaw raiding parties had long battled
the Osages in Arkansas, but the settlement of thousands of Cherokees near the Arkansas River in the second decade of the nineteenth century constituted a veritable invasion of lands the Osages
claimed as original inhabitants. Osages and Cherokees became
archenemies, and a fierce warfare, broken only by brief peaces
arranged by missionaries and territorial officials, constituted
Cherokee-Osage relations for the next few years.[29] According to
one missionary, warfare between the Osages and the Cherokees
broke out in the early nineteenth century when a party of Osages
wiped out a Cherokee hunting party. The Cherokees, wanting
peace, overlooked this killing and sent several of their chiefs and
principal warriors to the Osages to propose peace. The Osages
agreed. The two peoples smoked the calumet and exchanged gifts,
and the Cherokees went away thinking they had accomplished
their mission. But after traveling only a day or so, they sent out a
few hunters for game, and the hunters were attacked and killed by
a party of Osages who had been trailing them.[30] If the missionary's
story was true, then Cherokee culture demanded that blood
revenge be taken on the Osages. Unlike the Osages, for whom gifts
from the killer or his family could "cover the dead," if a non-
Cherokee killed a Cherokee, then death was the only payment.
With this mindset, Cherokee-Osage warfare in western Arkansas
and Missouri soon spiraled out of control.[31]

The Osages tell their own story of Cherokee treachery. In the
autumn of 1817, when most of the Osage men were out hunting
on the plains, five hundred Cherokees, along with a few Choctaws
and Chickasaws and several white men, attacked an Osage village
at Claremore Mounds near the Verdigris River. Knowing the warriors were gone and the village was filled with women, children,
and old men, the Cherokees killed thirty-eight Osages, captured
over a hundred, pillaged what they could, destroyed what they
could not, then set the village afire. Many of the captives were sent

back to the eastern Cherokees as gifts for their help with the raid.
The Cherokees boasted of their victory to the United States government and demanded they be given Osage lands as the spoils of
war. Secretary of War John C. Calhoun agreed with this reasoning
and in 1818 ordered the Osages to cede part of their land to the
Cherokees. Several, but not all, bands of Osages appeared in Saint
Louis that autumn for negotiations. The great chief Clermont,
spokesman for several Arkansas Osage bands, did not sign the
treaty, but enough chiefs did to make the United States recognize
it as valid. In it, the Osages made peace with the Cherokees and
signed away part of their land in return for the repatriation of the
captives taken in the Claremore Mounds raid. Still, peace was
elusive, because the Cherokees balked at returning the captives
and the Osages itched for revenge. In 1820 it all fell apart when
Skitok, son of Clermont, angry at the Cherokees' refusal to return
the captives, killed three Cherokee hunters on the Poteau River.
Attacks, raids, and thefts fired up once again.[32]

By 1820 the war caused a split among the Western Cherokees.
Chief John Jolly succeeded his brother, Talontuskee, as chief of the
Western Cherokees in 1817. Jolly advocated a negotiated diplomatic
peace with the Osages. More conservative leaders, such as Duwali
and war chief Takatoka, urged that the revenge killings continue.
Both men refused to attend a peace conference Jolly had arranged,
but the majority of the Western Cherokees supported Jolly's efforts.
Duwali, working within the traditional method of withdrawing if
he could not stomach a decision he opposed, led several hundred
Cherokees southwest into Texas, where they were soon joined by
several bands of Delawares, Chickasaws, and Choctaws.[33]

Jolly's peace efforts came to naught, and warfare continued,
with most observers betting on the Cherokees. As Little Rock's
Arkansas Gazette reported in December 1820:

> The Cherokees . . . are determined to drive them [the Osages]
> from their country, and possess it themselves. We also learn,

that the Shawanees [*sic*], and Delawares, now on their way
to this territory from Indiana, intend joining the Cherokees.
. . . The Osages are a bold and warlike people, but it is said,
they are badly supplied with arms and ammunition—their
principal weapons are bows and arrows; they have a few
muskets and shot guns, but make very little use of the rifle.
The Cherokees are said to be well supplied with every thing
necessary for a vigorous prosecution of the war.[34]

Osage chief Clermont now worked for peace and repeatedly
told officials at Fort Smith, which the government had established
in 1817 to bring peace between the two peoples, that his warriors
would not attack the Cherokees if the Cherokees would stay off
Osage lands. Officers of the 7th Infantry stationed at Fort Smith
promised to prevent Cherokee attacks but quickly found themselves powerless to stop them. The Osages found it difficult to take
revenge, as many Cherokees lived near Fort Smith, and the army
was just as anxious to stop Osage attacks as those of the Cherokees.
Only when the Osages could catch Cherokee parties on the plains
could they take the necessary revenge, and that they did whenever
they could.[35]

At the same time, northern Osages in Missouri, who had not
signed the agreement at Saint Louis or any other peace with the
Cherokees, now found themselves pulled into the fray. Even worse,
from the Osages' point of view, was that the numbers of immigrant
Indians in their area continued to grow, hunt on Osage lands, and
attack Osage parties and villages. By early 1824, near the Three
Forks region where the Neosho and Verdigris Rivers join the
Arkansas River at present-day Muskogee, Oklahoma, settlements
of Cherokees, Delawares, Shawnees, and Otos grew up on lands
claimed by the Osages. South of the Red River, but still within
hunting and attack range of the Osages, bands of Kickapoos,
Choctaws, Chickasaws, and Cherokees also settled and opposed
making peace. Even the Iowa Indians made a raid on the Osages.

Under this constant pressure, the Osages often struck back at the various Indian immigrants, as in 1824, when they attacked a Delaware hunting party. This brought retaliation by the Delawares, who brought in Shawnees and Kickapoos as allies. When Osage losses grew too great, they made a peace in Saint Louis with the Delawares, Kickapoos, Piankashaws, Weas, and Shawnees, though peace with the Cherokees remained elusive.[36]

If warfare and pressures on their lands were not enough, the Osages soon found their lifeways and traditions coming under attack by the United States' "civilization" program. In 1820 the United Foreign Mission Society established Union Mission on the lower Neosho River to help "civilize" the Arkansas Osages. The next year the society established Harmony Mission on the Osage River for the upper Osage bands. Other missions, such as Hopefield, Boudinot, and Neosho, soon appeared. Hoping to change the Osages into settled farmers, the men and women missionaries set up churches, schools, and farms to help transform Osage life. These efforts met with mixed success. The Osages, who already farmed a little, continued farming by the traditional method of letting the crops take care of themselves while they were away on the hunt—a method that flew in the face of the missionaries, who advocated capitalistic agriculture. Still, some Osages did set up a short-lived farming community near Hopewell Mission, but attacks by Cherokees and other Indians, pitiful harvests, and a cholera epidemic ended the experiment and sent the Osage families back to their bands. Churches did not seem to attract many converts, but a few Osages did send their children to the mission schools. The missionaries remained hopeful, for some Osages actually raised enough corn and melons in 1824 to sell to the soldiers at Fort Smith. As one missionary wrote, Osage Chief Pawhuska was one of those who went to Fort Smith to sell the crops. While there he met a Cherokee named Black Fox. Black Fox "entreated him to persevere in his agricultural pursuits—to be sure and educate his children, and take heed to the advice of the missionaries, for they were true friends to the Indians. He then showed him the clothes he wore, telling him they were spun and woven in his own house, and expressed the hope that Paw-hunk-shaw's [*sic*] wife would soon learn to make him clothes." Black Fox's advice apparently fell on stony ground, because Pawhuska gave up farming after one season and never went back to it.[37]

Whether the Osages became "civilized" mattered very little, because they stood in the way of the government's creation of an Indian Territory on which to settle the Southeastern Indians it was already beginning to remove. To the government, the Osages needed to make peace and give up their lands to make way for these removed Indians. An incident in 1823, when Skitok and other Osage warriors attacked a hunting party of whites and Quapaws on Osage lands near the Blue River, paved the way for removal of the Osages. The fact that four whites, including an army major, were killed outraged the United States government, and the military commander at Fort Smith demanded that the Osages surrender Skitok for trial. Skitok's father, Clermont, refused, insisting that the hunters had violated Osage lands. Still, he returned most of the hides and horses taken in the attack.

Believing Fort Smith was too far east to effectively cow the Osages, in April 1824 the government sent Major Matthew Arbuckle and five companies of infantry to build Cantonment Gibson, later Fort Gibson, near the confluence of the Neosho and Arkansas Rivers. Fearful of the soldiers now among them, and wanting to avoid a war with the government, Clermont took the highly unusual action of surrendering his son, Skitok, and five other warriors to the military.[38]

Being forced to give up their warriors to the United States government showed just how far Osage power had declined since the eighteenth century, and the reality of the situation must have come as a shock. With Cantonment Gibson in their midst, there was nothing Clermont and his Osages could do. Now the government played on this weakness and in 1825 directed the Osages to give up their lands in Arkansas and Missouri in order to make room for additional removed Indians from the east. At Saint Louis, Missouri, territorial governor William Clark demanded that Clermont and Pawhuska sign a treaty ceding their lands inside the Arkansas Territory and the state of Missouri all the way to the headwaters of the Kansas River. In return they received a small parcel of land, fifty by fifty miles square, within the northern part of their ceded land.[39]

Though they signed the treaty, the Osages refused to leave their lands, and the government, not wanting to force the issue, allowed them to stay but constantly urged them to move west. The treaty did not end the conflict between the Osages and the Cherokees, as rumors of wars between them and other immigrant Indians continued to circulate. For another decade or so Osage bands remained on their eastern lands. Only as more immigrant Indians arrived in the area during the 1830s did many Osages finally migrate westward, there to be confronted by the Comanches, Kiowas, and Wichitas. And even the Comanches by this time were complaining to the army about Cherokees and Choctaws stealing their horses and killing their people.[40]

By the 1820s the southwestern frontier of the United States was awash in immigrant Indians, with more on the way. In 1820 the government signed the Treaty of Doak's Stand, which gave the Choctaws land between the Arkansas and Red Rivers in Arkansas. In late 1824, Western Cherokee chief Takatoka led a delegation to Washington, D.C., in order to help negotiate the removal of the Shawnees, Delawares, Kickapoos, Peorias, Miamis, and Piankashaws from the east and resettle them near the Cherokees west of the Mississippi. According to Cherokee Chief John Jolly, the Cherokees felt that the successful removal of these peoples was "intimately connected with the preservation and future responsibility of the red people generally."[41] Though Takatoka died en route to Washington, the Cherokee delegation did bring back a deputation of Shawnees to inspect the country. In fact, the

Cherokees announced they wanted to form a confederacy with the Shawnees in which the Cherokees would adopt the Shawnees into their nation as citizens.[42] By 1828 the western territory was home to about six thousand Cherokees; eighteen hundred Delawares; twenty-two hundred Kickapoos; fourteen hundred Shawnees; fourteen hundred Weas from Indiana and Illinois; two hundred Piankashaws, also from Indiana and Illinois; and about seven hundred Creeks and seven hundred Choctaws.[43]

To accommodate all these Indians, and in hopes of removing the Southeastern Indians to the west, in 1825 the government created an Indian Country, which later came to be called Indian Territory. It was located west of Arkansas, Missouri, and Iowa. As Secretary of War James Barbour wrote in 1826, this area would be set apart for the exclusive abode of the Indians. Overseen by the United States, it would eventually result in "the extinction of tribes, and their amalgamation into one mass, and a distribution of property among the individuals." But, he said, "nothing is proposed to be done, in reference to the Indians, *without their own consent* [emphasis his]." He went on to guarantee that "the future residence of these peoples will be forever undisturbed—that there, at least, they will find a home and a resting place. And being exclusively under the control of the United States, and, consequently, free from rival claims of any of the states, the former may pledge its most solemn faith that it shall be theirs forever, and this guaranty is therefore given."[44]

With Indian Territory created, the white people of Arkansas began complaining about all the Indians living in their territory. To satisfy them, the government decided to move the Western Cherokees further west. In a treaty signed with them in May 1828, the government set the western boundary of Arkansas at its present location and provided seven million acres west of that line in Indian Territory to the Cherokees, including an outlet to the plains, all of which would be theirs forever. In return, the Cherokees would give up their land in Arkansas and remove west within fourteen months, and the government would pay for the improvements they had made to their land in Arkansas.[45] In what would be a model for future inter-Indian diplomacy, as they moved into Indian Territory the Cherokees, Shawnees, Mohawks, Delawares, Creeks, and others held a council to work out boundary disputes.[46]

Their move into Indian Territory now put the Cherokees even closer to the Osages and other peoples of the prairies and plains. Even with Cantonment Gibson on the Neosho River and Cantonment Towson, later Fort Towson, on the Red River, sporadic violence still broke out between these traditional southeastern Indians and the peoples whose lands they were moving onto. Now the Wichitas began to be resentful of the approach of the Cherokees, Delawares, Kickapoos, and others and began defending their land, attacking small parties of eastern Indians. Sometimes Wichita attacks spilled over onto the soldiers supposed to protect the Southeastern Indians.[47]

Despite this, the migration of Indians from the east to the west did not slow down. As pressure from American settlers grew in the east, many Indians, either individually, as families, or as larger groups felt it best to move west. For the first four decades of the nineteenth century, a steady stream of Southeastern Indians straggled toward Louisiana, Arkansas, Missouri, and now Indian Territory. Many of them wrote letters back home in hopes of convincing their kinspeople to join them there. The *Cherokee Phoenix* newspaper reported much of what these emigrant Indians had to say about Indian Territory, the abundance of game, and especially the "wild" Indians already living there. A Creek citizen named Benjamin Hawkins returned from the west to report that "emigrants are much pleased with their location, they finding game in the greatest abundance, and the surrounding tribes perfectly friendly. . . . We are induced to believe that the time is not far distant when the whole Creek nation will remove west of the Mississippi."[48]

Another Creek, Captain Thomas Anthony, also extolled the praises of the country, telling of a buffalo hunt in which a party of twenty-eight Creek migrants brought back the meat of twenty-four buffalo. "All the Indians are delighted with this country," Anthony wrote, "which is rich and well calculated for our peoples, who can live well by agriculture and hunting. We have no fears of their suffering, as the crops look well. We shall have roasting ears of corn in two weeks. . . . We have good gardens with cucumbers, lettuce, radishes, plenty of Irish and sweet potatoes, beans, peas, beets, watermelons, &c." Captain Anthony also told of having a council with the Delaware Indians, who presented beads and tobacco to the Creeks and who were "received in ancient form; and received presents of the same articles in return. . . . We do not anticipate difficulty with any of the Indian tribes. . . . There are, however, a number of Indians who do not respect the rights of any nation. That go upon a war expedition to gain the name and character of warriors, and will take any person's scalp and run the risk of the consequences."[49]

While the *Cherokee Phoenix* gave fair coverage to the benefits of Indian Territory, its official editorial position was against emigration and removal to the west, so it played up stories about Plains Indian outrages. It often ran stories about Osage or Comanche attacks, almost delighting in describing the "wild" or "savage" ways of the Indians living to the west of the country the Cherokees might one day inhabit. A letter from Young Beaver advised that emigration to the west was a very important thing for the Cherokees to consider. Having been to Arkansas, Young Beaver reported that all was not well for the Western Cherokees, especially in regard to other Indians there. "How many honest and innocent fathers and brothers have been laid low by the ruthless hands of more ignorant and vicious neighbors. Avarice and barbarity have deprived their social circles of many worthy members."[50]

Regardless of claims like Young Beaver's, now that Indian Territory had been established, and with so many Indians from the east emigrating west, the government urged those remaining in the Southeast to accept lands in the West. Wanting this emigration to be voluntary, the government sponsored several expeditions of western exploration in which parties of Southeastern Indians could inspect the area, choose the lands they wanted, and then, it was hoped, go back east and convince their kinspeople to migrate. In the summer and fall of 1828, a large contingent of Choctaws, Chickasaws, and Creeks went to explore Indian Territory and were gone for over six months. The Choctaw delegation included Subagent David W. Haley; Tapenahumma, chief of the Choctaw southern district; Captain Asetahumma, also of the southern district; Captain Ofihumma, or Red Dog, of the western district; and Captain Joseph Kincaid, Peter Pitchlynn (who later became the principal chief of the Choctaws), and interpreter Daniel Nail of the northern district. The Chickasaw delegation included Subagent John B. Duncan, Levi Colbert, Ishtematahka, Emmebba, Immatahishto, Ahtocowah, Ishtayahtubba, Bahkahtubba, Thomas Sealy, Isaac Love, Elapaumba, Charles Colbert, J. McLish, interpreter Benjamin Love, and three white men, who went as friends and advisors of the Chickasaws, as well as a few black slaves. The Creek delegation included Subagent Luther Blake, Doe Marthla, Tuskeneha, Choeste, and interpreter Harper Lovett, who died two weeks after they left Saint Louis. Along with hired men and camp helpers, the expedition totaled over forty men and sixty horses.[51]

The exploring party, as they toured the eastern part of Indian Territory, encountered both immigrant and native Indian peoples. They spent five days with the Shawnees and met Tenskwatawah, once known as the Prophet, brother of Tecumseh, who had been defeated by William Henry Harrison at the Battle of Tippecanoe Creek in Indiana in 1811.[52] In his diary of the trip and in several letters to his family in Mississippi, Peter Pitchlynn made many observations about the character of the Prairie and Plains Indians he encountered. In almost all cases he felt they were of a lower caste. When he met the Kansas Indians, Pitchlynn, ever the acculturated progressive, wrote his father that "you never saw such people in your life. Their manners and actions are wild in the extreme. They are in a state of nature and would be a curiosity to any civilized man."[53]

The Osages, whose reputation for war reached back to the Southeast, concerned Pitchlynn most. The exploring party finally met them in November 1828 at the Osage Agency in eastern Kansas. At the Osage villages the explorers met Pawhuska, whom they called White Hair. All members of the exploring party realized that peace had to be made with the Osages or their people would never be safe. Pitchlynn made a speech to Pawhuska in which he advocated peace and explained his vision of what Indians should become, saying, "It is a fact that our nations have been, at times, in enmity with each other. . . . But we have been lectured by our Great Father, the President, to be at peace with all nations, and teach our young men how to work and advised them to pursue the ways of the white men."[54] The council succeeded, for as Pitchlynn termed it, they spent several days together talking and eating and "made a white road and turned forever the tomahawk."[55] The Osages seemed to want peace as much as the Southeastern Indians did and also made eloquent speeches in favor of it.

Ironically, years later, when Pitchlynn was an old man, he gave an entirely different account of this council with the Osages. Rather than a meeting of the minds of peoples who wanted peace, Pitchlynn now portrayed the Osages as blood-thirsty and menacing and said that he only managed to bring about a peace by threatening the Osages with Choctaw power. The *Cherokee Advocate* printed an account of this council in 1877, almost fifty years after it happened, and in it Pitchlynn admonished the Osages to make peace because there were plenty of Choctaw warriors back in Mississippi who would like to "obtain a few hundred of your black locks." Pitchlynn warned the Osages that when the Choctaws migrated to this area, they would be within two hundred miles of the Osages, and if peace were not made then, the Osages would "hear the whoop of the Choctaw and the crack of their rifles. Your warriors will then fall, and your wives and children shall be taken into captivity." According to the article, Pitchlynn explained to the Osages how the Choctaws had already adopted the "customs of civilization," were living as farmers, and had established schools and churches. "He advised the Osages to do the same; to give up war as an amusement, and the chase as a sole dependence for food, and then they would become a happy and prosperous people. This was their only means of preservation from the grasping habits of the white man . . . and, though they might throw away their eagle feathers, and live in permanent cabins, there was no danger of losing their identity or name."[56] It is doubtful Pitchlynn actually made a speech like this to the Osages. Still, the sentiments expressed in the article, that the Southeastern Indians were already "civilized" and the Osages were "savages" who needed to become "civilized," certainly confirmed Pitchlynn's beliefs in 1828 and those of most citizens of the Five Major Tribes in 1877.

After making peace with the Osages, it came time for the exploring party to head further west. Most members of the party hesitated to go too far onto the plains, because they feared the Indians living there. They protested that their horses were tired and that it was too late in the year for an adequate exploration. They were assured that all would be well, and Pitchlynn, along with a small party, ventured further west. He did not like what he saw and complained that it was all prairie and totally devoid of game, but he was hopeful of finding buffalo, elk, and bear on the Canadian River. Still, he was happy to report that near the Arkansas River he found huge amounts of cane, a material the Choctaws used for making baskets and a host of other utensils. Though it was not as large as the cane found on the Tombigbee River, it was just as thick. While Pitchlynn's diary and letters do not mention any contact with the Plains Indians, the 1877 article in the *Cherokee*

Advocate says the party did have some "severe" skirmishes with the Comanches. He might well have had a few encounters with them, for while on this trip to the plains Pitchlynn admitted he did not have much time to keep up his diary or write letters. No matter, the explorers were back in the Southeast by early 1829, and all were adamantly against their peoples migrating west.[57] As one Creek chief, Nehah Micco, wrote to the secretary of war in 1831, the Creeks viewed the western country as "a graveyard. The country we now occupy is healthy, and plentifully rich for us to make aplenty. Our attention is now entirely to labor; our game is gone; we make aplenty of corn, and raise fine hogs and beef cattle."[58]

While many Southeastern Indians viewed the western country with fear and trepidation, other Indian peoples saw it as a land of opportunity. Centuries before, Apaches, Comanches, and Kiowas had migrated down onto the Southern Plains. The Iroquoian expansion in the seventeenth century had sent the Osages to the west, where they vied for control of the country with the Caddos and Wichitas already living there. By the late eighteenth and early nineteenth centuries, remnants of shattered tribes from the Northeast, such as bands of Shawnees, Kickapoos, and Delawares, began moving toward the Southern Plains. Added to this mix were large bands of Cherokees, Choctaws, Chickasaws, and Creeks who hoped to migrate west to get away from the American influence and preserve their ancient ways. With so many Indians moving toward the plains, the United States government, during the 1820s, decided that this would be an excellent place to put the Indians until they were ready to assimilate into American society. Initially, the government hoped the large number of Cherokees, Creeks, Chickasaws, and Choctaws remaining in the Southeast would voluntarily move west the way so many of their kinspeople already had. But Indian leaders, for the most part, refused. By the 1830s the government had decided that, whether the Indians wanted to or not, they must be removed to Indian Territory, and during that decade it forced on them treaties by which

they exchanged their land in the east for lands in Indian Territory. There they would have to live in proximity to the Plains
Indians, whom these Southeastern Indians felt were dangerous
and savage.

CHAPTER THREE

WHERE THE TRAIL
OF TEARS ENDS

*These wild Indians depend almost altogether upon the chase
for support, and their glory is war. We are anxious to pursue
a different course. Our object is to cultivate the land, to
support our families by our industry, and to preserve the
peace not only with our white, but with our red brothers.*

CREEK CHIEF ROLEY MCINTOSH
October 29, 1831

With the election of Andrew Jackson as president and passage of
the Indian Removal Act in 1830, the United States government
compelled the Five Major Tribes to sign removal treaties in which
they exchanged their lands in the east for lands in Indian Territory.
It mattered little that most of the treaties were signed under some
form of duress and that usually only a small fraction of the people
signed them over the objections of the majority. Once signed, the
government began removing these Indians to the west over what
became for many the "Trail of Tears." Forced removal for the Civilized Tribes began with the Choctaws in 1830 and ended with the
Cherokees in 1838–39. Removal of any one of the Five Major Tribes

was not done in a single expedition and should not be thought of as such. Southeastern Indians had been straggling west for years, and now some, seeing the future all too well, left before the government could remove them, while a few managed to stay behind after the Trail of Tears. Even the government's removal was often done in stages over a period of months, and in some cases, years. No matter; while the Southeastern Indians had raised many objections to removing to the west, one of the greatest was their fear of living in such proximity to the "wild Indians" of the plains. To overcome this objection and speed their removal, the government guaranteed to protect them from all enemies.[1]

So throughout the 1830s the peoples of the Civilized Tribes took their assigned places in Indian Territory. The Cherokees settled in the northeastern part of what is today Oklahoma, with the Cherokee Outlet lying roughly between the thirty-sixth and thirty-seventh parallels and extending from the Arkansas border to the one-hundredth meridian. The Creeks and Seminoles settled south of the Cherokees, initially sharing lands roughly between the thirty-fifth parallel and the Canadian River, their territory also extending west as far as the one-hundredth meridian. Most of the Creeks lived in the eastern part of the their territory, with the Lower Creeks on the Arkansas River and the Upper Creeks on the Canadian River. The Seminoles were assigned lands further west, in the central part of present-day Oklahoma, between the Canadian River and the North Fork of the Canadian. They eventually separated their lands from those of the Creeks in a treaty signed in 1845. The Choctaws and Chickasaws received land between the Canadian River in the north and the Red River on the south. Though they held the lands in common, the more populous Choctaws took land in the eastern part of their territory, while the Chickasaws received land further west, virtually on the frontier with the Plains Indian peoples. As one Chickasaw woman claimed, "The Choctaws gave the western part of the land allotted to them to the Chickasaws because they were afraid of the Comanches who were their neigh-bors to the west." It would not be until 1855 that the Chickasaws separated their land and government from those of the Choctaws.[2]

By early 1832, eastern Indians in Indian Territory numbered 2,500 Creeks; 6,000 Choctaws; 3,500 Cherokees; 3,000 Delawares; 1,800 Kickapoos; 1,500 Shawnees; 400 Piankashaws, Kaskaskias, and Peorias; 350 Weas; and 340 Senecas.[3] As they took their place in Indian Territory, these removed Indians had to reunify their nations, rebuild their societies, and find some way of dealing with their Plains Indian neighbors.

In fact, it was this fear of the Indians to the west that almost upset the government's placement of the removed Indians in Indian Territory and caused serious land quarrels among the dif-ferent removed nations. From the start, the Creeks, many of whom believed that Indian Territory would prove nothing more than a cemetery for them, demanded land in the eastern part of Indian Territory because of their fear of the "wild tribes." The Creek exploring parties had accepted lands west of the Verdigris River and north of the Canadian River. But when the first removed Creeks arrived in Indian Territory, their agent settled them east of the Verdigris and north of the Arkansas River in the northeastern part of Indian Territory because it was easier to provision them by way of the Arkansas River than the Canadian River. Also, they would be closer to the protection provided by Cantonment Gibson. Unfortunately, this was on lands claimed by and designated for the Cherokees. The Cherokees were not happy with Creek squatters on their land and demanded that the government oust the Creeks from Cherokee territory. To make matters worse, by 1831 about one-third of the entire Creek Nation lived on land claimed by the Cherokees. Wth more emigrants on the way, the government urged the Creeks to expand further west. Instead of moving closer to the "wild" Indians or leaving Cherokee lands, the Creek chiefs suggested that they exchange their promised lands west of the Verdigris and north of the Canadian with the Cherokees for the

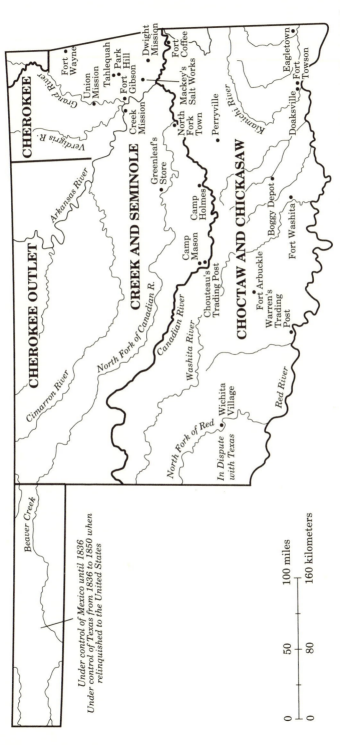

Map 2. Indian Territory, 1830–55. (Map from W. David Baird and Danney Goble, *The Story of Oklahoma* [University of Oklahoma Press, 1994])

lands the Creeks now occupied east of the Verdigris. The Cherokees would not agree, and it would take years to get this settled.[4]

While trying to keep as far east as possible, the Creeks also
demanded that the government coerce the Plains Indians into
making a peace with them. Appealing to the President, Creek
chiefs Roley McIntosh, Chilly McIntosh, and others explained that
the Creeks were "subject to depredations from small bands of
those Indians who live on our southern and western frontiers,
which keeps us in continual alarm for the safety of our people,
more particularly our women and children. These small bands
generally make their attacks at night, and before the alarm can be
given, their escape is almost certain as they are so well acquainted
with the country." To remedy this, the chiefs suggested that the
government appoint a friend of theirs, Colonel Auguste P. Chouteau
of Saint Louis, as a commissioner to hold councils with the "wild"
Indians in order to make a peace.[5] To protect themselves until
peace could be secured, the Creeks asked for the government to
supply them with rifles.[6]

The removed Indians had good reason to be fearful, for the
Plains Indians did raid their homesteads. The Osages continued to
cause trouble for the Cherokees and Creeks, especially as the herds
of buffalo dwindled on their small reservation and they were
reduced to virtual starvation.[7] Besides the Osages, Pawnees, Wichitas, Comanches, and Kiowas, as well as other western Indians, also
raided far to the east.[8] Essentially, the Southeastern Indians had
been removed to within striking distance of Indian peoples who
felt that their long-claimed territory was being invaded by these
removed Indians and who were ready to defend it. They also
viewed warfare and raids as a way to acquire wealth, status, and
power. Removed Indians had at one time felt this same way, but
for many of the progressives, war for wealth, status, and power
was "uncivilized." Besides, the Creeks' defeat in 1814 by Andrew
Jackson had convinced many of the futility of war and had hastened
their acculturation to an American life-style.

For the Comanches and Kiowas, who had never been defeated by whites, the 1830s were flush times, and they were at the height of their power. The Spanish had been ousted from North America. The Mexicans proved ineffectual in dealing with them. The Texans were busy with their own revolution and independence. The Americans were far to the east. Traders periodically visited them, bringing them guns, ammunition, and other manufactured goods in exchange for hides and horses. And there were plenty of buffalo to hunt. Even such semisedentary peoples as the Wichitas and Pawnees lived this good life with little interference. Then, onto the eastern margins of their territory came large numbers of agriculturally oriented removed Indians who would provide both problems and opportunities for the Plains Indians.

As the Creeks and Choctaws so accurately pointed out, the initial relationship between the removed Indians and the Plains Indians was one of violence. Several things contributed to this. First, the Plains Indians saw these removed Indians as invaders. Warfare to take territory or deny other peoples the use of its resources was not uncommon among the Plains Indians. When the Comanches entered the Southern Plains during the late seventeenth century, they fought the Apaches for control of it, finally wresting it from them after years of conflict. The Plains Indians resented the large numbers of Southeastern Indians settling on lands they had long seen as their own and struck back. The Wichitas were particularly incensed at the government's assignment of the Choctaws and Chickasaws to lands along the northern bank of the Red River, which completely ignored the fact that the Wichitas had been living in that area for hundreds of years. Until they learned how to appeal directly to the government for redress, they fought back in the only way they knew.[9]

Another problem between the two different types of peoples was one of kinship, or rather, lack of it. No matter whether they were a Plains hunter-gatherer or a Southeastern agriculturalist, the family was the most basic and most important unit of society.

From birth, each individual was part of a large extended family and enveloped in an extensive web of kinship. Indian peoples recognized three types of kinship: blood kin, affinal kin, and fictive kin. Blood kin were those people biologically related to a person, such as mother, father, sister, brother, and so on. But even this was not as simple as it appears. All Southeastern Indians were members of matrilineal clans in which a person's blood relatives were only those on his mother's side. Therefore, a Choctaw father was not really his children's "blood" kin. Conversely, since a person could not marry someone of his or her own clan, all members of the same clan, no matter how distant, could be considered blood kin.[10] Neither Comanches nor Kiowas possessed clans of this sort, as most Plains Indians lived in small, roving bands isolated from others and thus making clans unnecessary and unwieldy. Still, kinship was equally important among them, and a person could not marry anyone considered kin. The Comanches considered as blood kin those people extending three generations senior to them and two generations junior to them. For the Kiowas, it was not much different.[11]

Affinal kin were those people related by marriage, such as husbands and wives. Because Southeastern Indians used a matrilineal descent system, men essentially married into a woman's family and often even into her and her parents' household, though this did not mean he was necessarily subservient to them. A wealthy Southeastern man might even be able to take several wives. Among the Comanches and Kiowas, plural marriage was common and often anticipated and preferred. On the plains, life could be short, and it was entirely possible for a wife or husband to lose his or her spouse to any number of mishaps. If a Comanche or Kiowa man's wife died, he was expected to marry his wife's sister. Similarly, if a Comanche or Kiowa woman's husband died, it was expected that the dead man's brother would marry her. In this way the widower received another wife as his helpmate and reconnected to his in-laws' family, and the widow as well as the dead man's in-laws were once again provided for. Because it was so well understood in Comanche and Kiowa society that brothers from one family might marry the sisters of another family, brothers- and sisters-in-law might share sexual favors with each other. Since a man knew that if he died his brother would marry his wife, he often "shared" his wife with his brother. Conversely, a wife, knowing that if she died, her husband would take her sister as a wife, often shared her husband with her sister. So for Comanches and Kiowas, marriage groups made up of brothers and sisters from different families took the place of clans, with a woman calling her spouse and his brothers "husband" and her sister's children "son" or "daughter."[12]

Fictive, or ritual, kinship also played an important role with both Southeastern and Plains Indian peoples. In this instance, people who were not related through blood or marriage considered themselves kin. Among the Kiowas, young men might develop such a close relationship that they would call each other brother and treat each other's children as sons or daughters.[13] The Caddos, though agriculturalists, used the term *tesha* to denote a person not related by blood or marriage but who was thought of as a brother or sister.[14] The most common example of fictive kin was the adop- tion of outsiders by a family. Once adopted, they became recog- nized members of the community. This is an important point, because both Southeastern and Plains Indians normally viewed all peoples as either kin and community members or as strangers and nonkin. Strangers were dangerous and unpredictable, and since no kinship bonds existed with them, they were fair game for attacks, thefts, and swindles. Therefore, it behooved strangers to make kin- ship ties with other Indian peoples, and conversely, it was certainly in the best interests of a person to make kinship with powerful strangers. Southeastern and Plains Indians went to great lengths to adopt strangers into their families, often using elaborate adop- tion ceremonies, which included gift giving, pipe smoking, dancing, food sharing, and other rituals.[15]

All kin, no matter whether they were blood, affinal, or fictive, had reciprocal social obligations they were expected to uphold. Essentially, kin took care of kin and were supposed to do so in a generous and hospitable fashion. People expected to be fed by their kinspeople, be given gifts of various things, receive good counsel and advice, be protected from enemies, and even obtain active military assistance if needed. As seen among the Comanches, a brother might share the favors of a man's wife. Among the Caddos, if a person's tesha were in danger, that person was obligated to stand by the tesha even if it meant certain death. And if the tesha asked a person for any possession he owned, then that person was bound to give it. If refused, the relationship broke on the spot. Still, the burdens of kinship were not light and often onerous. Some people tried to manipulate the kinship bonds in their favor and some tried to avoid them altogether, but for the most part kinship obligations were taken seriously and usually upheld.[16]

Over the centuries, because of their close contact and their position within the same trade network, various bands and communities of Comanches, Kiowas, Wichitas, and Caddos had developed kinship bonds and alliances. Now, as the removed Southeastern Indians settled in Indian Territory, these Plains and Prairie Indians saw them as strangers and invaders. Violence often erupted, usually in the form of raids. A Comanche raiding party was usually only three or four young men; Kiowa raiding parties were normally a little larger. A young man wishing to make a raid would call all the other young warriors together and pass around a pipe, and all who wished to go with him took a draw upon the pipe. Men who had already distinguished themselves on raids had no problem recruiting companions, because it was believed that his "medicine" was good. For the raid, the men decked themselves and their favorites horses out in paint and feathers and made a circuit of the village, cantering before every lodge. If successful, the men would come back with a large drove of horses, captives, or metal goods.[17] A raid also gave them an opportunity to show their bravery.

Therefore, raiding was actually an economic activity, and from a successful one warriors gained wealth, prestige, status, and power. Raids, though, usually led to retaliatory attacks, and if someone was killed in a raid, then there was the obligation to take blood revenge on the killers or their people.

When it came to conflict between the Plains Indians and the removed Southeastern Indians, it was usually the Comanches, Kiowas, and Wichitas making the raids, and retaliation and blood revenge were taken by the Cherokees, Choctaws, Creeks, Chicka- saws, Delawares, Shawnees, and Kickapoos.[18] As one government official explained it: "The intercourse between those Prairie Indians, and the citizens of the United States, and with our Indians, as we may term them, has been little else than a series of mutual intrigues, and acts of destruction upon each other's property and persons."[19] Raids became so bad that the Choctaws, Cherokees, and Creeks demanded that the government create three new military posts north of the Red River.[20] Peter Pitchlynn, now a chief of the Choc- taws, tried his own hand at making peace with the Comanches and Kiowas when he made a three-month-long buffalo hunt on the plains in 1834, but his overtures failed.[21] Other officials, realizing that it might take more than talk to stop the raids of the western Indians, suggested replacing the mounted rangers then patrolling the frontier with dragoons.[22]

In August 1832, to avenge some of the raids upon their own peoples, a band of about one hundred Cherokees, Creeks, and Delawares decided to make a strike on the Comanches. The Creek chiefs managed to stop the participation of all their people, save one, in the raid. Down on the Red River, instead of finding the Comanches, the war party attacked a small band of Wichitas who had not been involved in any raids, killing three and capturing two. One of those killed was a young girl of thirteen. She had initially been taken prisoner, but she had been killed when a couple of Cherokees squabbled over who owned her. Killing her had put an end to the argument. The Creek government wanted to arrest and

try their man who went on the raids. When the Cherokees heard
of this, they taunted the Creeks as cowards and threatened them
with war if they did not support attacks on the western Indians. In
reality, Cherokee anger at the Creeks may not have been so much
over Creek refusal to fight the western Indians as over their con-
flicting land claims.[23]

The great muddle of Indians in Indian Territory, the problems
over land claims, but especially the raids and counterraids between
the Plains Indians and the removed Indians, finally brought government action. In 1832, Secretary of War Lewis Cass created the
Stokes Commission, which was composed of former North Carolina
governor Montfort Stokes, H. L. Ellsworth, Reverend J. F. Schermer-
horn, and Colonel Samuel C. Stambaugh, who served as secretary.
Cass charged the commission with a number of duties. These
included solving the land disputes between the Cherokees and the
Creeks, scouting out locations at which to put future removed
Indians, convincing the Osages to remove to Kansas, investigating
Indian education, and seeing if the Indians would exchange their
present annuities, which they held in perpetuity, for more limited
annuities of about twenty years. But the main object was to make
peace with the Plains Indians and convince them to stop raiding
the removed Indians. A party of mounted rangers would escort
them in their travels, and the commander at Fort Gibson was
ordered to comply with any requisitions the commissioners made
and furnish them whatever they required. The assistant commis-
sary at Fort Gibson would be ordered to supply any provisions for
the Indians the commissioners felt were needed.[24]

The Stokes Commission got under way in 1833 and began trying
to untie the Gordian knot of Indian problems. The Osage problem
seemed the most serious, and the commissioners first turned their
attention to preventing Osage attacks and convincing the Osages
to go live on the reservation designated for them. By the early 1830s
many Osages still squatted on lands claimed by the Cherokees, and
Osage warriors continued raiding Cherokee, Creek, and Choctaw

farms and hunting parties. Plains Indians had their own complaints about the Osages. In 1833, known by the Indians as the "year of the falling stars" because of brilliant meteor showers, a band of Osages attacked a Kiowa camp while most of the men were away hunting. The Osages captured the Kiowas' sacred tai-me medicine bag and took a few prisoners, but killed most of the women and children, cut off the heads of the dead, and left them in metal pots for the Kiowa men to find. The Kiowas have ever since known this place as Cut Throat Gap.[25] Still, it was the removed Indians who complained the most about the Osages and demanded that the government force an Osage peace. Despite numerous councils, the raids continued unabated, although almost all Osage annuities went to pay claims made against them by the Cherokees and Creeks.[26]

The Stokes Commission met with the Osage chiefs and principal men at Fort Gibson in March 1833. In deference to Cherokee complaints that the Osages still lived on lands that had been given to the Cherokees, the commission tried to convince the Osages to sign a new treaty. They explained that all the land the Osages presently lived on had been guaranteed to the Cherokees and that the Osages should now leave the reservation given to them in the 1825 treaty and accept a new one in Kansas along the Neosho River. Almost to a man the Osage chiefs refused, saying that the land in Kansas was worthless, that they wanted to remain on their present lands, and that the United States government had yet to keep any of the promises made to them. Black Dog, one of Clermont's principal men, summed up the Osage point of view by saying, "You want our land for another nation. I suppose you owe them something, and wish to pay them with our land. Now, I believe our great father has much money; and if you owe these Indians anything, pay them out of that money, and not with our land, which will make us poor and miserable."[27]

The Osages' refusal to sign a new treaty was a blow to the commission and angered the Cherokees. The Cherokees, Choctaws, and Creeks still complained that their people were being murdered by the Osages, and it was with great difficulty that Stokes and Colonel Matthew Arbuckle, commander of Fort Gibson, prevented a war from breaking out between the Osages and the Cherokees in May 1833. Still, if the commission could not resolve the problem of the Osages living on Cherokee land, they were able to arrange a peace between the Pawnees, Otoes, and Omahas and the Osages, Creeks, and Cherokees. With this small success the commission turned its attention to making a peace with the Comanches, Kiowas, and Wichitas.[28]

Creating a peace between the Indians of the Southern Plains and the removed Indians and the United States was a necessity if the government's vision for Indian Territory was to become a reality. And the government had a grand vision. The way the United States saw it was that as removed Indians moved into Indian Territory, they would create their own governments. These governments would form a General Council. The council would create an Indian multinational police force, which, backed by the United States Army, would support the governments and council and enforce the laws by arresting lawbreakers belonging to any of the various nations represented in the council. Eventually, the President would appoint a territorial governor and secretary. At some point, when enough removed Indians had settled in Indian Territory and the Plains Indians had made peace and adapted to "civilized" ways, the United States would convene a conference with the all these Indian chiefs, and they would create an Indian confederacy. Still, the government recognized that the biggest hindrance to this was the Plains Indians. Until they could be induced to make peace and adopt farming, the army would have to keep troops stationed at Fort Leavenworth, Fort Smith, Fort Gibson, and Fort Towson. The forts could also be instrumental in getting the Plains Indians to become "civilized," as farmers around them could show the Plains Indians how to farm and raise stock. But all this hinged on peace between the Plains Indians and the removed Indians.[29]

Some members of the commission hoped the Comanches, Kiowas, and Wichitas would come to Fort Gibson in eastern Indian Territory for a council. Montfort Stokes was skeptical. He considered the Comanches the "Arabs of the great prairie," and to get them to come to Fort Gibson one "might as well attempt to collect last year's clouds. . . . They are all out on their fall hunt; they are at war with the Delawares, the Shawnees, and the Osages, who are now out upon the same great western prairie; and they are compelled for their own safety to keep their bands together."[30] Instead, Stokes, showing an insightful knowledge of Indian diplomacy, believed the Comanches would see through any promises made to them and could only be approached with large quantities of presents, something the commission did not have on hand. The best way, Stokes believed, would be for the government to purchase a few of the Comanches and Kiowas held captive by the Osages and to restore them to their people. Along with this the government should throw in a few suitable presents and provide a contingent of dragoons to escort the Indians safely to and from Fort Gibson. If this were done, it would show the good will of the United States government, and the Indians might be induced to come and make peace.[31]

The government saw merit in Stokes's recommendation. In the summer of 1834, Brigadier General Henry Leavenworth, commander of the Left Wing of the Western Department, and Colonel Henry Dodge, commander of the Regiment of Dragoons that had been created the year before to replace the mounted rangers, led about five hundred dragoons and collateral personnel to the plains. Their objective was to meet with the Comanches, Kiowas, and Wichitas and urge them to make peace. Along with them went eleven Osages, eight Cherokees, six Delawares, and seven Senecas serving as guides, hunters, interpreters, and representatives of their nations with authority to make peace with the Plains Indians. Hoping to induce the Plains Indians to make peace, the expedition brought along two Indians girls, one an eighteen-year-old Wichita and the other a fifteen-year-old Kiowa, who had been captives of the Osages. Famed painter George Catlin tagged along and provided some of the earliest visual records of the Indians of the Southern Plains.[32]

From a soldier's point of view, Dodge's Expedition, as it was called, was a disaster. General Leavenworth was injured during a buffalo hunt and soon died. The dragoons, dressed in woolen uniforms, suffered terribly in the plains' heat, with more than three hundred men and one hundred horses dying or falling too ill to perform their duties. From a diplomatic point of view, the expedition was a tremendous success. On July 21 the expedition reached a Taovaya Wichita village of over two hundred lodges on Red River. Lieutenant T. B. Wheelock, who kept a journal of the expedition, was impressed with the Wichitas' cornfields, which he described as "well cultivated, neatly enclosed, and very extensive, reaching in some instances several miles. We saw also here, melons of different kinds, squashes, &c."[33] Although the Taovaya principal chief was not there, over the next couple of days Weterrashahro, chief of the Waco Wichitas, whose village was nearby, met in council with Dodge. Weterrashahro exchanged a white boy the Wichitas had captured the previous spring for the captured Wichita girl, whose village this was. Dodge urged the Taovayas to make peace with the removed Indians. Afterwards, each of the representatives of the Osages, Cherokees, Delawares, and Senecas made a short speech, declaring their peoples' desire for peace with the Wichitas. Dodge asked the Taovaya chief to accompany him back east in order to meet the President, but the Taovaya demurred, saying it would be difficult to pass through the thick timber that separated them from the white men. Still, "the Great Spirit has seen us, as we see now the white men, Cherokees, Osages, Delawares, and Senecas, as friends; we hope to remain so."[34]

Suddenly the council was almost disrupted when a band of twenty or thirty Kiowas dressed for war raced into camp. They had heard Dodge had Osages with him, and the Kiowas, still angry over the Osages' beheading of Kiowa men, women, and children in the previous year's raid, came to kill them. Dodge managed to calm the Kiowas when he returned the Kiowa girl to them, and soon more bands of Kiowas and Comanches arrived until there were over two thousand Plains Indians at the Taovaya village. In council with Weterrashahro, the Waco chief; Tawequenah, chief of the Comanche band; and Titchtochecha, chief of the Kiowa band, Dodge distributed presents to the chiefs and urged them to make peace with the removed Indians and to come with him to the East. All agreed, and when Dodge and his expedition started back toward Fort Gibson, Weterrashahro and two Taovaya warriors, Titchtochecha with fifteen Kiowas, and Tawequenah with five Comanches headed back with him, though all the Comanches save one soon left the troops and returned home.[35]

The expedition arrived back at Fort Gibson on August 24, the lone Comanche and the Wichita and Kiowa representatives still with it. On September 2 a three-day council between these Indians and the leaders of the Osages, Cherokees, Creeks, and Choctaws began. As they had on the plains, the removed Indians and the Plains Indians embraced, shook hands, smoked the pipe, exchanged gifts, and reiterated their desire for peace. Clermont of the Osages, initially cool to making peace with the Kiowas, eventually came around. The Kiowas now took this opportunity to ask Dodge if he could recover their sacred tai-me medicine bag, which had been taken by the Osages the year before. Dodge said he would try. He also explained that he did not have the authority to make a treaty with the Kiowas, Comanches, and Wichitas at present, but that federal commissioners would visit them in buffalo country next year to arrange one. He distributed gifts and medals and sent them back to their peoples to announce the visit. Still, it was the first time leaders of the removed Southeastern Indians met face-to-face with representatives of the Southern Plains Indians. Unfortunately, many of these representatives of the Plains Indians died of cholera on their journey home. Two of the surviving headmen believed they had been poisoned by Stokes, swearing they had seen the poison darting from his spectacle-covered eyes.[36]

In August 1835 a great council was held at Camp Holmes, which was specially constructed for this council not far from present-day Lexington, Oklahoma. The purpose, as Montfort Stokes understood it, was to arrange a peace between the United States and the Comanches and between "them and the Indian nations near them, and liable to suffer from their depredations, which include the Choctaws, Creeks, Cherokees, Osages, Senecas, and Quapaws."[37] Stokes was nervous, because he had received information that the Mexican government in Texas was preparing to make an attack against the Comanches and their allies using as auxiliaries Cherokees, Shawnees, Kickapoos, and Delawares living south of the Red River in Texas. If true, this would certainly upset any chances of making peace between the Southern Plains Indians and the removed Indians. Still, Stokes was not sure if the information was accurate and went on with the council anyway. When the council began in late August, over seven thousand Comanches, Kiowas, and Wichitas were encamped around the council grounds, while the chiefs and scores of representatives from the Choctaws, Creeks, Cherokees, Osages, Senecas, and Quapaws accompanied Stokes and General Matthew Arbuckle.[38]

For the removed Indians this was the chance to make peace with the Plains Indians who had caused them so much trouble, and they were not going to let it slip through their fingers. On August 22, Mushalatubbe, a chief of the Choctaw Nation, addressed the Plains chiefs, saying, "The talk we have had with each other, I like. It is a good one. I hope there will be no more killing of each other. If there be any killing, let it be by the falling of the limbs of trees."[39] Roley McIntosh, first chief of the Creeks, echoed these sentiments, saying:

> Brothers. . . . We are all of one color. . . . When we reached our new homes we heard of you in the west. We heard of

your way of living. Our forefathers used to live in the same way. We now live differently. . . . Our people will now travel the road from one town to another. They will be open and clear. With all the different people we have made peace, we have made roads to these houses. We will now extend these roads to your towns. . . . I give you this tobacco. When you go home, I want all your warriors to smoke of it, and when the white smoke ascends, altho [sic] I shall be at home and not see it, it will be the same as if I was present. These white beads are the emblem of peace, when you go home you must let all your people draw them through their hands. It will be the same as if I was shaking hands with them.[40]

Similar speeches urging peace were made by Black Dog, head warrior of Takhala's band of Osages; Thomas Brant of the Senecas; and Heckaton, chief of the Quapaws.[41]

On 24 August 1835, representatives of the United States, Comanches, Wichitas, Cherokees, Creeks, Choctaws, Osages, Senecas, and Quapaws signed a peace treaty. The Kiowas, who had begun the council, had left a few days earlier without signing the treaty, probably because of the hard feelings they still harbored against the Osages. The treaty also stipulated that there would be free intercourse between the signatories and safe passage through each others' territories, that the Comanches and Wichitas would treat other removed Indians who had not signed the treaty as friends, and that if any difficulty arose among those Indian peoples who had signed the treaty, such as murder or horse and cattle theft, then the other tribes, or the United States, would try to see justice done. Two years later, the Kiowas, Kiowa-Apaches, and Tawakoni Wichitas signed an almost identical treaty with the United States, Creeks, and Osages at Fort Gibson on May 26, 1837.[42]

On the surface the treaties were merely ones of peace, with no mention of land cessions by the Comanches, Wichitas, and Kiowas to the United States or to the removed Indians. Still, the Comanches,

Wichitas, and Kiowas probably did not realize the full implications of the treaty and that by signing it they had theoretically given up thousands of square miles of land they traditionally had claimed as their own. When the Southeastern Indians signed their removal treaties with the United States, they exchanged their lands in the East for lands in the West. Never recognizing Plains Indian owner-ship of the land, and basing their own claim to ownership on the Louisiana Purchase, the United States "gave" the Southeastern Indians lands in Indian Territory. Technically, Cherokee, Creek, Seminole, Choctaw, and Chickasaw lands extended west to the one-hundredth meridian, while the Comanches, Kiowas, and Wichitas claimed lands as far east as the Cross Timbers, which lay mainly between the ninety-sixth and ninety-seventh meridians. By making peace with the removed Indians, promising not to molest them or their property and guaranteeing free access and passage through their country, the Comanches, Wichitas, and Kiowas, in the minds of U.S. officials, essentially recognized the removed Indians' right to the land. One of the Wichita chiefs, Kosharoka, may have had an inkling of what the treaty actually meant when during the Camp Holmes council he said, "There is one thing I have to ask of you. I do not want any one to settle here [in the Camp Holmes vicinity]. If they do they will drive off the game, and this is the only place we have to come for it." The Southern Plains Indians and the removed Indians probably went away from the council certain in the knowledge that the lands they claimed were recognized and respected by the other.[43]

It did not take long for the Comanches to realize differently. In late December 1835, Stokes received word that the Comanches had torn up the Camp Holmes treaty and contemplated attacking the Coffee Trading House located on the upper Red River. The reason, as Stokes was told, was that the Comanches felt the government had been very stingy with the presents given to them at Camp Holmes. The three hundred dollars' worth of goods given out to Comanches and Wichitas was not nearly what they expected or needed. Second, the "treaty had laid open their hunting grounds to our friendly Indians who were killing up their game."[44]

While the Cherokees, Creeks, Choctaws, Chickasaws, and Seminoles might have legal claim to the land in the eyes of the United States government, it was smaller nations, such as the Delawares, Shawnees, and Kickapoos, who were crowding the Southern Plains Indians and actually settling on lands claimed by them. These three nations, particularly the Delawares and Shawnees, once lived far to the east in New Jersey, Pennsylvania, and Ohio. Over the years, warfare and migration had fractured these nations into several separate and autonomous bands. As early as 1790, large bands of Shawnees and Delawares had moved to the area near Cape Girardeau, Missouri, where bands of Kickapoos soon joined them. Some bands moved to the White River of northern Arkansas. In the early 1820s, a portion of the Missouri and Arkansas Shawnees, Delawares, and Kickapoos migrated into Mexican Texas, and many eventually settled in eastern Texas and near the Red River. By 1825, other bands of Missouri Shawnees, Delawares, and Kickapoos migrated further west to the Kaw River in present-day Kansas. In 1832 the remaining Missouri Shawnees, Delawares, and Kickapoos signed a treaty with the government that extinguished their claims to land in Missouri and removed them to the Kaw River reservations in the northeastern corner of Kansas. Some bands of Shawnees, Delawares, and Kickapoos from Kansas, unhappy with their land there, migrated south onto the lands of the Five Major Tribes. About the same time, a mixed contingent of Shawnees and Senecas from Ohio removed to present-day northeastern Oklahoma. Essentially, then, by the mid-1830s three large but separate divisions of Shawnees, Delawares, and Kickapoos existed: one in Kansas, one in Indian Territory proper, and one in eastern Texas.[45]

It was mainly the Shawnee, Delaware, and Kickapoo bands in Texas that caused the most problems for the Plains Indians and the Southeastern removed nations. Many Texas Shawnees, Delawares and Kickapoos crossed the Red River and hunted on lands claimed by the Comanches, Wichitas, Chickasaws, and Choctaws. Later, during the Texas Revolution and in the anti-Indian feelings that swept across Texas after its independence, many of these bands left Texas of their own accord to settle in Indian Territory, often on lands the United States government had already designated for other Indians.

Over the next few years problems between the Plains Indians and these removed Indians became even more heated. In early 1836 several Comanche chiefs complained that the Delawares were hunting on their land and had gone so far as to kill one of the Comanches' principal men. The Comanches wanted to abide by the Camp Holmes treaty, their chiefs declared, but if the government could not or would not stop these injustices, then they were determined to take up arms against the Delawares. Equally bad, the chiefs pointed out, was that a small combined party of Choctaws and Quapaws robbed three of their lodges and stole twenty-two horses and mules. The Comanches wanted their complaints laid before the commissioners at Fort Gibson and demanded restitution for the outrages as stipulated in the treaty. The Tawakoni Wichitas and Waco Wichitas had their own complaints, but mainly about the Osages. They were determined to go back and retake land the Osages had pushed them from several years before.[46]

By 1837 things had gotten so bad that a war between various Indian nations appeared imminent. In January, Comanche chief Ishacoly, who had been the principal Comanche signatory of the 1835 Camp Holmes treaty, visited the Chouteau trading house located at Camp Holmes, since renamed Camp Mason, and vented his anger. He felt he had received numerous insults and injuries from the whites since the signing of the treaty and was determined to return in the spring and destroy the trading house. He also warned the Osages not to be there when he returned or they would receive similar treatment. P. L. Chouteau, subagent for the Osages and proprietor of the trading house, investigated Ishacoly's threats and found that the chief meant what he had said. Already the

Delawares were preparing for war with Ishacoly's Comanches. Recently a Delaware man and his family, along with a couple of Waco Wichitas, had visited Ishacoly's camp to trade, but the Delawares had barely escaped with their lives. Only the intercession of the Wichitas had saved them, but not before the Comanches took the family's horses. A Shawnee trading band received similar treatment. In response to Ishacoly's threats, scattered bands of Delawares began uniting to form stronger camps, while many sent their women and children north to the safety of their relatives in Kansas.[47]

Even government officials realized that the problem stemmed from the fact that that part of the plains was now a virtual common hunting ground. Some officials had predicted this situation and urged that "all emigrating Indians should be restrained, as far as possible, from those buffalo and beaver-hunting expeditions" on the plains.[48] These lands had long been occupied by the Comanches and Wichitas, who believed that only they had the privilege to hunt on them. The Creeks and Choctaws, by right of government grant, owned a large part of the country, while the Delawares, Shawnees, and Osages also considered it their right to hunt there. It was only natural "that depredations upon the property of each other will take place, which must soon lead to collisions."[49]

Though Texas had gained its independence the year before, tense relations between it and Mexico still ran high, and the United States feared Indians might be drawn into the continuing conflict. To prevent this, the government felt it best to uphold Ishacoly's claims. William Armstrong, acting superintendent of the Western Territory, instructed his agents to tell the Delawares, Shawnees, and Osages they were wrongly intruding onto Comanche territory and should return to their own country. Similarly, Choctaw and Creek hunters were told that although they might have the legal right to hunt on that part of the plains or search for stolen horses there, they should also return to and remain on their own lands in eastern Indian Territory until things could be worked out. At the same time, the Comanche grievances should be redressed, but it should also be explained to them that the United States had purchased this land from the various tribes and guaranteed the exclusive right to it to the removed Indians, who intended to settle and farm it. Even with all this, Armstrong worried that war might still break out, because the Delawares might not take his instructions with good grace. He considered them some of the best warriors on the plains, disposed to war, and people given to hunting over a large territory extending as far as the Trinity River in Texas. The Osages could also cause problems, as the Comanches held them "in great terror."[50]

While the Comanches complained about the removed Indians' hunting on lands they claimed, conversely, the Choctaws and Chickasaws complained about the Plains Indians', as well as other removed Indians', hunting on lands that "legally" belonged to them. The area around the Washita and Blue Rivers, which lay in the area ceded to the Chickasaws, seemed particularly bountiful and attracted Delaware, Shawnee, Kickapoo, Osage, Wichita, Caddo, and Comanche hunters.[51]

If trespassing hunters galled the Chickasaws and Choctaws, bands of both removed and Plains Indians flooding onto their lands from Texas scared them. In 1838, Mirabeau Lamar defeated incumbent Sam Houston for the presidency of the Republic of Texas and decided to do something about the large number of Indians living there. Bands of Comanches, Kiowas, Wichitas, Tonkawas, Caddos, and others had lived in Texas long before any white person had ever set foot there. Beginning in the late eighteenth century, bands of eastern Indians, such as Delawares, Shawnees, Kickapoos, Creeks, Choctaws, Chickasaws, and Cherokees, had settled in Texas. During his two-year tenure as president, Houston, who had once lived among the Cherokees, made numerous treaties with the Indians in which he tried to achieve peace by guaranteeing the Indians the rights to their lands. Lamar possessed a different view of Indian relations, believing that Houston's policy of reserving lands for the Indians limited white settlement

and therefore white economic prosperity. Knowing his consti-
tuents' belief that whites were racially superior to Indians, and
claiming that the Indians were agents and allies of Mexico, Lamar
promised to exterminate them. This helped secure his election, and
once inaugurated as Texas' second president, he instituted his
policy, initiating several wars with Indians. By 1840 almost all the
removed Indians in Texas had been forced into Indian Territory.[52]

Now Indians expelled from Texas settled on Chickasaw and
Choctaw lands, where they plundered ranches and farms of other
removed Indians. This posed a highly dangerous problem with the
new Republic of Texas. Many Texans already hated Indians and
always suspected they might side with Mexico in an attempt to
retake the former province. The Indians themselves fueled this
suspicion when a contingent of about eighty Cherokee, Caddo,
Delaware, and Kickapoo warriors visited Mexico City, received
weapons and rations, and killed six Texans on the road from Mier
to San Antonio. Even worse, bands of Delawares, Shawnees, and
Kickapoos who had been expelled from the republic now launched
raids into Texas from Chickasaw and Choctaw territory. As one
government official pointed out, these Indians "run into the Republic of Texas, kill and plunder the inhabitants and then flee into the
Choctaw nation where they kill the cattle and hogs and steal the
horses of the Choctaws and Chickasaws."[53] Although the Texas
government officially complained to the United States about these
raids, Texas settlers tried to solve the problem on their own.
Ignoring the international boundary, twice in the late summer of
1841 a heavily armed company of about eighty men crossed the
Red River, but instead of catching the Delaware, Shawnee, or Kickapoo raiders, they killed two Chickasaws and attacked several
Chickasaw homes.[54]

As bad as attacks by Texans were, Chickasaw agent G. P. Kingsberry worried mainly about the raids made by the Indians coming
out of Texas: "The different tribes of Indians, as they are driven out
of Texas, will have no place to go to and I think there is great

danger of the desperate and rascally men of the various tribes forming themselves into a separate band for the purpose of robbing and plundering the Indians . . . on this frontier." Already, the Chickasaws, he pointed out, "are now exposed to the depredations of all those wild roving tribes of Indians, and have already lost a considerable quantity of stock, and live constantly in fear of losing more." He reminded the government that it had promised to protect the removed Indians and suggested that some of the forts in eastern Indian Territory be moved farther west. Also, a fort should be erected on the Washita River to protect the Chickasaws and Choctaws and serve as a first line of defense against any warlike Indians who might approach the removed Indian settlements.[55]

As Delawares, Shawnees, Kickapoos, Caddos, Quapaws, Comanches, and others flocked to Chickasaw lands, thefts, raids, and killings were not far behind. The Chickasaws declared that until these people were removed from their territory, the Chickasaws would never be able to extend their settlements to their western boundaries. Kingsberry ordered the Shawnees, Delawares, and other removed Indians to leave Chickasaw lands and return to their own territory. But he did not think they would ever leave unless the army sent a company of dragoons to force them.[56]

Kingsberry was right; they would not leave. In fact, the Delawares, Kickapoos, and Shawnees made threats of their own, saying that if they were forced off this land, before they left they would plunder the country. Not only that, they had made alliances with the Comanches, Wichitas, and Caddos and so could raise as many warriors as the Choctaws could. But they would wait until they saw what the Choctaws planned to do before they made any move.[57] The Choctaws and Chickasaws were not intimidated, and the Choctaw General Council, which included representatives of Chickasaws, ordered the Delawares, Shawnees, and Kickapoos to leave their lands by March 1, 1841. If they did not, the Choctaws and Chickasaws would raise five hundred warriors to make them leave.[58] Many Choctaws looked forward to this "brush," certain that they would "put it on to them."[59]

Hoping to prevent any hostilities, General Matthew Arbuckle at Fort Gibson promised the Delawares, Shawnees, and Kickapoos that if they left the Chickasaw and Choctaw lands and went back to their respective lands, he would provide them with provisions.[60] When this failed, the army set up a council between the Choctaws and Chickasaws and the Delawares, Shawnees, and Kickapoos in May 1841. The Delawares, Shawnees, and Kickapoos initially refused to leave, saying they would "make bullets whistle" before they would go. Captain B. D. Moore, who set up the council, asked the Choctaw chiefs how long it would take them to furnish warriors to help the dragoons remove the Indians. Only a few days, the Choctaws answered. The next day, the Delawares, Shawnees, and Kickapoos returned to the council and announced they would leave the lands in thirty days.[61]

While war had been averted, bad feelings remained among all involved. Rather than going back to Kansas where most of their peoples lived, the Delawares and Shawnees were going north only to Creek country, where they were welcomed, while the Kickapoos were removing northeast to the Cross Timbers. What with all the bad feelings; the influence the Delawares, Shawnees, and Kickapoos had with the Plains Indians; and the wealth of the Choctaws and Chickasaws, government officials felt it was only a matter of time before actual hostilities broke out. To prevent this, William Armstrong, the head of the Western Superintendency of the Office of Indian Affairs, urged that a fort be established at the mouth of the Washita River and a contingent of dragoons stationed there.[62]

If the Chickasaws and Choctaws felt they had solved their intruder problem by getting the Delawares, Shawnees, and Kickapoos to leave, they were sadly mistaken. In fact, when Captain B. D. Moore and his dragoons arrived at the mouth of the Blue River to hold the council, they found large bands of Caddos, Quapaws, Cherokees, and Coushatta Creeks living in the area. Moore explained that they were on lands claimed by the Chickasaws and Choctaws and gave them until November 1, 1841, to leave. He was not worried too much about the Cherokees, Creeks, and Quapaws, as they all had reservations established for them and could return to them. The Caddos posed a much thornier problem. About two hundred Caddo men, women, and children lived north of the Red River near Fort Towson, but they had no lands to return to. In 1835 the United States government had persuaded the Caddos to give up their lands in Louisiana and Arkansas, but instead of providing them with lands in Indian Territory, the government merely stipulated that they remove to Mexican Texas. With the Texas Revolution and Texas' refusal to recognize Indian lands, the Caddos now had no home. As Captain Moore saw it, if the Caddos had no land to call their own, "they will be continually harassing our frontier and intruding on the lands of the border Indians. They are at war with Texas, and not on the most friendly terms with Mexico, consequently have no other refuge." Since they were inclined to agriculture and "civilization," he suggested that the government assign them a small tract of land on the Red River west of the Washita.[63] Nothing came of Moore's suggestion, and it would be another twenty years before the Caddos got their land.

If other Indians hunting and settling on their lands outraged the Chickasaws and Choctaws, horse and stock theft plagued the country and angered all peoples in Indian Territory. Government officials urged the Indians to report any horse thefts to their agents or government authorities, who would then handle restitution, and not just steal horses from someone else to make up for their losses.[64] Delawares posed a problem for the Comanches, as did the Pawnee Mahas from Kansas and Nebraska, but the Osages seemed to steal horses from everyone. Southeastern removed Indians, such as the Creeks, constantly complained about Osages stealing their horses and cattle. Northern removed Indians, such as the Kickapoos and Delawares, also complained and sometimes retaliated by killing Osage raiders. Comanche chief Tabaqueena, one of the signatories of the Camp Holmes treaty, reported that the Osages, whom they now considered friends, often came to their country to hunt, but when they left they frequently took Comanche horses.[65]

Tabaqueena's complaints spurred the government to investigate his charges. A. P. Chouteau, who often served the government
as an intermediary with the Plains Indians, spoke with Osage chief
Clermont, who admitted the charge was true but blamed the horse
thefts on young men of both his and Black Dog's bands. According
to Chouteau, Clermont explained to him that the chiefs had little
or no control over the young men, and "it is not in their power to
prevent them from repeating the acts." While the Osages wanted
to continue their friendship with the Comanches, he did not believe
he and his chiefs could prevent the young men from stealing
Comanche horses in the future. Clermont proposed to Chouteau
that an example be made of the young men and suggested they be
arrested, confined in cells at Fort Gibson, or even better, "be compelled to ride on a wooden horse during the day and confined to
the cells at night." Chouteau believed this treatment might have
the desired effect and recommended it.[66]

One of the problems of Clermont and other Plains Indian chiefs,
and something that often frustrated those people who had to deal
with those nations, was that a Plains Indian chief's power was
extremely limited. While certain families may have been looked
upon as ones that traditionally produced leaders, in reality a Plains
chief gained power not so much from heredity but through prac-
ticing such virtues as bravery, fortitude, generosity, and wisdom.
If a man eventually displayed all these virtues, the people of the
band bestowed power upon him and he governed through his
moral authority. His power increased as word of his virtues grew;
as his success in raids, hunting, and diplomacy continued; and as
he became recognized as a man who provided for his people. By
this, more and more people would be attracted to his band and the
easier it became for him to sway the opinion of other bands and
chiefs. Since his people conferred power upon a chief that he
maintained by his success, it could be withdrawn by continued lack
of success. This meant that a chief's power was severely limited. He
could rarely order his people to do or not do something, but only

advise. This was one reason chiefs had trouble keeping in line young men, who saw raids and horse thefts as ways to increase their status and display their own virtues. Because the chief could coerce his followers only at certain times, as when actually on a raid or hunt, any persons or groups who disagreed with the chief's policies could withdraw to another band or even form their own band and strike out on their own. Because of this, there were scores of Comanche, Kiowa, and Osage bands and chiefs. And for peace to take place, it would have to be made with each band of every nation, and even then it could not be guaranteed as long as chiefs could not control their young men.[67]

This proved a problem as large numbers of eastern agriculturally oriented Indians settled in Indian Territory during the 1830s and came into contact with large numbers of hunting-gathering Indians of the plains. Before this, the two peoples had little contact with each other and so developed few kinship relations. So as they came into contact, each viewed the other as strangers. The Plains Indians saw the removed Indians as invaders, while the removed Indians viewed the Plains Indians as warlike savages. Raids, revenge killings, and retaliatory attacks flickered along this Indian-Indian frontier for years. By the end of the decade, some removed Indians, such as the Delawares, Shawnees, and Kickapoos, who were actually rather similar to the Caddos and Wichitas in that they were bands that combined hunting and gathering with agriculture, began to make peace with the Plains Indians. The Five Major Tribes, who had already developed republican governments and written constitutions, found they had little in common with these peoples nor with the Comanches and Kiowas on the plains. Tired of these "wild" Indians settling on their lands, stealing their horses, and attacking their settlements, during the 1840s and 1850s the Five Tribes embarked on a policy of holding councils in which they could make peace with the Plains Indians while teaching them how to become "civilized."

CHAPTER FOUR

COUNCILS, TRADE, AND CAPTIVES

*The Creeks have, at considerable expense, taken great pains
to conciliate the prairie tribes, and in my opinion, their efforts
should be encouraged and assisted by the government.*

WILLIAM ARMSTRONG
September 30, 1844

As the last Cherokees straggled into Indian Territory in 1839,
Indian removal came close to an end. Over the next two decades,
the Five Tribes created an amazing renaissance. They re-created
their national governments, reestablished their newspapers, and
rebuilt their schools and churches. It did not always come easy,
because there were serious political and social problems to overcome. Each of the Five Major Tribes split over who had the legal
authority to govern their nation, those people who had signed
removal treaties and voluntarily come to Indian Territory, or those
who had held out until forced to leave the Southeast over the Trail
of Tears. For the Cherokees, these schisms developed into a virtual
civil war.[1]

Also, divisions still existed between the progressives, who
wanted to reenter the market economy as soon as possible, and the

traditionalists, who hoped to reestablish their ancient ways without the meddling influence of whites. Despite traditionalists' desire to remain true to their old ways, progressive notions of economic prosperity dominated. As William Armstrong noted about the Choctaws in 1842, many "live in comfortable houses, and with very few exceptions even the poorer class have good substantial log cabins. They own large stocks of horses, cattle, hogs, and sheep. This constitutes the wealth of those who may be termed the poorer class. It is rare indeed to find a family that has not a good supply of stock. The richer class, in addition to stock, own many of them a number of slaves. These are engaged generally in cultivating cotton." The Choctaws, he pointed out, also had mechanics, blacksmiths, millers, and other craftsmen, while their farmers often grew corn to supply the troops at Fort Towson.[2] For the progressives, who actually ran the national governments of the Five Tribes, the only way to protect their peoples from the Plains Indians was to make exchange relations with them and invite the Plains chiefs to attend councils where they could arrange peace.

Over the next several decades, councils became the main way the Five Civilized Tribes tried to ensure peace with the Plains Indians. Chickasaw agent G. P. Kingsberry had proposed the notion of regular grand councils in 1837. He suggested that Indian Territory have a single superintendent who could settle the small problems that might arise between nations and that a general council be held every two years in which delegates of all the Indian nations would assemble, meet with government representatives, and discuss their needs. "The wild Indians of the north and extreme west could here meet his more civilized brethren of the south, and, seeing the beneficent effects of civilization in the improved conditions of these Indians, he might be induced to follow their example, and cultivate the arts of civilization himself."[3]

The first real attempt at a full-blown council among the various removed and Plains Indians came in October 1837. It was a failure from the start. First, the council was held too late in the year for the

Plains Indians to attend. For the Comanches and Kiowas, the council would have had to be held during the spring, late summer, or early fall, because they hunted buffalo during the summer, while during the winter they might be on a hunt or making raids against their enemies. Also, the Osages, Choctaws, and Chickasaws refused to attend.[4]

Two years later, in 1839, the Cherokees got wind that some Comanche bands wanted to hold another council with the government. The Cherokees saw this as an opportunity to bring about the council they had so wanted.[5] A bit of good fortune now came to the Cherokees' endeavors. In early June, a small contingent of twenty-four Comanche and Kiowa men and women arrived at Fort Gibson. Colonel A. P. Chouteau had planned to escort them to Washington, D.C., to meet the President. Unfortunately, Chouteau had died several months before, and now the Comanches and Kiowas refused to go. So the Cherokees played host to these representatives and apparently pitched their idea of holding a council with them in the late summer. To entertain them, the Cherokees and Choctaws held a stick ball game in which "the wild Indians were highly delighted," while Acting Superintendent of the Western Territory William Armstrong gave them gifts of blankets, cloth, and other goods worth almost seven hundred dollars.[6]

The Cherokees' council opened at Tahlequah, the Cherokee capital, in early September 1839. While details about it are sketchy, it appears that representatives of eleven Indian nations attended, mainly those Indians living in the eastern part of Indian Territory: the Five Major Tribes, smaller nations of removed Indians such as the Senecas, and such Prairie peoples as the Osages and Quapaws. Apparently no Plains Indians attended, because Tahlequah was too far east for these people to feel comfortable. Still, the council was important because it created an Indian multinational organization, a sort of Indian confederacy or United Nations. Cherokee John Looney was elected principal chief of the organization, while Roley McIntosh was elected second chief. Cherokee Joseph Vann was named head war chief and theoretically would be in command of the warriors and young men of all the attending nations. While the organization possessed little real power, and the attending nations were bound to it merely through the friendly feelings they had toward each other, it represented the United States government's vision for Indian Territory and laid the foundation for future cooperation among the Indian nations. Ironically, the large gathering of Indians in far northeastern Indian Territory terrified the citizens of Arkansas, and rumors flew that the Indians were preparing for a war upon the whites. Army troops rushed to Cherokee Territory in preparation for battle. Fortunately, Montfort Stokes explained the situation, calmed everyone's nerves, and sent the soldiers back home.[7]

This multinational Indian organization represented an attempt by the Five Tribes to bring some order to Indian Territory—something it needed, because during the 1840s numerous bands from scores of different Indian nations settled onto lands the Five Tribes claimed as their own. Despite the army's forcing various Indian bands off Chickasaw and Choctaw lands in 1841, the problem was back the next year. In 1842 at the behest of the United States government, Ethan Allen Hitchcock, a former army major general, toured Indian Territory to report on conditions there. He counted a large band of Shawnees from Texas living on Chickasaw lands on the Blue River, while about 175 Caddos lived in the Choctaw Nation. The Canadian River formed the boundary between the Creeks and the Chickasaws and Choctaws, and the Creeks had invited many of these bands of removed Indians to settle in the western part of their lands to serve as a barrier between them and the Comanches, Wichitas, and Kiowas. On the Canadian, just north of the confluence of Little River, lived another band of about 700 Shawnees, while near them were about 1,500 Kickapoos. Also about fifteen miles north of the Little River confluence lived 250 Quapaws and 600 Piankashaws, the latter also known as Miami Indians. The Piankashaws had been adopted by the Creeks and were regarded as part of the Creek Nation. Their chiefs attended the Creek General Council sessions, and the Creek chiefs had donated $120 from the previous year's Creek annuity for their upkeep. Hitchcock also found a family of Natchez Indians living in Creek Territory near the Arkansas River, while on the Blue River in Chickasaw country lived one or two families of Biloxi Indians.[8]

Though most of these Indians did not actually live on Chickasaw lands, the Chickasaws claimed they often attacked their homes and farms. The Chickasaws also complained that Comanches; Kiowas; the various Wichita bands, such as the Wacos, Taovayas, and Tawakonis; Caddo bands, such as the Hainais and the Caddos proper; and even some Creek Coushatta bands lived out in the westernmost parts of their lands and robbed and killed their citizens.[9] In response to Chickasaw complaints and their demands for protection, the United States established Fort Washita on the Washita River about fifteen miles north of its confluence with Red River. With this protection, Chickasaw families began moving into that area.[10]

Indian problems in Texas also caused headaches for the Chickasaws. Although Texas president Mirabeau Lamar's Indian wars expelled a number of immigrant Indians out of Texas and into Indian Territory, they also brought about almost constant warfare with the Comanches while costing the Texas treasury about $2.5 million. Texas citizens, now tired of Lamar's exterminationist policy, reelected Sam Houston as president in 1841. But Lamar had started something that could not easily be stopped, and the Comanches were particularly angry after the Council House Fight in 1840, in which Texas Rangers gunned down over thirty Penetaka Comanches, including twelve chiefs, during a peace conference in San Antonio. The Comanches, Kiowas, and Wichitas saw this as evidence of Texan treachery and a declaration of war against them. From that point on, most Comanche, Kiowa, and Wichita bands became implacable foes of the Texans, distinguishing between Americans, whom they liked, and Texans, whom they hated.[11]

The Comanches, Wichitas, and Kiowas now stepped up their raids against Texas settlements. The Comanches appealed to the Osages to join them in their attacks on Texas. Texans, as they had in the past and in violation of international law, sometimes made counterraids into Indian Territory, but also tried to garner their own Indian allies. If this were not bad enough, in 1842, Mexican forces raided into Texas, briefly capturing San Antonio. Not wanting to fight both the Mexicans and the Indians, and fearing the Plains Indians might side with Mexico, in June 1842, Major James R. Oneal of Texas appealed to the Chickasaws and Choctaws to join them in fighting the Plains Indians. Pointing out that these Indians had committed attacks in both Texas and the Chickasaw and Choctaw Nations, Major Oneal said, "We must arise and put them to the sword for they are a people that has forgotten God." He urged the Choctaws and Chickasaws to "rub up your guns, prepare yourselves with ammunition, rouse up your warriors, by your bugles, and we will teach those rogues and murderers that this policy is bad and we will let them know that we well resent their wicked deeds."[12]

Keeping peace among the Indians in Indian Territory being paramount to the United States, Chickasaw agent A. M. Upshaw urged the Chickasaws to ignore Oneal. Joining Texas in attacks on the Plains Indians, Upshaw pointed out, would bring the severest displeasure of the President. Whenever their warriors are needed, the President would call upon them. But they must never go to war until he called. If any Indians were to commit depredations in their nation, they should inform him or the officers at Fort Washita or Fort Towson, who would take steps to recover their property. Upshaw instructed the Chickasaw chiefs to tell their warriors "to stay home and attend to the cultivation of their corn, cotton, wheat & oats, attend closely to their horses, cattle, and hogs. Use no ardent spirits. And in a few years they will become intelligent, prosperous and happy."[13] While the Chickasaws possessed valid complaints against the Plains Indians, they may well have feared more an invasion by the Texans. Still, they took their agent's advice and did not join the campaign.

Fear of an escalation of the war between the Plains Indians and the Texans and the effects it might have on all the peoples of Indian Territory led Creek chief Roley McIntosh to call a "grand council." It was held in May 1842 on Deep Fork River in the Creek Nation, near present-day Eufaula, Oklahoma. Representatives from sixteen Indian nations attended, including the Creeks, Seminoles, Choctaws, Chickasaws, Kickapoos, Shawnees, Delawares, Senecas, Piankashaws, Osages, Quapaws, Caddos, Taovaya Wichitas, Kichais, Tawakonis, and Pawnees. The Cherokees were not officially represented at the council, but some of their principal men did attend the gathering. General Zachary Taylor, William Armstrong, and agents for a few of the Civilized Tribes represented the United States. Visibly absent were the Comanches and Kiowas. Still, about twenty-five hundred people attended, with an encampment stretching more than two miles. The Creeks, as hosts of the council, provided the twenty-five thousand pounds of beef and ten barrels of flour it took to feed everyone.[14]

Creek chief McIntosh hoped this council would provide a means by which the Plains Indians and the removed Indians might become acquainted each other, make peace, and adopt some rules on the restoration of stolen property. Pipes were smoked and speeches made, and all agreed to friendship. Superintendent Armstrong addressed the representatives and again urged them to refrain from getting involved in the affairs of Texas and not to take sides in the almost continuous raids and counterraids between Mexico and Texas that took place in the years after the Texas Revolution. General Taylor spoke to the representatives concerning whites held captive by the Plains Indians. The Kickapoos, Shawnees, and Delawares informed him that several were in the hands of the Comanches. He then announced that the government would pay a ransom for all white captives brought to Fort Gibson. Taylor's policy would have unforeseen consequences in the years to come.[15]

Particular attention was paid to the Wichita Taovayas, Kichais, and Tawakonis, as they lived closest to the frontier of the Civilized Tribes. The representatives of these three Wichita communities all stressed their desire for peace with Texas and asked Creek agent James Logan to arrange a ceasefire with Texas. Logan forwarded their request to Texas president Sam Houston. In return for their peaceful overtures, the chiefs of the Taovayas, Kichais, and Tawakonis, once the council ended, were escorted to Fort Gibson, where they received $206 worth of gifts from the government.[16]

The Creek influence at the council was conspicuous. Because the Creeks hosted the council, their delegation sat in a place of honor just outside the council house. In front of them sat their allies at the council, such as members of the remaining Civilized Tribes. The Cherokees were not officially attending the council, so their representatives could not sit in front of the Creek chiefs. The Seminoles, allied with the Creeks, could have sat in front of the Creeks, but their chief, Cooacochee, or Wild Cat, chose to remain aloof and did not take part in the ceremonies. So in front of the Creeks sat the chiefs of the Chickasaws and Choctaws—and also the Caddos.[17]

The Caddos had always been considered one of the Prairie peoples, similar to the Wichitas, Quapaws, and Osages, who used both horticulture and hunting and gathering. They were some of the first Indians east of the Great Plains to acquire horses and so had developed a strong plains orientation. They often went on buffalo hunts and became close friends and trade partners with the Wichitas and Comanches, but during the last years of the eighteenth and early years of the nineteenth centuries they fought fierce wars with the Choctaws and Chickasaws. Though they had long contact with the Spanish, French, and Americans, as late as 1819 American agents considered them wild, savage, and uncivilized. In 1835 they had signed a treaty with the United States in which they gave up their claims to land in Louisiana and Arkansas and agreed to move to Mexican Texas. Essentially, this treaty left them homeless, and it split them. Some bands moved to Texas to be near their Hasinai Caddo cousins, some briefly went to Mexico, and some moved to Indian Territory, where they settled north of the Red River near the Wichitas but on lands claimed by the Chickasaws. Now it appeared that the Caddos were gravitating away from the Comanches and their plains orientation and back toward the Southeast and a life-style espoused by the Five Civilized Tribes.[18]

The Creeks exerted their influence with the Caddos a few months later in July 1842, when the Creek chiefs appealed to those Caddos living in Indian Territory to be peaceful, reminding them that the Texans "are furnished with ammunition and guns, and the Indians, being poor, have none." The Creeks went on to advise the Caddos not to join with other Indians in attacks on Texas, to "have nothing to do in their wars and . . . not meddle in no way with either side." The Caddos in Indian Territory accepted the Creeks' advice, and they met with three Texas commissioners at Boggy Depot in Chickasaw Territory, made a peace treaty, and promised to try to convince the other Plains Indians also to make peace with Texas.[19]

By calling the grand council and drawing the Caddos into their orbit, the Creeks, of all the Five Major Tribes, appeared to be taking the lead in arranging diplomatic relations with the western Indians. Even the Plains Indians seemed to realize this. During the council, Black Dog's Osages had shown up with about twenty stolen horses. The Creeks admonished them to quit stealing horses, or they would be punished and the stolen horses would be taken from them. After the council, Black Dog's band went out to hunt buffalo on the plains and there stole about thirty horses from the Kiowas. The Kiowas immediately came to Creek chief Roley McIntosh for satisfaction. McIntosh sent messengers to the Osages demanding the return of the horses, which Black Dog did.[20]

Even Mexico recognized Creek influence with the Plains Indians and sent a representative to the Creeks in hopes of getting them to persuade the Plains Indians to side with Mexico against Texas. The Creeks refused Mexico's entreaty. In fact, Chief Roley McIntosh went so far as to urge the United States to annex Texas as a "means of civilizing a portion, if not all of the wild tribes of Indians who roam along our western border," thereby protecting the settlements of the Civilized Tribes.[21]

The Creeks' efforts to influence and pacify the Plains Indians occasionally suffered setbacks. Sometimes the Creeks themselves overplayed their hand. For years they had strongly warned the Wichitas and Caddos that their raids into Texas would bring retribution and that Texans would cross the Red River to attack them. When Texas sent a large delegation to the Wichitas in hopes of making peace, the Wichitas, remembering the Creeks' warning, thought the Texans had come to attack them. When they found out it was for peace, the Wichitas accused the Creeks of lying to them about the Texans.[22]

Even worse, an incident showed the Creeks that they might not have had as much influence with the Plains Indians as they hoped. In early February 1845, the Creek inhabitants of Toatprofker Town on Little River in the western part of the Creek Nation discovered signs that a large party of Plains Indians was nearby. Not recognizing the signs as coming from Indians they normally dealt with, the Creeks believed it was a raiding party come for their horse herds. Creek warriors began tracking the party, which now showed signs of trying to evade them. The Creeks eventually caught up with the alleged raiders, who took refuge on a rocky cliff. The Creeks attacked and killed maybe four, maybe six of the raiders, while four or five survivors escaped. The Creeks suffered one man wounded. A passing Kickapoo identified the alleged raiders as Pawnees.[23]

Now the confusion began. Rumors circulated that the Pawnees were returning with six hundred warriors to take revenge upon the Creeks for killing their men. Creek chief Roley McIntosh promised the Pawnees that if they attacked, the Creeks would give them "the greatest thrashing that ever fell on heartless marauders."[24] A few days later, a party of Osages approached a Creek town on the Arkansas River in the eastern part of the Creek Nation to buy corn

and to trade. Rumors now flew that the raiding party had not been
Pawnees alone, but that Osages had also been along and that a combined force of Pawnees and Osages had destroyed a Creek settlement on Little River, had defeated a Creek army, and were mas-
sacring Creeks on Red Fork. Now they had come east to take further
revenge. With the town's men attending council in the nearby
town and with no one to provide correct information, the women
panicked. A mass exodus began toward Fort Gibson.[25] James
Logan, agent for the Creeks, not believing the Creeks could be so
excitable, described the scene: "Here was to be seen a crowd of the
poorer class of women on foot, loaded down with their children
and bundles containing valuables; here a line of wagons laden
with the property of the richer class, with their Negro drivers, &c.,
&c., and their owners and their families on horseback . . . the rivers
were literally covered with canoes, laden with women, children,
&c., &c., all wending their way to Fort Gibson."[26] It took two days
to realize that the rumors were false and before the Creeks warily
went back to their homes.[27]

According to Logan, not only had the rumor of a party of six
hundred Pawnees attacking the Creeks been false, but the story of
Osage complicity also turned out to be untrue. Logan visited Osage
chief Black Dog, and while Black Dog admitted that he had once
had a misunderstanding with the Creeks, it had been a while ago,
everything had been cleared up, and none of his people had
attacked, or planned to attack, the Creeks.[28] Even the identity of the
raiding party the Creeks had attacked came into question. Since
the Osages had been discounted, now it was questioned whether
they had actually been Pawnees. General Matthew Arbuckle at
Fort Gibson did not believe it had been the Pawnees, because they
lived on the Platte River and seldom, if ever, ventured south of
the Arkansas River. Instead, suspicion now fell on the Tawakoni
Wichitas, as several people in the western part of Indian Territory,
including some Choctaws living on the Canadian River, pointed
the finger at them. As the Wichitas were often incorrectly referred

to as "Pawnees," it was believed that this might have been how the Pawnees mistakenly were implicated.[29]

If the Tawakoni Wichitas could cause this much trouble and confusion, then the Creeks felt it was time to hold another council to iron out their problems. It was again to be held on Deep Fork River in early May 1845.[30] But the Creeks quickly realized this council was not going to be what they hoped, for the Comanches adamantly refused to attend. The Comanches said they had heard that the object of the Creek council was to form a league to destroy their Osage allies and other Indians of the prairies and plains. To counter this, they were planning to hold their own council with these Indians on the Great Salt Plains—about thirty-five miles northwest of present-day Enid, Oklahoma—during the same time as the Creek council. In fact, the six-man delegation the Creeks sent to the Comanches to invite them to the council were roughly handled by the Comanches, barely escaping with their lives, while their horses and equipment were confiscated. Without the Comanches, the Kiowas would not attend, and on the other side, the Cherokees refused to send delegates to the council.[31]

Nevertheless, the council got underway in the second week of May. The removed Indians at the council included the host Creeks, Seminoles, Choctaws, Chickasaws, Shawnees, Delawares, Piankashaws, Kickapoos, and Peorias. The last five, because they lived west of the Five Tribes' settlements, served as barriers between them and the Plains Indians. A few days later, while the council was in progress, representatives of the Winnebagos, Chippewas, Ottawas, and Menominees arrived. The only Prairie or Plains Indians to attend were the Quapaws, Osages, and Caddos. Cherokee agent Pierce Butler, Creek agent James Logan, as well as several army officers, a reporter from the *Arkansas Intelligencer*, and scores of spectators from the surrounding area also came to witness the proceedings.[32]

From the start, the greatest issue was the Comanches' absence and the report that they had planned a council of their own with the Indians of the plains and prairies. According to the Creek delegation that had gone to the Comanches, the Comanches believed the Creeks had been telling them lies. Also, they thought "that the buffalo had got too far from them by smelling the cattle, hogs, &c. of the Creeks and others upon the border, [and] that they got too hungry before they could reach them."[33] The Comanche message made suspicion fall upon Echo Harjo, the one man of the Creek delegation who could speak Comanche. Harjo had spent long periods of time with the Comanches, long enough to learn their language. He may have had ideas of his own on where the Comanches' loyalties should lie, as he had escorted the Mexican representative to them when Mexico had made its small foray into Texas in 1842 and had tried to get the Comanches on Mexico's side. The other members of the Creek delegation to the Comanches intimated that Harjo may well have intentionally given a bad interpretation. This could not be verified, and it had been Harjo who had saved the delegation from being put to death by the Comanches. Still, suspicions about him continued.[34]

When the Osage delegation arrived, the Creeks questioned them about the supposed Comanche council on the Great Salt Plains. Osage principal chief Bell Ringer replied that he did not know of any agreement to go to the council, but the Comanches had sent them the "broken days": sticks painted red that indicated the number of days until the council and served as an invitation. Bell Ringer said the same invitation had been sent to fifteen other nations, but he did not know why the Creeks were not invited. Osage chief Black Dog said that the Comanches planned on inviting the Creeks as soon as the grass got about a foot high. According to Black Dog, along with the Comanches, representatives from the Kiowas, Taovayas, Tawakonis, Caddos, Wacos, Kichais, Osages, Cheyennes, and Otos planned to attend. The object of the council was to create an alliance to make war upon the Pawnees, who were viewed as enemies by all these peoples.[35]

Although Black Dog assured them they would be invited to join the alliance, the Comanche council and proposed alliance disturbed the Creeks, who thought it might be used not so much against the Pawnees, but against the Creeks' westernmost settlements. To try to ensure a peace with the Comanches, the Creeks turned to their new allies on the plains, the eight-man Caddo delegation led by Chief Chowawhana. Cherokee agent Pierce Butler described the Caddo chief as small but "striking" and with "great personal beauty & commanding appearance." Dressed in a feather turban and silver bands, the Caddo chief, according to Butler, gave a moving speech in which he deplored the past, and future fate, of the "Red Man." The past "had been gloomy; the future prospect worse. Hostility among themselves, destruction of the race and ruin of their children." Chowawhana approved this council, though, and when he returned home he would tell his people about it; they were "honest and true to the object of this council." The Caddos said they would be emissaries for the Creeks to the Comanches, and Chief Addebah agreed to carry some tobacco encircled with white beads to them. Osage chief Black Dog agreed to carry similar emblems of peace to the Pawnees.[36]

The remainder of the council, which ended May 16, was taken up with speeches guaranteeing peace, smoking of the pipes, feasting, hand-shaking, and embracing. The *Arkansas Intelligencer* reporter noted that Creeks shook hands and the Osages grasped the other person near the elbow, while the Caddos embraced "with an old-fashioned country hug." But even these displays of friendship could cause problems. One of the members of the Osage delegation was a medicine man who claimed to be invulnerable to all types of poisonous animals and insects. To prove this, he wore a live snake tied in his hair. The snake was about a foot long, and its head often played about his forehead and neck. During the Caddo embracing ceremony, this did not cause any problems at first, as the Osage medicine man, being well over six feet tall, towered over most of the Caddos he greeted. Then came one Caddo chief who matched his height. The *Arkansas Intelligencer* reporter wrote that "as their heads came in contact, Mr. Snake presented the graceful bow of his neck to the astonishment and utter confusion of his co-hugger, who drew back, exclaiming 'BOOH!,' and has, I fear, for a season put an end to this time-honored custom of his race."[37]

Still, the absence of the Comanches, Kiowas, and Wichitas at the council bode ill. Relations between them and the Shawnees, Delawares, Kickapoos, and Five Major Tribes alternated between peace and war. The Delawares frequently seemed to be at odds with one Plains Indian nation or another. A Delaware party of fifteen, while trapping otter on the headwaters of the Kansas River in the summer of 1844, were wiped out by a large band of Lakotas and Cheyennes. The Delawares also complained that the Wichita Taovayas continually stole their horses. After one foray, the Delawares gave chase, caught up with the Wichitas, killed two of them, and got their horses back.[38] The Kickapoos and Comanches had problems of their own. The Comanches still complained about the Kickapoos' hunting on Comanche lands and finally captured and briefly detained one of the trespassers, the son of a Kickapoo chief. This only angered the Kickapoos all the more.[39] Pawnees still raided south but were usually driven back empty-handed by the Creeks, Kickapoos, and Quapaws. Conversely, the Pawnees complained that they were the victims, being constantly attacked by their enemies.[40] This constant "feuding" among various Indian peoples distressed United States officials, who viewed it as a brake on the "civilization" process. Unfortunately, they realized there was little they could do. Government officials were coming to realize that the chiefs actually possessed little power in suppressing war parties. As Thomas Harvey, superintendent of Indian affairs, recognized, there were many things that made Indians go on raids, "and probably not one of the least inducements is the indulgence of military ambition, as nothing gives a young warrior more éclat than success in taking scalps."[41]

Once again, the Creeks decided to try to end these feuds by holding another grand council, but this time with the Comanches, Kiowas, and Wichitas. The hopes of the Creeks had been encouraged by a party of Wichitas who had visited Roley McIntosh in June to promote friendly feelings between them and the Creeks. Also, during the summer the Cheyennes had met at Bent's Fort with United States officials and representatives of the Delawares to make amends for killing the Delaware trapping party the year before.[42] Now the Creeks sent out their invitations for a council to be held on the Great Salt Plains in either October 1845 or in May or June 1846. The Comanches accepted the invitation. Apparently, though, the fall was too soon to get everything in order, so it was scheduled for the coming spring.[43]

Before the Creek council could come off, the United States government stepped in. In late 1845, Texas joined the Union. For years many bands of Comanches, Kiowas, and Wichitas had considered the Republic of Texas their enemy. They distinguished between Americans and Texans, hated the Texans with a white hot rage, and raided them with all their power. Now the government needed to make the Southern Plains Indians realize that Texans were now Americans. It had been a decade since Dodge's expedition and the Treaty of Camp Holmes, so a new treaty had to be made. The government appointed Pierce M. Butler and M. G. Lewis to go out to the plains in early 1846 to meet with the Comanches, Kiowas, Wichitas, and any other Southern Plains Indians who would meet with them. The objective was twofold: get them to stop raiding into Texas and make a firm peace between them and the removed Indians living in Indian Territory.[44]

Butler and Lewis asked the commander at Fort Gibson for a troop of dragoons to escort them, but they were refused. Instead, they turned to the Five Tribes for assistance. Two Cherokees, three Chickasaws, two Creeks, and two Seminoles, along with their interpreters, cooks, and packers, volunteered to accompany the two commissioners. As they moved south, small bands of Kickapoos and Delawares volunteered to serve as guides to Texas, while even a few whites joined, including a reporter from the *Arkansas Intelligencer*. In the meantime, the commissioners sent messages to the various Southern Plains Indians to meet them during the January full moon at Comanche Peak, a large hill on the Brazos River about fifty miles southwest of present-day Fort Worth, Texas. From the start, things seemed to go awry. The commissioners and their party got lost between the Brazos and Colorado Rivers and wasted valuable time wandering aimlessly around northern Texas. Heavy rains swelled the rivers, delaying them even further and making them miss the appointed date. Even worse, they found that many of the Indians they hoped to meet had never received their messages. The commissioners now sent out new runners to inform the Indians that the council would not take place until the March full moon.[45]

Cherokee representative Elijah Hicks accompanied Butler and Lewis and kept a journal of their travels. Hicks had been delegated by the Cherokees to make peace between them and the peoples of the Southern Plains. He, another Cherokee, William S. Coodey, and Seminole chief Wild Cat had made up one of the parties the commissioners sent out to try to locate the Indians a second time for the conference. Hicks and Coodey, both very much progressives, had been impressed and somewhat amazed by Wild Cat, a Seminole traditionalist who seemed like everything they were not. According to Hicks, Wild Cat entertained them with stories about his exploits during the Seminole War. Wild Cat said he was impressed with the bravery of the American army officers because every time the Seminoles fired on the troops, the troops would panic and the officers "would use the sword liberally on them and force them into lines." Still, Wild Cat did not care for Americans, or white men in general, and according to Hicks, he often made "witty remarks of the whites." Wild Cat said that during the war he once captured an American soldier near Saint Augustine. When the soldier realized he was captured, he grabbed Wild Cat's arms and said "friend." As Hicks recorded the story, Wild Cat replied, "I am hold of you, & [a] friend also, and then [I] slayed him."[46]

Hicks, Coodey, and Wild Cat returned to the commissioners' camp on the Brazos River. Soon bands of Texas Caddos, Tonkawas, and Lipan Apaches arrived, and on February 22 the delegation held an impromptu council with these Indians. Wild Cat addressed them, saying he was glad to shake their hands and that all the commissioners wanted to do was prevent crimes, horse theft, and war between them and the United States and removed Indians. He also pointed out, probably with some irony, the benefits of dealing with the United States. The removed Indians, he said, now lived in comfort and raised corn, cattle, and hogs while peace reigned throughout Indian Territory, enabling them to travel in safety. The commissioners may have gotten some intimation of what they were up against when after Wild Cat's talk the Tonkawas and Lipans merely replied that while it was a good talk, they were not the ones stealing horses, but some other people. They then all smoked the pipe, and the council ended with nothing signed or agreed to. Soon after, Comanche chief Buffalo Hump arrived at the camp and informed the commissioners that they were not far from Comanche Peak, and he had over two hundred of his people camped there awaiting them.[47]

On March 4, 1846, the expedition finally reached Comanche Peak, where it remained for the rest of the month as various peoples and parties arrived or departed almost daily. Things there also got off to a slow start. Some of the Comanche parties had been raiding into Texas and, remembering the Council House Fight of 1840, refused to come in without a guarantee of safety. Still, large numbers of Comanches, Taovayas, Wacos, Kichais, Tonkawas, Caddos, and Plains Apaches met with the commissioners and the delegates from the Cherokees, Creeks, Chickasaws, Seminoles, Delawares, and Kickapoos, but with not much actually accomplished. Numerous councils were held, with much pipe smoking and speech making. Hicks and other representatives from the Civilized Tribes addressed the Plains Indians, urging them to make peace and take up farming. The Plains Indians expressed an interest in dealing with the Five Tribes and even making a treaty with the government, but they were wary. They reminded the commissioners that they had previously signed treaties with the governments of both the United States and Texas, but neither had lived up to their promises; therefore, they could not sign another treaty without first consulting their people. They also suggested they leave Comanche Peak and meet at Council Springs, near present-day Waco, Texas, in April. The commissioners agreed and sent out more runners to bring in more Indians to the treaty conference, while most of the Indians who had been at Comanche Peak accompanied the commissioners' party to Council Springs.[48]

Things did not get much better for the commissioners at Council Springs. Lewis fell ill. Then the Mexican-American War broke out. This filled the commissioners' party with apprehension as they wondered if the Plains Indians would side with Mexico. Fearing this, the governor of Texas sent two messengers asking the commissioners to use all their power to keep the Indians under control and peaceful toward the new state. The war and the need to keep the Plains Indians friendly placed the commissioners in a weak bargaining position. Because of this, as the two commissioners pointed out, they "had not only to make many promises, but were at once compelled to make profuse presents and resort to unusual expenditures of money, to secure themselves and divert and detain the Indians."[49]

Over the long months of the treaty negotiations, Cherokee delegate Elijah Hicks recorded his observations of and interactions with the Plains Indians. And he did have many interactions with these peoples of the plains. A Tonkawa woman often cooked breakfast for him and his party. He got into an argument with Waco chief Shot Arm, attended the wedding of a Lipan Apache woman and a Kichai man, and was present at many of the dances performed by the various Indian peoples, including one the Cherokees held.

Hicks was a keen observer of what went on around him. He watched as the Caddos and Tonkawas gambled, playing the hand game, in which two teams of four players sat and faced each other. One team took a bullet and tried to hide it among them in their hands, singing the whole time. The other team tried to guess who had it. Four arrows were bet per game. He also looked on as a group of twelve Comanche and Kichai boys, about twelve to fourteen years of age, participated in a kick-boxing match. Of course he attended many feasts, pipe-smokings, and other ceremonies.[50]

Still, Hicks was a Cherokee progressive, and though he may have addressed a Comanche chief as "brother," he certainly viewed all these Plains peoples as being very different from him. As he recorded the activities of the Plains Indians, the tone of his journal ranged from pleasant surprise to condescending amusement to outright racism. Hicks enjoyed the "sweet voices" of the women singers; made a few snide remarks about their ceremonies, dances, and dinner manners; and firmly believed that the Tonkawas were "the lowest of human beings in North America."[51] Hicks saw himself as different from the Plains Indians around him, and the Comanches may well have agreed with his self-assessment. After one speech made by Hicks, in which he urged the Comanches to make peace, he recorded Comanche chief Pahucah's reply that "he came a long way to see his white brothers the Cherokees & Creeks." This is a cryptic sentence, Hicks writing what someone said about him. It could have been merely bad grammar, or he may have actually recorded how Pahucah viewed him. But possibly by that time Hicks actually saw himself as more white than red.[52]

Finally, on May 15 the commissioners managed to get a treaty signed, but only with the help of numerous interpreters and delegates from the removed nations and Civilized Tribes. The Plains Indian signatories included twenty-four Comanche chiefs and principal men as well as chiefs from the four Wichita communities: the Wacos, Tawakonis, Kichais, and Taovayas. The remnants of the old Caddo chiefdoms of eastern Texas and western Louisiana also signed. This included a band of Caddos as well as the Hainais and Nadacos. These "Caddos" were originally from Louisiana but had moved to Texas in 1835 and were related to those Caddos then living on Chickasaw lands on the Red River. The Hainais and Nadacos were originally part of the Caddoan Hasinai chiefdom of eastern Texas and by now were called, respectively, "Ionies" and "Anadarkos" by the Americans. The treaty itself was one of peace, the main points being that these Indians would recognize American authority, stop raiding into Texas, quit stealing horses, and remain at peace with all Indians who were then at peace with the United States. They were also to give up all their non-Indian captives in return for all their people being held captive by Texas. In return, the United States promised to give all the signatory nations ten thousand dollars' worth of presents at some future date. Also, blacksmiths, schoolteachers, and preachers of the gospel would be sent among them to show them the road to civilization.[53]

Unfortunately, all their work came to naught, for the United States Senate refused to ratify the treaty. Not comprehending the intricacies of Capitol Hill checks and balances, many of the Plains Indians grew angry over the government's reneging on providing the promised presents.[54] Officials in Washington never seemed to realize that not providing the goods and annuities severely eroded the power of the chiefs to control their own people. For the people of the Southern Plains, manufactured goods, once luxuries, were now necessities. Guns, as well as metal edged weapons and tools, were essential in warfare, hunting, and buffalo hide production. Women now used metal cooking utensils and tools in all areas of camp life. Intricately beautiful designs of glass beads, sewn on with metal needles, now covered the ceremonial clothing of Plains Indian men and women, and their prestige rose with the magnificence of their clothing. Status and prestige also came with the ability to possess and give away many of these manufactured goods to kinspeople and friends. So chiefs negotiated for these goods when making treaties, their own power rising by being able to supply these things to their people. But when these goods never came, their people lost confidence in their wisdom and abilities. People began to pay attention to what the chiefs' rivals had to say—maybe to those who had opposed the treaty from the start or to those who said they knew other ways of delivering the goods. Young men now might ignore the advice of the chiefs, and urged on by their families' need for manufactured goods and their own desire for status, would raid the farms, ranches, and wagon trains of settlers in Mexico and Texas and of the removed Indians in Indian Territory.

Captain Randolph Marcy, who made several exploring expeditions across the Southern Plains, understood the importance of gift-giving and tried to get the United States government to make it an official policy:

> The Indians of the plains are accustomed, in their diplomatic intercourse with each other, to exchange presents, and they have no idea of friendship unaccompanied by a substantial token in this form: moreover, they measure the strength of the attachment of their friends by the magnitude of the presents they receive; and I am firmly convinced that a small amount of money annually expended in this way, with a proper and judicious distribution of presents, would have a very salutary influence in checking the depredations upon the Mexicans. In a talk which I held with a chief of one of the bands of prairie Indians, I stated to him that the President of the United States was their friend, and wished to live in peace with them. He replied that he was much astonished to hear this; for, judging from the few trifling presents I had made his people, he was of opinion that the "Big Captain" held them in but little estimation.[55]

Sam Houston, the governor of Texas, also realized the importance of giving the Indians gifts and the serious situation Texas faced with the refusal of the Senate to ratify the treaty. He immediately dispatched Texas Indian agent Robert Simpson Neighbors and other representatives to convene a council with the Indians who had signed the treaty. Bands of Comanches, Lipan Apaches, Caddos, Hainais, Nadacos, Kichais, Tonkawas, and even some Cherokees showed up at Council Spring in October 1846. The Comanches, Wacos, Tawakonis, and Taovayas were split, with some bands arriving for the council while others refused to come, declaring themselves enemies to Texas and the United States. Neighbors handed out over seven thousand dollars' worth of goods to the Indians, impressing upon them that these presents were essentially redeeming the promises made at the last council by Butler and Lewis and they should still continue to wait for the U.S. government to fulfill its promises. Neighbors deemed the council a success, with the Indians continuing to uphold the peace.[56]

Not willing to make peace and let it go at that, Neighbors began investigating why so many of the Wacos, Taovayas, Tawakonis, and Comanches were so hostile to the government. He made an amazing, yet disconcerting, discovery. In almost every case the clues led to small parties of Shawnees, Delawares, and Kickapoos, who "visited the prairie tribes this fall for the purpose of trade, and found it much to their interest to keep those wild bands hostile, as their plunder afforded a profitable source of traffic." Neighbors soon identified Jim Leplow and Black Cat of the Shawnees and Jim Ned and his party of Delawares as the main instigators. Leplow and his Shawnees had recently gone to a Wichita village and purchased a large number of horses stolen from Texas settlers. Many of the chiefs reported the bad influence these bands had on their people. Comanche Chief Santa Ana complained that he always experienced great difficulties in restraining his warriors after a visit from Jim Leplow. According to Santa Ana, Leplow would tell his people that the whites were preparing to wage a war of extermination upon them and that the United States government would never keep the promises made to them in the treaty. The nonratification of the treaty seemed to prove Jim Leplow correct in the minds of many Comanches.[57] If the bad counsel was not enough, Neighbors soon uncovered a racket involving the trade of stolen horses and captives that implicated the Plains Indians; the Delawares, Shawnees, Kickapoos, and Osages; and even some members of the Civilized Tribes.

As the Five Tribes settled into their Indian Territory homes during the 1830s and '40s, some of their people initiated trade with the Plains Indians to the west, exchanging manufactured goods for horses, mules, buffalo hides, and other pelts. This was an ancient trade, existing long before Europeans ever arrived in the western hemisphere. During the Mississippian cultural tradition, Caddos from along the Red and Arkansas Rivers and Pueblos from the Pecos and Rio Grande had created exchange relations with those peoples then living on the plains. During the eighteenth century, French traders from the Mississippi and Red Rivers and the Spaniards from Texas and New Mexico introduced manufactured goods to the Indians of the prairies and plains. In the early nineteenth century, American traders from newly purchased Louisiana replaced the French and Spanish. Now, the removed Indians and the Five Major Tribes in Indian Territory merely continued the trade.

One of the most renowned of these Five Tribes traders was Jesse Chisholm, a Cherokee. He is probably most famous for blazing the Chisholm Trail, which was, during the early 1860s, one of the first cattle trails from Texas to Kansas. Chisholm was born about 1806 in Tennessee, the son of a Cherokee mother and a Scottish father. Not long after his birth, his family moved west as members of the Western Cherokees. He spent a typical Cherokee boyhood, but possessed an affinity for languages, speaking Cherokee, Caddo, English, and probably also Comanche and Creek. By the late 1820s Chisholm lived with Chief Duwali's Texas Cherokees, and in 1830 he participated in a raid on the Wichita Tawakonis in retaliation for their killing some Cherokees. Chisholm made his first contact with the Plains Indians proper in 1834, when he served as an inter-

preter with Dodge's expedition to the Comanches, Kiowas, and
Wichitas. Two years later he married a Creek woman, built a home
at the confluence of Little River and the Canadian River near the
Edwards trading post, and began trading with the Plains Indians,
an occupation he continued until his death in 1868.[58]

Undoubtedly, Chisholm made fictive kinships with many of
the Plains Indian peoples and was welcomed virtually every-
where he went. He gained tremendous influence among the
Comanches, who looked upon him as a trusted brother who upheld his social obligations and as an advisor whose counsel could
be relied upon. Because of his understanding of the Plains Indians
and his influence with them, Chisholm came to serve as a diplo-
mat. The Five Tribes, the Republic of Texas, and the United States
all clamored for his services. He attended almost every major
council held with the Plains Indians during the 1840s and 1850s.
Soon after Butler and Lewis made their treaty in May 1846, Chisholm helped escort a party of fifty Comanches, Taovayas, Wacos,
Tawakonis, Kichais, Caddos, Nadacos, Lipan Apaches, Tonkawas,
Delawares, and Creeks to Washington, D.C. Despite his diplomatic efforts, Chisholm remained first and foremost an entrepre-
neur in the Indian trade.[59]

Jesse Chisholm was only the most famous of the traders to come
out of the Five Major Tribes. Many others also tried their hand at
the trade and had some success at it. Even Seminole chief Wild Cat
made trading expeditions to the Plains Indians. But the main
towns of the Cherokees, Creeks, and Choctaws were far to the east,
and most of these peoples with an entrepreneurial bent turned to
the burgeoning plantation economy, growing cotton or corn or
supplying horses and mules to farmers throughout the South.
Besides, the Cherokees, Creeks, Choctaws, and Chickasaws soon
found that rather than deal directly with the Comanches, Wichitas,
and Kiowas, they could more easily deal with the Delawares,
Kickapoos, and Shawnees, who served as intermediaries with the
Plains Indians.[60]

As bands of Delawares, Kickapoos, and Shawnees settled along the Canadian River in the 1830s, the Chickasaws might complain about them, but the Creeks welcomed them as buffers against Plains Indian raiders.[61] Here, between the settlements of the Civilized Tribes and the roving bands of Plains Indians, the Shawnees, Kickapoos, and Delawares developed a prairie life-style that incorporated both horticulture and hunting-gathering. They lived in small settled hamlets. Their women grew corn and other foods, while the men hunted buffalo on the plains to the west. This mixed life-style closely resembled that of the traditional Prairie Indians of the area, such as the Caddos, Quapaws, Osages, and Wichitas.[62]

During the eighteenth century, these traditional Prairie Indians, particularly the Caddos and Wichitas, had been intermediaries between the French and Spanish outposts in Louisiana and Arkansas and the Comanches, Lipan Apaches, and other Plains Indians. Caddos and Wichitas were part of a Southern Plains trade network connecting the Europeans and the Comanches. Caddo and Wichita villages served as entrepôts, where Euroamerican traders met and did business with the Indians from the prairies and plains. With the growth of American farming populations in Louisiana, Arkansas, and Texas in the 1830s, and the collapse of the Caddo chiefdoms about the same time, the traditional Southern Plains trade network shattered. The Caddos' 1835 Louisiana land cession divided them into several bands, with some living in Texas and others in Indian Territory. By the mid-1840s, both these Caddo divisions abandoned much of their Plains connections, returning more to agriculture as they had in the days before horses arrived. Politically and economically, they found themselves slowly drawn into the orbit of the Civilized Tribes. Similarly, the Wichitas were also divided, with some bands, such as the Taovayas in Texas, willing to settle down and devote more time to agriculture, while the Wacos, Tawakonis, and a few others moved toward a more plainslike life-style and became closer allies of the Comanches.[63]

As the old trade network deteriorated, the Comanches still needed a sure supply of manufactured goods, particularly guns and ammunition. But they could no longer rely upon their long-time Caddo and Wichita trade partners, who were beginning to pursue different interests. At the same time, the Five Tribes wanted buffalo hides, but more importantly, horses and mules. American farmers needed ever more horses and mules, as did Forty-Niners heading out on the California Gold Rush. While the Five Tribes tried to make peace with the Plains Indians, they needed partners to facilitate this trade. As the Plains Indians and the Five Tribes reached out toward each other to trade, they found a vacuum that had once been occupied by the Caddos and Wichitas. Now the Shawnees, Kickapoos, and Delawares along the Canadian River filled the void, and a new Southern Plains trade network developed. Shawnees, Kickapoos, and Delawares acquired guns, whiskey, and other manufactured goods from white or Civilized Tribes traders, then passed these on to the Plains Indians. They received buffalo hides, horses, and captives from the Plains Indians and exchanged these with the Civilized Tribes and American traders further east.[64] Captain Randolph Marcy reported that the Kickapoos "form a commercial communicating medium between the white traders and the wild Indians, and derive a profitable trade, while they indulge in their favorite amusement, the chase."[65] As always, kinship facilitated trade and exchange, so the Shawnees, Delawares, and Kickapoos sometimes solidified their trade relations with the Plains and Prairie Indians through marriage and adoption.[66]

This increase in trade also increased the number of raids made by the Comanches, Kiowas, and some Wichitas into Texas. Since capturing and breaking wild horses on the plains was time-consuming, the Plains Indians raided Texas settlements and ranches instead. Major Ethan Allen Hitchcock, who toured Indian Territory in 1842, pointed out that the Delawares and Shawnees had extensive relations with the Comanches. Through them, Hitchcock said, "the Comanches have received ammunition & other supplies in the way of trade, which have assisted them in prosecuting their predatory excursions among the white settlements in Texas."[67]

With the demand for horses and mules so great, the Shawnees, Kickapoos, and Delawares sometimes made their own horse raids. Caddo and Wichita communities in Texas complained about being the targets of these Indians and insisted that Texas allow them to retaliate. Even Shawnee, Delaware, and Kickapoo trade partners, such as the Comanches, Chickasaws, Choctaws, and Creeks, found their own horses stolen by them.[68]

Despite these losses, trade relations remained paramount. With the Plains Indians' constant need for guns and manufactured goods, they not only forgave the Shawnees, Kickapoos, and Delawares for a few horse thefts but welcomed them and any other traders, such as Jesse Chisholm, to their camps. In early 1847 the Comanches sent out word that they had plenty of mules and buffalo skins to trade and would trade with anyone who wanted to. In response, a great trade fair convened during the summer of 1847 on the Great Salt Plains, which was considered a neutral ground. Representatives from the Comanches, Kiowas, Osages, Seminoles, Creeks, Cherokees, Quapaws, Delawares, Shawnees, and other nations attended. Numerous hides and horses changed hands, with one twenty-dollar gun exchanged for one or two mules worth sixty dollars. The Osages alone took twenty-four thousand dollars' worth of guns, powder, lead, blankets, and other goods to the fair and came home with fifteen hundred head of horses, worth sixty thousand dollars. While horses, mules, and hides for manufactured goods constituted most of the exchanges, it would not have been surprising if several captives were also "traded."[69]

Just as horses were a major component of this new Southern Plains trade network, captives also made up a lucrative share. Before the coming of Europeans to the western hemisphere, captives were merely a by-product of warfare. No matter whether their captors were hunter-gatherers or agriculturalists, most captives were taken back to the captors' villages or camps, where they were ritually tortured to death to end the grief of those people who had lost kinspeople of their own. Some few became slaves, living with the family of their captor and doing the same work as the members of his household. With capitalist agriculture not then in existence among the Indians, and since the captor was forced to feed his slaves, there was little profit in keeping large numbers of them, who only drained a family's resources.[70]

The coming of Europeans and their demand for labor in the mines or on their sugar and tobacco plantations made the taking of captives profitable. Like horses or hides, Indian slaves became commodities demanded by the English, French, and Spanish. With this demand, Indians made raids with the purpose of taking captives in order to exchange them for manufactured goods. In the Southeast, during the seventeenth and early eighteenth centuries, the Cherokees, Creeks, Choctaws, Chickasaws, and other peoples, particularly the Yamasees, became inveterate slave takers, with raiding parties reaching as far as the Caddo villages on the Red River. Most captives were then marched back to Charleston, South Carolina, from where they were shipped to the sugar islands of the Caribbean to work away the remainder of their short lives. Slave raids became so bad that many smaller nations of the Southeast were virtually wiped out or their survivors driven out of the area. In the English colonies of the Southeast, demand for Indian slaves slackened considerably by the 1730s as African slaves, which colonists believed a better investment, became more plentiful. By the early nineteenth century, as the progressives of the Civilized Tribes entered the market economy, they began purchasing black slaves to work on their own farms and plantations. Many of these black slaves came with them on their removal to Indian Territory.[71]

On the Southern Plains, similar slave raids took place, and Indian slavery lasted a bit longer than it did in the English colonies. Though Spain had from the earliest days of the Conquest officially disapproved of Indian slavery, it had allowed it in cases of war captives or if a slave were bought from an Indian master. After the Pueblo Revolt of 1680, Spanish colonists, now unable to enslave the Pueblos but still needing Indian laborers, used to their benefit the natural animosities among the various Indians on the Southern Plains. While Lipan Apaches might be made into slaves, during trade fairs when all Indians were invited to the New Mexican settlements, the Lipan Apaches offered Comanche, Wichita, and Caddo captives to the Spanish. The French in Louisiana also needed laborers, and the Comanches, Wichitas, and Caddos provided them with Apache captives. By the late eighteenth century, a large Apache slave population had grown up among the French settlements on Red River. As the English did, the Spanish found that Indian slavery often caused more warfare and problems than it was worth, and once Spain took control of Louisiana in 1769, it officially banned the practice. By the 1790s Indian slavery had virtually died out among the Euroamericans on both sides of the Southern Plains.[72]

Though Euroamericans did not need any more Indian slaves, the Indians of the Southern Plains found new incentives for taking captives. One reason was to replenish their disease-ravaged populations. Before 1820, at least thirty epidemics swept through the villages and camps of the Indians living on or about the Southern Plains. Smallpox took the greatest toll, but measles, cholera, malaria, whooping cough, and influenza did their own damage.[73] One way for the Southern Plains peoples to overcome these losses was to adopt outsiders into their families and bands. These adoptees, mainly women and children, usually started out as captives taken in raids who then served as slaves. They included other Indians peoples; Hispanics from New Mexico, Texas, and Old Mexico; and later, Anglo-Americans from Texas. Their status changed from slave to family member as women eventually married and the children grew up to take their places in Southern Plains society. Beginning life as an adopted captive proved no real hindrance for most boy captives, as many eventually became respected warriors and war leaders. When painter George Catlin accompanied Major Dodge's 1834 expedition to the Wichita villages, he painted the portrait of a Comanche war leader named His-oo-sán-chees. Much to his surprise, he found out that His-oo-sán-chees was actually a Mexican, Jesús Sanchez, who had been captured by the Comanches as a young boy.[74]

The growth of Southern Plains Indians' horse herds spurred the taking of boy captives who could serve as herders. During the first half of the nineteenth century, no other Indian nation possessed as many horses as the Comanches and Kiowas. A successful warrior might own between fifty and two hundred. As late as 1867, the Kwahadi Comanches of the Texas Panhandle, with a population of two thousand, owned over fifteen thousand horses and about four hundred mules.[75] Even Prairie Indians might possess a considerable number. While attending the 1846 council at Council Springs, Cherokee delegate Elijah Hicks reported that a Caddo village's horse herd covered the hills as far as he could see.[76] The job of watching over the horses usually went to young boys about ten to thirteen years of age. With so many horses, there just were not enough boys to mount an adequate guard on them. So during raids, young boys became valuable prizes. As the boys worked, they learned Plains culture, and a family eventually adopted them.[77] The growing buffalo hide trade also brought an increase in the taking of captives. Comanches, Kiowas, and Apaches depended heavily on the buffalo. So did such Prairie peoples as the Caddos, Wichitas, Osages, and Quapaws and removed Indians such as the Kickapoos, Delawares, and Shawnees. While they served as the main source of food for the Comanches, Kiowas, and Lipan Apaches, buffalo also provided a host of tools and utensils, everything from clothing and building materials to glue to cookware. Hides and robes were particularly valuable, some becoming veritable *objets d'art*, with intricate designs of beads and paint applied to them. Indians of all nations prized these, and they became important commodities for exchange. Among the Five Major

Tribes, the United States, and the rest of the increasingly indus-
trialized world, buffalo hides served whenever leather was
needed—in later decades as belts to turn machinery. With the
demand for buffalo hides growing, the Plains Indians determined
to supply it, willing to exchange buffalo hides for manufactured
goods. Since each Plains Indian ate about six buffalo a year, when
the demands of the hide trade are added to this, then any given
Plains Indian hunter might have killed an average of forty-four
buffalo per year. It fell to the women to skin, tan, and, if need be,
decorate these hides, all of which was time-consuming work. Since
a man's wife did most of the hide work, it did not take long for
Plains men to realize that the more wives they had, the more hides
they could produce and the more manufactured goods they could
receive. This began an increase in polygamy among Plains societies.
There also became a need to take more female captives who could
either become wives or at least be put to work on buffalo hides.[78]

With all these considerations in mind, the Indians of the Southern
Plains stepped up their raids into Texas and Mexico and by the
early 1830s counted a considerable number of Anglo and Hispanic
women and children among them. As previously pointed out,
Indian peoples often took captives from each other, and it would
not be wholly unexpected, though no less distressing, for an Indian
man, woman, or child to be taken captive by another Indian
people. Osages had often taken Caddos captives in the eighteenth
century and had taken several Kiowas girls captive in their 1833
attack at Cut Throat Gap. Whites took their own share of Indian
captives, such as the Comanche women taken at the 1840 Council
House Fight. The Comanches agitated for years to get their women
back, and they were finally returned to them during the 1846 treaty
negotiations with the United States representatives at Council
Springs.[79] Still, no the matter ethnicity of the captive, or who captured whom, the experience of captivity could be brutal. From the
start there was the sheer terror of being taken and possibly seeing
friends and relatives killed before one's eyes. Captured adult males

were often tortured to death, while adult women sometimes experienced torture and rape.[80]

Anglo men seemed to have a horror, perhaps justifiable, of being captured by the Plains Indians, some even going so far as to commit suicide in order not to fall into Indian hands.[81] They were equally horrified at the idea of Anglo women and children captives and so went out of their way to recover them. Even the Civilized Tribes seemed to take on this feeling that being held captive by the Plains Indians was a fate worse than death. In 1837, Choctaw Principal Chief Peter Pitchlynn took another tour of the Southern Plains. While there, he met a camp of whites and fell into conversation with a young white woman who had been held captive by the Taovaya Wichitas. She related her sad story, which was filled with episodes of cruelty and abuse. Pitchlynn was very sympathetic, and the story so impressed him that he wrote it down word for word in his journal. Pitchlynn, though an Indian himself, could not count the Taovayas as being in the same class as his Choctaws, and he opined that the Taovayas were "the most cruel Indians to prisoners than any tribe with which I am acquainted. It is the custom of all the Indians east of the Mississippi to adopt prisoners into their families and to treat them with affection."[82]

Ironically, the families of Anglo captives, the citizens of Texas, and the U.S. government unwittingly fueled the taking of captives by Plains Indians. Their desire to recover them created a scam from which the Plains and Prairie Indians, the Five Major Tribes, and the Shawnees, Delawares, and Kickapoos, all profited. When the Comanches, Kiowas, and Wichitas took captives in Texas and Mexico, the U.S. government offered a ransom for their return. In 1842, General Zachary Taylor, then at Fort Smith, heard of some white children who were held prisoner of the Comanches. He told a party of Kickapoos that if they would bring the children to Fort Gibson, he would pay them two hundred dollars for each child. The Kickapoos returned with one of the children, an eleven-year-old boy, and received their two hundred dollars. Taylor promised the same amount for the boy's sister.[83] Payment of cash for captives quickly became standard operating procedure of the government at forts in Indian Territory. Texan and Mexican families of captives also offered their own rewards for the return of their children.[84]

With the taking of captives once again profitable, a pattern developed. The Comanches or Kiowas raided into Texas, New Mexico, or Old Mexico, where they took captives. Some of them were adopted into the band, while others became items of exchange, often passed from individual to individual and band to band and sometimes from one nation to another. Gillis Doyle, a Texas boy who had been captured by the Comanches, told Cherokee trader Jesse Chisholm, who hoped to ransom him, that he had "several times changed masters, from one tribe to another."[85] Then, knowing of the ransom offered by the United States government or by the families of the captives, trading parties of Osages, Kickapoos, Shawnees, Delawares, and even the Civilized Tribes went out to the Comanches and "purchased" these captives. In one incident, a party of Chickasaws and Kickapoos met a Comanche party led by Chief Tichetonuhte and found a Texas boy named George Wilson held captive by an old Comanche man. They gave the old man forty beads, eight yards of cloth strouding, ten pints of gunpowder, twelve bars of lead, sixteen yards of blue grilling (sic), half a dozen paint pieces, six plugs of tobacco, four butcher knives, six coils of brass wire, and twelve yards of cloth called "Choctaw Stripe" for the boy. For helping arrange the exchange, they gave Chief Tichetonuhte a pony, a rifle, and six plugs of tobacco. This amounted to about five hundred dollars' worth of goods.[86] Once purchased from the Comanches, these captives were then taken back to eastern Indian Territory, where they were then turned over to the authorities or their families for the ransom money offered.[87]

Still, the ransoming of captives was not as easy as it might appear. Many captives did not want to leave their Plains families. For boys, the Plains life-style was often fun and filled with adventure. Horseback riding, hunting, camping, and being doted on by the women made some boys unwilling to return to a life of hard-scrabble farming. Some women, who had been captured as girls and reared as Indians, had made lives for themselves. They had married Indian men, given birth to children, did not want to leave their families, and so tried to avoid being ransomed.[88] At the same time, some people recognized that the ransoming process smelled like a shakedown. In 1845 the *Arkansas Intelligencer* of Van Buren, Arkansas, was scandalized to learn that the Osages possessed twenty white children that they had purchased from the Comanches. The paper reported that the Osages would ransom these captives only for horses or merchandise. "Occasionally, they bring one into the settlement to barter off," with one man purchasing a pretty eleven-year-old girl for a horse. The paper demanded that the government investigate the process.[89]

If the need for manufactured goods made the Comanches, Wichitas, and Kiowas more willing to take captives and then ransom them, then the growing need for servants and slaves in eastern Indian Territory also made the Civilized Tribes more willing to purchase captives. While white captives could usually rely upon family members or the United States government to put up enough money for a ransom, many Mexican captives did not have this luxury. Some Hispanic captives wound up as servants or slaves of Five Tribes families, either through Kickapoo intermediaries or through trading parties from the Five Tribes themselves. One government official at the Chickasaw Agency reported that nearby lived a little Mexican girl. She had been captured by the Comanches, ransomed by the Kickapoos, and then purchased by a Chickasaw man in exchange for a mule. "She is now . . . a slave, badly clothed and indifferently cared for in every respect. She has been so long a prisoner and slave as to have lost all knowledge of her relatives."[90] Even Jesse Chisholm owned a few Mexican servants he had ransomed from the Comanches.[91]

The African-American slaves held by the Civilized Tribes and the Civilized Tribes' need for additional slaves made them both

victims and beneficiaries of captive ransoming. Comanche, Kickapoo, Delaware, and Shawnee raiding parties sometimes took black
slaves from the Five Tribes, particularly from the Chickasaws.
Later, these same captive slaves would be ransomed back to the
Chickasaws for between $150 and $250. On the other hand, black
slaves taken on raids in Texas would then be sold to the Five
Tribes. Sometimes the slave's Texas owner might come to retrieve
his property, but if not, these African-American captives became
the property of the Civilized Tribes.[92]

So it was their vested interest in this lucrative trade of horses,
mules, hides, and captives that dictated the diplomatic efforts of
the Kickapoos, Shawnees, Delawares, Osages, and even some
members of the Five Tribes. War between the Plains Indians and
Texas and the United States was more profitable than peace, which
would severely hamper their economic activities. It paid to spread
rumors among the Comanches, Wichitas, and Kiowas that the
United States wanted to take their land or kill them all.[93]

In the minds of the Comanches, Wichitas, and Kiowas, there
appeared to be truth in what the Kickapoos, Delawares, and Shaw-
nees told them. Though the Five Tribes, particularly the Creeks,
during the 1840s had initiated council after council with the Plains
Indians and had even served as intermediaries between them and
United States negotiators, the councils had never lived up to the
Plains Indians' expectations. White settlers out of Texas and citizens of the Five Tribes still moved into territories claimed by the
Comanches and Wichitas. The buffalo, the mainstay of Plains
Indian economics, were already declining on the Southern Plains.
While the trade in horses and captives brought in valuable
manufactured goods, it also brought on increased violence with
the Texans. As these pressures increased over the next few decades,
the Indians of the Southern Plains would find various ways to deal
with them. This would reshape their relations with the Civilized
Tribes and other removed Indians.

Peter P. Pitchlynn, principal chief of the Choctaw Nation, who advocated Indians' adoption of American culture. (Courtesy Western History Collections, University of Oklahoma Libraries)

George W. Grayson, principal chief of the Creek Nation, who later served as a lawyer for the Wichita Indians. (Courtesy Western History Collections, University of Oklahoma Libraries)

Members of the Choctaw Light Horse in 1893. A combination police force and national guard, they often fought Comanche raiders. (Courtesy Western History Collections, University of Oklahoma Libraries)

Students and faculty at Bloomfield Academy, a Methodist school for Indian girls in Chickasaw Territory, 1870. (Courtesy Western History Collections, University of Oklahoma Libraries)

Cherokee and Delaware leaders in 1866 negotiating the joining of Delawares with the Cherokee Nation. (Courtesy Western History Collections, University of Oklahoma Libraries)

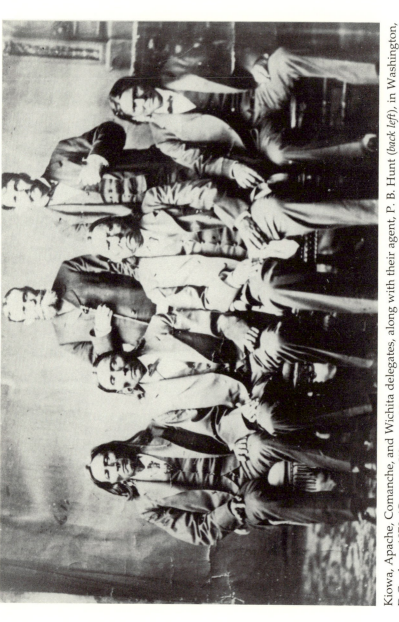

Kiowa, Apache, Comanche, and Wichita delegates, along with their agent, P. B. Hunt (*back left*), in Washington, D.C., about 1870. (Courtesy Western History Collections, University of Oklahoma Libraries)

Comanche women and child in front of a buffalo tepee in Indian Territory, about the early 1870s. Meat and hides dry on nearby racks. (Courtesy Western History Collections, University of Oklahoma Libraries)

Wichita village on the reservation, about 1900. Note the completely thatched traditional grass houses, arbors covered only on top, log cabins, and tents. (Courtesy Western History Collections, University of Oklahoma Libraries)

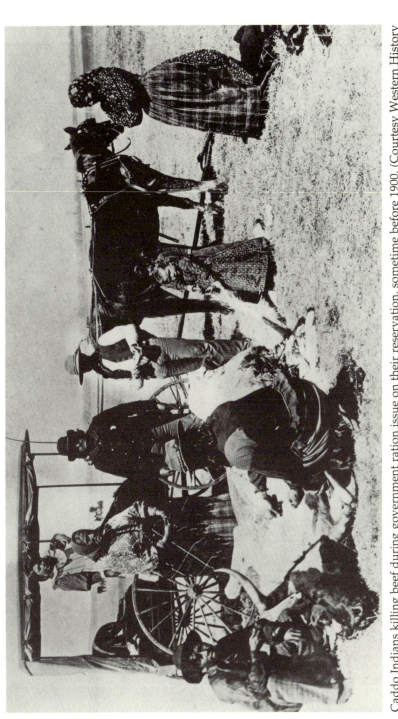

Caddo Indians killing beef during government ration issue on their reservation, sometime before 1900. (Courtesy Western History Collections, University of Oklahoma Libraries)

Indian scouts of Troop L, 7th Cavalry. *Left to right:* Jack Watse-momsoakawat (Comanche) Arko (Comanche), and Charlie Ohet-taint (Kiowa). (Courtesy Western History Collections, University of Oklahoma Libraries)

CHAPTER FIVE

IN THE SHADOW OF
THE WHITE MEN

You will imagine the surprise of the Principal Chief and Head Men [of the Wichitas] upon being informed that the government of the United States . . . had actually sold and guaranteed to the Choctaws the whole of the territorial limits of the Wichita Nation.

TOSHAQUASH
second chief of the Wichitas, July 19, 1854

Beginning in the late 1840s and continuing for the next several decades, the frontier line of white settlers finally caught up with the peoples living in Indian Territory. Mineral strikes in the far West drew thousands of emigrants across the Southern Plains. The expanding farming frontier sent just as many to the margins of the Great Plains in Texas and Kansas. To protect these migrants and settlers, a line of army forts from Kansas to Texas steadily advanced westward during these decades. As the need for a transcontinental railroad became apparent, army exploring and surveying parties ventured out to the Southern Plains. When the country finally exploded into Civil War in the 1860s, the peoples of Indian Territory could not avoid being pulled into it. As whites settled around the peoples of Indian Territory and the Southern Plains, they strongly affected the Indians' relations with each other, often exacerbating suspicions and reinforcing differences. Instead of unifying the removed Indians and the Plains Indians, white encroachment increasingly set them at odds with each other.

Achieving unity among all the Indians of Indian Territory would have been difficult in the best of times. Making it harder was that the Civilized Tribes, who saw themselves as the pinnacle of acculturation and the ideal of what all Indians should strive for, had not developed a unified approach to dealing with the Plains Indians. By the 1850s the Cherokees had the least to do with the Plains Indians. Their problems with the Osages diminished as the Osages gradually moved further west. As the easternmost of the Civilized Tribes, and with a large Indian buffer west of them, rarely, if ever, did the Cherokees see a Comanche, Kiowa, or Pawnee raiding party make its way into the Cherokee Nation. So, over time, the Cherokees had less and less to do with the Plains Indians. The Creeks and Seminoles, then joined under a single government, took a friendly, almost paternalistic attitude toward the Plains Indians. During the 1840s the Creeks had taken the lead in sponsoring councils with the intent of arranging peace with the Plains Indians and improving relations with them. These good relations between the Plains Indians and the Creeks were facilitated when mixed-blood Cherokee trader Jesse Chisholm married the daughter of James Edwards and his Creek wife, who ran Edwards's Store at the confluence of the Little and Canadian Rivers. The store, with its strong Creek connection, supplied goods, including whiskey, to the various Indian peoples in the area.[1]

The Seminoles also developed good relations with the Plains Indians. As the Seminoles moved into Indian Territory during the 1840s, the Creeks assigned them to the western part of their lands, making the Seminoles the westernmost of the Five Major Tribes and closest to the Plains Indians. Seminole chief Wild Cat quickly made alliances with the Kickapoos, Wichitas, and Comanches, and in turn these Indians found Wild Cat to be one of the few people who, they believed, dealt truthfully with them. Comanches and Wichitas often visited Wild Cat at the Seminole Agency, where he urged them not to bother the Forty-niners crossing the plains. If they did, it would only bring the wrath of the United States down on them, something he had personally experienced during the Seminoles Wars in Florida. Still, he gave the Plains Indians several warnings when it came to dealing with whites. Be wary of promises made by the United States, because the whites would lie to them, especially when it came to their land. Be careful when accepting gifts from whites, because whites often equated the giving of gifts with the Indians' giving up their land. If need be, the whites would take their land by force. Just look at how the growth of the white population in Texas was depriving the Indians in that state of their land, he pointed out. Wild Cat, though, wanted his Seminoles to have a government separate from that of the Creeks. Tired of constantly being overruled by the Creek majority in their combined council, in late 1849 or early 1850 he led a large number of Seminoles, Kickapoos, and blacks to the Mexican side of the Rio Grande. There he died in 1857 of smallpox, but descendants of these people remain on the border of Mexico and Texas to this day.[2]

Unlike the Creeks and Seminoles, the Chickasaws and Choctaws took a hard approach in dealing with the Plains Indians. They saw their western neighbors as savage inferiors, trespassers, and raiders and wanted as little to do with them as possible. In 1849, when Congress once again floated the idea of uniting all the Indian nations between the Red and Platte Rivers under one government, Peter Pitchlynn of the Choctaws argued against it. Pitchlynn acknowledged that the bill arose out of an earnest desire to do what was best for the Indians, but in reality it would only introduce "discord, dissensions, and strife among them." According to Pitchlynn, all the various Indian nations in and about Indian Territory were different, had different treaties with the United States, had land tenure differently, and were all independent of each other. Not only that, but he also pointed out that they were all at different levels of "civilization; some being nearly wholly civilized, others partially so, and others, again, retaining the wandering habits of their fathers, may be termed hunter tribes." And as for a republican form of government for all these different peoples, Pitchlynn saw no hope for it. Who would elect delegates from the Plains Indians? And how would they be elected? Would they be willing to give up hunting to exercise their franchise? Would the Plains Indians be willing to enact laws against murder and robbery? Pitchlynn thought not. The bill never saw the light of legislation.[3]

Pitchlynn's belief in the superiority of the Civilized Tribes and the inferiority of the Plains Indians was not a lone conviction but was often echoed by other Choctaws and Chickasaws. As they had so often in the past, the Choctaws and Chickasaws continued to complain to the United States government about the Plains Indians' intrusion upon their territory. Chickasaw leaders insisted that the government protect them and their property and that if any of these Indians "really have any right (which we deny) to the country, we hold that the United States is bound to extinguish that right in our favor." In answer to Chickasaw complaints, the army built Fort Arbuckle on Wild Horse Creek in 1851.[4]

Some whites, such as Captain Randolph Marcy, gave weight to the Choctaw-Chickasaw demands for the government to remove the Comanches from their lands in present-day western Oklahoma. Marcy claimed that the western lands were excellent for farming but were of no use to the Choctaws and the Chickasaws, as that region was within range of the Comanches. Because of this, few Choctaws and Chickasaws ventured into it, preferring to remain upon their very fertile lands on the Red and Canadian Rivers. He further noted that the Choctaws "have thrown aside their primitive habits in a great degree, and abandoned the precarious and uncertain life of the hunter for the more quiet avocation of the husbandman. They look upon the wild Indian in much the same light as we do, and do not go among them; indeed, there is but little in common with them and the wild Indians."[5]

Some of the Prairie Indians were not ready to accept the Choctaw and Chickasaw claims to the land at face value and stressed their own rights to the land. For centuries the Caddos had been Prairie peoples with close connections to the Comanches and Wichitas. In fact, the Caddos had created such bonds of kinship, exchange, and alliance with the Plains Indians that Caddoan was often spoken by the Comanches and Kiowas and was a Southern Plains lingua franca.[6] But over the past few years, the Caddo band living in Indian Territory had increasingly been moving into the political orbit of the Civilized Tribes. Now, the chief of the Indian Territory Caddos, George Washington, visited Chickasaw agent Kenton Harper in late 1851 to discuss his peoples' land claim. Washington explained that years before, his people had been driven out of Texas, and under the leadership of his father, Chonen, who was then chief of the band, they moved to Indian Territory. His father appeared before the General Council of the Choctaws and asked them for land, and the Choctaws gave them a strip of land on the Washita River in the western part of the Choctaw-Chickasaw territory. Washington produced a certificate signed by George Folsom, one of the Choctaw district chiefs, which guaranteed the Caddos this land. Not only that, Washington pointed out, but the Choctaw agent had long known and approved of their living on this land. In fact, Washington said, the agent promised them that the government would provide them with plows, axes, hoes, wedges, froes, ovens, pots, skillets, kettles, and even their own blacksmith shop. Harper, who detailed his talk with Chief Washington, wrote that the chief said, "His people wished to farm . . . they wished to do like the neighboring tribes, who had good fences and good fields. He asked to be informed when his people would get those things which . . . had been promised them." Harper also believed that the Caddos had a good claim, as even some Chickasaws recognized the accuracy of what Chief Washington said. The agent believed that the government should give them the tools promised and that they should not be forced off the land. "Indeed, some of the Chickasaws contend that their presence so far has been rather a benefit. That they have served to check inroads of other wild tribes, of less [exemplary] habits—and that they would be sorry to see them removed."[7]

As with the Caddos, the consequences of white immigration onto the Southern Plains and the examples of the Civilized Tribes began to split the Wichitas. A Prairie people who used both buffalo hunting and horticulture, the Wichitas, like the Caddos, had long maintained close relations with the Comanches. But now, while some Wichita communities chose to remain closely attached to the Comanches and hostile to the encroaching whites and removed Indians, others adopted practices associated with the Civilized Tribes. Not long after the Caddos demanded recognition of their settlement rights, some Wichitas also officially questioned the legality of the government's giving Wichita lands to the Chickasaws and Choctaws.

The second chief of the Wichitas, Toshaquash, using Cherokee Jesse Chisholm as his interpreter, informed United States officials of what he saw as Wichita lands. The area north of the Red River and west from the confluence of the False Washita and Washita Rivers, all the way to the 102nd meridian, "has been owned and occupied by the Wichita Tribe of Indians for the last four generations." Toshaquash said his people were surprised to find out that their land had been given to the Choctaws and Chickasaws. Now he wanted the United States to know that the Wichitas had never "bartered or sold any portion of their country to the United States." He proposed that government commissioners fairly and amicably settle this land dispute so the government could fulfill its obligation to the Choctaws, but also "so that our people may remain unmolested in the peaceable possession of that part of their country now occupied by them." In return for that part of the Wichita land that the government gave to the Choctaws and

Chickasaws, Toshaquash directed the United States to pay the Wichitas "its equivalent in agricultural implements, seeds, stock, goods and money; and further to take under the care and protection of this government the remnant of our said tribe and attach us to this superintendency. We need the advice and practical teachings of the white man in the productions of the earth and of manufactures that we may learn to feed and clothe our children as do the fathers of the white children so that our nation may be preserved and in their preservation learn to appreciate and to enjoy the blessings of civilization."[8]

As it had with the Caddos and Wichitas, the effects of increased white migration to the Southern Plains forced the Comanches to create a barrier against this migration. When the Comanches first arrived on the Southern Plains in the late seventeenth century, they battled the Lipan Apaches for control of the area. Driving the Apaches from the plains forced the Comanches to make kin-based political, military, and economic alliances with the Wichitas and Caddos. During the second half of the eighteenth century, when Spain tried to strengthen its settlements in New Mexico, Texas, and Louisiana and negate Comanche power through stricter Indian trade policies, the Comanches responded by allying with the Kiowas and Kiowa-Apaches then moving onto the Southern Plains. As whites in Texas and removed Indians in Indian Territory began settling on the margins of Comanches lands, in 1840 the Comanches strengthened their position by making an alliance with the Southern Cheyennes ranging north of the Arkansas River. Shoring up this barrier, in 1851 the Comanches allowed the remnants of their old enemies, the Lipan Apaches, to spend the winter near the Wichita Mountains.[9]

This Comanche alliance was not wholly unified, as some Caddo and Wichita bands were already deserting the alliance and moving into the Civilized Tribes' sphere. Nor was the alliance under the control of any single Comanche chief or division. As historian Tom Hagan has pointed out, a Comanche warrior might still steal a

Kiowa pony, but all the chiefs of the alliance knew not to let these petty incidents get out of hand to fracture the alliance.[10] Even the Comanches themselves, composed of five major divisions and maybe just as many minor ones, were not unified, nor had they ever been. The southernmost Comanche division, the Penatekas, lived in Texas and had been in association with whites the longest. They had been the ones to sign the 1846 treaty with the United States and had long been involved in trade with the Euroamericans. By the 1850s, some Penatekas were willing to try the reservation life the United States was urging upon them. Even U.S. officials divided the Comanches into "southern" or "lower" Comanches, the Penatekas, whom they viewed as more or less peaceful, and "northern" or "upper" Comanches, who lived north of Red River and committed most of the raids into Texas. Some Texans would not agree with this last assessment.[11]

Still, this Plains alliance was formidable, and the Indians' worry over the dwindling number of buffalo cemented it. By 1850 even the most optimistic Comanche could see that buffalo numbers were not what they once had been. Diseases such as anthrax and brucellosis; wolves that took four out of every ten calves; periodic floods, fires, and droughts; and overhunting by Texans, overland trail emigrants, removed Indians, and even the Plains Indians themselves through their involvement in the hide trade all made serious inroads on the buffalo population.[12] In fact, it may have been the scarcity of buffalo that made Caddo Chief George Washington and Wichita Chief Toshuhquash opt for a life of farming over one of hunting. How the Plains Indians rationalized the shrinking numbers of buffalo is not known; probably they blamed it on overhunting by whites and removed Indians. Whatever the reason, the Comanches, Kiowas, Kiowa-Apaches, Southern Cheyennes, Lipan Apaches, and some bands of Wichitas increasingly refused to tolerate hunting parties made up of peoples not part of their alliance that ventured west of a line about even with the Brazos River.[13] Even U.S. officials recognized that many Comanche attacks were in "retaliation for the destruction of their buffalo, timber, grass, &c., caused by the vast number of whites passing through their country without their consent."[14]

Comanche, Kiowa, and Wichita suspicions now increasingly affected their relations with the removed Indians. Reports circulated of battles between those Plains tribes and the Delawares, Shawnees, Kickapoos, and even the Sacs and Foxes—with varying outcomes. Rumors circulated of a huge battle in 1854 west of Fort Riley, Kansas, in which, it was alleged, a hundred well-armed Sac and Fox buffalo hunters held off a thousand bow and arrow–wielding Comanches. The Sacs and Foxes so often prevailed in battles with the Comanches that one government official stated that "the very sound of the name of Sacs caused a panic among those very bands of Comanches long considered so terrible upon the frontiers of Texas."[15] In many cases the army unwittingly fueled these suspicions by using Delaware, Shawnee, and Kickapoo guides on its explorations of the Southern Plains.[16]

Black Beaver, a Delaware, became the most famous of these guides, leading Captain Randolph Marcy's expedition to Santa Fe in 1849. According to Marcy, who seemed awed by the Delaware, Black Beaver had spent five years in California and Oregon and two years among the Crow and Blackfeet Indians; had trapped along the Gila, Columbia, Rio Grande, and Pecos Rivers; and had crossed the Rocky Mountains at various points. Not only could Black Beaver fluently speak Comanche and most other Prairie Indian languages, but he also taught Marcy how to identify Indian camps by the configurations of lodge poles and campfires. On any given evening Marcy and Black Beaver might discuss the roundness of the earth, steam engines, or even the workings of the telegraph. For years after, Black Beaver served as one of the most important Indians in the western part of Indian Territory.[17]

Sometimes suspicions of the Plains Indians fell upon trading parties from the Five Tribes. In May 1852 a party of Chickasaws went on an expedition to the Wichitas and Comanches to trade goods and ponies for mules and hides. Along the way they encountered a small party of Osages, who offered to serve as guides. On June 10 the party met a band of Comanches, and the trading commenced. At some point the Osages and Comanches came to believe that the Chickasaws were spies for the United States and that a company of soldiers was fast closing in for an attack. In later depositions the Chickasaws claimed it was all a ploy by the Osages to kill them and take their goods, while the Osages vehemently denied anything of the sort. The Comanches and Osages, either in panic or fury, attacked the Chickasaws, killing the black slave who managed the horses, and took all their goods. The Comanches took the Chickasaws back to their camp, where, according to the Chickasaws, the Osages demanded they be killed. The Comanches disagreed and the next day allowed the trading party to return to Chickasaw territory minus all its property. The traders filed claims with the government against the Comanches and Osages, but these were still being haggled over as late as 1868.[18]

Although one trading party may have been saved, raids and counterraids between Comanches and Kiowas and Chickasaws and Choctaws continued as they always had. Still, when the United States decided to make another treaty with the Comanches, Kiowas, and Kiowa-Apaches to stop raids along the Santa Fe Trail, the Chickasaws and Choctaws took the opportunity to try to make their own peace with the Plains Indians. For about three weeks during the summer of 1853, delegations of Comanches, Kiowas, Kichais, Creeks, Delawares, Shawnees, Chickasaws, Choctaws, and the United States met at Fort Atkinson in Indian Territory. The much-respected Jesse Chisholm served as interpreter. Major Thomas Fitzpatrick, Indian agent for the Upper Platte and Arkansas Rivers, represented the United States and distributed twenty thousand dollars' worth of blankets and other gifts to the Plains Indians in attendance. On July 27, 1853, Fitzpatrick signed a treaty with sixteen chiefs from several bands of Comanches, Kiowas, and Kiowa-Apaches. In return for eighteen thousand dollars' worth of goods and agricultural implements a year for ten years, they would allow the government to put roads through their territory and build forts to protect these highways. They also promised not to raid into Mexico anymore and to give up their Mexican captives. Nothing really came of the treaty, as the next year the Senate amended it so that the eighteen thousand dollars, instead of being given directly to the Indians, was to be put into a fund to help place the Plains Indians on farms, something most Comanches scoffed at. The Comanches, Kiowas, and Kiowa-Apaches also did not give up their Mexican captives, nor did they stop raiding into Mexico.[19]

Little is known of what peace negotiations, if any, transpired between the Plains Indians and the other Indian peoples attending the conference. Apparently nothing was resolved, for not long after the council ended, Choctaw-Chickasaw agent D. H. Cooper proposed creating a strike force of about eighty Choctaws and Chickasaws. The force would scour the area around Fort Arbuckle for "marauding Comanches" and protect the surveying party that was then fixing the boundary between the Choctaw and Chickasaw districts.[20]

While relations between the Plains Indians and Prairie Indians and the Civilized Tribes might range from very friendly to very hostile, with the ubiquitous Delawares, Kickapoos, and Shawnees thrown into the mix, anything might happen. By the early 1850s bands of Delawares, Kickapoos, and Shawnees lived in Kansas, Indian Territory, and Texas. These three peoples were so closely associated with each other that they often intermarried.[21] Settlers in Texas and Kansas, as well as the Chickasaws and Choctaws, wanted them removed. Comanches and Kiowas sometimes traded with them, sometimes raided them, and in turn were sometimes raided by them. Caddos and Wichitas also had varied relations with them, from sometimes friendly, even to the point of living in the same villages, to being the subjects of their raids. The United States saw them as useful guides, interpreters, scouts, and military auxiliaries and compared them much more favorably to such peoples as the Wichitas.[22]

The government wanted to find a permanent home for all these various bands, hoping, for example, that the Delawares might be located among the Five Major Tribes. This came to naught when the Cherokees and Creeks refused to give up any of their land to create a Delaware home.[23] Though nothing had been decided upon concerning a permanent home for all the various bands of the Delawares, Kickapoos, and Shawnees, in 1854 the United States signed treaties with the Delawares and Kickapoos in Kansas that extinguished their title to all their lands in that territory. Essentially expelled from Kansas, these Kansas Delawares and Kickapoos now had to find homes among the Five Tribes or the Plains Indians.[24]

In Texas the federal government also took steps to deal with the Delawares, Kickapoos, and Shawnees, as well as all Prairie Indians living in that state. In 1854 the government created two reservations. The Brazos Reserve became the home for bands of Caddo Nadacos (Anadarkos), Hainais (Ionies), and Kadohadachos (Caddos); Wichita Wacos and Tawakonis; and Tonkawas as well as Shawnees and Delawares still living in Texas. The Clear Fork of the Brazos Reserve was created for the Texas bands of the Penateka Comanches, who manifested a desire to settle down and begin farming.[25]

Similar things were taking place in Indian Territory. Increasingly, bands of Caddos, Kickapoos, Wichitas, Quapaws, and Biloxis applied to the Chickasaw agent for supplies and provisions.[26] In early 1855 some bands of "southern" Comanches—probably Penatekas—appealed to the Creeks to intercede for them with the United States. These Comanches, who claimed all the land between the Arkansas and Red Rivers stretching from the Creek and Choctaw Nations to the Rocky Mountains, were having trouble finding buffalo. According to Thomas Drew, head of the Southern Superintendency, several thousand of these "southern" Comanches "are fully impressed with the agricultural life from witnessing the prosperity of the Creeks." Drew said they now wanted to take the first steps toward "civilization" by receiving a grant of land somewhere between the Red and Arkansas Rivers.[27] And something that might assist in this "civilization" process was a discovery made by a scientist who accompanied Captain Marcy on his trip across the plains—gum mesquite. Drew believed gum mesquite could become a substitute for gum arabic, then used to seal envelopes. Gum mesquite could also be used as clothes starch and would provide income and support to the Prairie Indians, who could easily gather and sell it.[28]

While the Penateka Comanches were asking for a land grant in western Indian Territory, nine chiefs and head men of the Wichitas were appealing directly to the President for a guarantee to the Wichita Mountains so they could settle down and take up agriculture. Esauewah, spokesman for the Taovaya Wichitas, reported that the Wichita Mountains had always been their land, and the government had no right to give it to the Choctaws without consulting the Wichitas first. Depriving them of their land had made them wanderers and outcasts and had driven many of their young men to commit depredations that they would normally not have done.[29] Major George Andrews, commander of Fort Arbuckle, supported the Wichitas' appeal, reporting that there were eight hundred Wichitas ready to give up hunting and follow "the good example of the Choctaw and other Indians" if they would be given their old home among the Wichita Mountains.[30]

The requests by the Wichitas and Penateka Comanches and the constant complaints of the Choctaws and Chickasaws seemed to make an impression on the government. In 1855 the United States mediated a treaty between the Choctaws and Chickasaws, effectively separating the two nations. The Chickasaws now set up their own government and had their own land assigned to them. But part of this treaty also stipulated that the Chickasaws and Choctaws would lease to the United States all their lands between the ninety-eighth and one hundredth meridians. Called the Leased

District, this land was designated to be the permanent home of the Wichitas and any other Indians the government wanted to put there. In return, the government promised to remove all other Indians from Choctaw and Chickasaw lands. Choctaws and Chickasaws, though, still had the right to settle in the Leased District should they decide to do so. Out of this, two years later in 1857, the government created the Wichita Reserve.[31]

Despite the creation of the Leased District and a Wichita Reserve, hundreds of Caddos, Wichitas, Shawnees, Delawares, and Kickapoos remained on Chickasaw lands. The Chickasaws and Choctaws demanded they be removed to the Leased District, but the government had made no plans for their removal. Wichita agent A. H. McKisick pointed out that many of these Indians, such as the Kickapoos, Delawares, and Shawnees, had been "born on this soil and have never been off it."[32] He appealed to Chickasaw Governor Cyrus Harris to allow them to remain on their lands until reserves in the Leased District could be created for them.[33]

Still, the three reserves—the Wichita Reserve in the Leased District and the Brazos and Clear Fork Reserves in Texas—did provide a home for many Indians who had, theoretically, been landless up to that time. In 1857 a census was taken of the three reserves. The Brazos Agency in Texas totaled 982 Indians: 235 Caddos, 218 Anadarkos (Nadacos), 162 Wacos, 199 Tawakonis, and 168 Tonkawas. The main spokesman for the Indians on the Brazos Reserve was Anadarko chief Iesh, known to whites as José Maria. Three hundred eighty-seven Penateka Comanches lived on the Clear Fork Reserve in Texas.

At the Wichita Agency in Indian Territory, Agent McKisick reported nine hundred Wichitas, probably Taovayas, and three hundred Kichais living in proximity on Rush Creek—all led by Chief Esauewah. The Taovayas and Kichais, longtime allies, had become so close and intermarried that McKisick considered them now one people. Three hundred Wacos and Tawakonis lived together on the Canadian River. Three hundred sixty-five Caddos,

Anadarkos, and Ionis (Hasinais) were scattered along the Washita, Red, and Kiamichi rivers and, as McKisick reported, lived in a deplorable state, destitute of everything. About twenty-five hundred Kickapoos, Shawnees, and Delawares lived on the Canadian and False Washita rivers, while six hundred Comanches lived near the one hundredth meridian. The Comanches told McKisick they did not want to live in Texas.[34]

While the three reserves provided homes for many Prairie Indians, their boundaries could not break kinship bonds or stop the obligations of reciprocity so long a part of Indian life. Officials grew worried as peoples from one reserve visited their kinspeople on another. Sometimes people from one reserve just picked up and left to go live on another. Sam Houston appealed to the secretary of the interior to ensure that the Indians on the Wichita Reserve in Indian Territory be placed under the same regulations as those on the two Texas reserves. According to Houston, those Indians on the Wichita Reserve often mingled or traded with the Indians on the Texas reserves. If those Indians of the Wichita Reserve "should receive annuities and roam at large, it will cause the Indians in Texas to quit their reserves & betake them to former habits of stealing & killing on our borders. . . . Those Indians, if not confined in reserves, mite [sic] steal horses in Texas, and with the Indians in Arkansas, find a nearby market for stolen property."[35]

Particularly galling to government officials was the constant intercourse between the Clear Fork Reserve Comanches and the "northern" Comanches, who still roamed free across the Southern Plains. Texas Indian Superintendent Robert Simpson Neighbors predicted that the Comanche reserve would never be successful until the government got the "northern" Comanches to come live on the reserve. "The intercourse between them and the Indians on the reserve is constant and uninterrupted, and whenever an Indian on the reserve commits a crime, or there is the least difficulty, they prepare immediately for flight, to join their northern brothers." Neighbors believed the only way to stop this was to convincingly defeat or overawe the Comanches with military force. "Their chiefs have but little control, and I have never known them to make a treaty that a portion of the tribe do not violate its stipulations before one year rolls around." Until all the Comanches were defeated and put on reserves, he said, the raids would continue.[36]

There may have been something to what Neighbors said. The problem was that there were large numbers of Indians living on three reserves, while another large number of Indians still roamed free, adamantly against living on a reservation. Those living on reserves now became scapegoats for anything done by those Indians who remained free. Settlers near the reserves constantly blamed the reserve Indians for any crime committed. For the most part, this was misplaced blame. Most reserve Indians, such as the Caddos, Anadarkos, Wacos, Kichais, Tawakonis, and such, were thoroughly peaceful and merely wanted to live a quiet farming life. The Comanches on the Clear Fork Reserve proved more prob- lematic. In some cases Comanches and Kickapoos used the reserves as a sort of "oasis" or "way station" in which they might go live for awhile, draw rations, or rest up and then leave and join their free kinspeople. Sometimes these same free Indians, such as "northern" Comanches, Kiowas, and even some bands of Wichitas, might raid into Texas or Indian Territory and then seek refuge on one of the reserves. Some Texans firmly believed that blame for the robberies committed in that part of Texas could be laid at the door of the "northern" Comanches, who were aided and abetted by their reserve kinspeople.[37]

Events during the spring and summer of 1858 revealed the hopeless confusion resulting from the swirling mix of "civilized" Indians, reserve Indians, free Indians, Texas Rangers, U.S. Army troops, and white settlers and freebooters living in such close quar- ters. It also indicated the shifting alliances and agendas that had been developing among the various Indians peoples in Indian Territory during the previous few years. In March 1858 a band of Comanches attacked some Delawares and Kickapoos living near

Fort Arbuckle. Delaware chief Black Beaver rallied his warriors and fought off the Comanches, killing four.[38]

The Comanches' attack made Douglas Cooper, agent for the Choctaws and Chickasaws, worry that his charges would be next to be set upon. He reminded his superiors that the recent 1855 treaty pledged the United States to protect the Choctaws and Chickasaws from attacks by other Indians, then pointed out the exposed position his charges occupied. To remedy this, he recommended the government keep a large supply of guns and ammunition nearby so he could arm the Choctaws and Chickasaws for their own defense when necessity dictated. Cooper went even further, suggesting that a Choctaw and Chickasaw police force be created and "that such a force would be far more effective in preventing the introduction of intoxicating liquors among the Indians, in giving security to the life and property, and for the enforcement of the laws of the United States."[39] According to Cooper, about one hundred men could be formed into a force that could be called up at minute's notice. They would furnish their own horses and would be paid between one hundred and two hundred dollars a year, depending on the time they remained on duty. To drive this point home, Cooper pointed out that this force could be used to remove the Kickapoos who kept intruding on Chickasaw lands. Also, he had heard from some Cherokee traders that Mormons were trying to stir up the Kiowas, Wichitas, and other Indians into making an attack on the U.S. supply trains going to Utah.[40] Acting Commissioner of Indian Affairs Charles Mix, still not able to differentiate between Choctaws and Comanches, refused Cooper's request.

The United States' Mormon Expedition in 1858 stripped Indian Territory of most of its troops. With the troops gone, many Indian and white settlers feared the Comanches, Kiowas, and Wichitas would take the opportunity to attack. Even Jesse Chisholm, just returned from a trading expedition to the Comanches, believed the Plains Indians were up to no good. Wichita agent A. H. McKisick felt Brigham Young himself was stirring up the Plains Indians and had so frightened the Choctaws and Chickasaws that most had fled east of Fort Arbuckle. But if war actually broke out between the Comanches and the Choctaws, Chickasaws, and whites, he believed the Delawares and Kickapoos would side with the Civilized Tribes and the United States government.[41]

With every raid, theft, or murder that took place that spring and summer in Texas or Indian Territory being blamed on the Indians, white outlaws went on a crime spree. Agent Cooper had long admitted that the country was filled with lawless, freebooting whites, and with the army away, they seemed to get even worse. When Robert Love, a Chickasaw, told Cooper that the Comanches had killed some cattle and stolen a corral of horses down near Red River, Cooper commented, "I doubt very whether the thieves were Comanches. Every murder and theft on the border will now be charged to them."[42] Even the reserve Indians became targets of white horse thieves. Superintendent Neighbors reported that forty head of horses had been stolen from the Indians on the Brazos Reserve. The thieves rode shod horses, and that made him believe they were white men.[43] Other Texas reserve officials reported that white men dressed like Indians often committed crimes, even murdering soldiers.[44]

Most Texans had already made up their minds about the raids and theft. It was the Comanches, and that was that. So in mid-May 1858, Texas Ranger Captains John S. "Rip" Ford, leading a hundred Rangers, and Lawrence Sullivan "Sul" Ross, leading about 112 Caddo, Shawnee, Tonkawa, and Kichai warriors from the Brazos Reserve, disobeyed U.S. law, invaded Indian Territory, and attacked a Kotsoteka Comanche camp on the Canadian River. The Rangers' Indian auxiliaries charged in first and performed extremely well. In the battle, the combined force of Indians and Rangers killed Kotsoteka Comanche chief Iron Jacket, who got his name because he wore an old Spanish coat of mail. They also claimed they killed seventy-five other Comanches, captured three hundred horses, and took eighteen women and children captive. In turn, they lost two killed and three wounded. Happy with the results, they raced back to Texas with their spoils.[45]

Immediately, varying reports of what happened circulated among the Indians. According to the Comanches, the Texans and Brazos Reserve Indians made an unprovoked attack on a relatively undefended camp in Comanche territory near the Wichita Mountains. Most of the Comanche warriors were out hunting buffalo, and the camp contained only a small party of men, women, and children left there to guard the horses. Only five Comanches had been killed in the raid, but the Rangers and Indians had managed to take three hundred horses and some of their women and children. The young men immediately returned from the hunt and gave chase. Although they could not catch up with the attackers, a few of the prisoners did manage to escape.[46] The Delawares believed that the Texans got the wrong Indians and killed seventy-three Comanches who actually lived on Texas' Clear Fork Reserve. As the Delawares saw it, "The white folks fattened the Comanches & now they have killed 73 of them."[47]

Retaliation came quickly, as Iron Jacket's surviving Comanches needed to replenish the horses stolen by the Texas Rangers. Over the next few weeks Chickasaw farms lost over sixty horses.[48] The surveying party charged with marking the line between the Chickasaws' western boundary and the Leased District also found itself besieged. According to surveyors A. H. Jones and H. M. C. Brown, between two thousand and three thousand very angry Comanches roamed the area, threatening to attack the surveyors. The Comanches, under the leadership of Penateka chief Potsanaquahip, whom whites called Buffalo Hump, along with his Kiowa and Cheyenne allies, also made a small raid upon Fort Arbuckle in hopes of getting the ammunition stored there. The fort was weakly defended, because the Seventh Infantry had been sent to Utah. To its rescue came Chickasaw-Choctaw agent Douglas Cooper, who reinforced the few men at the fort with ten Chickasaw men under the

immediate command of Chickasaw governor Harris W. Moncrief.
The Comanche threats delayed the survey for almost a year, and
it would not be completed until July 1859.[49]

Despite Commissioner Charles Mix's refusal to create a
Chickasaw-Choctaw police force, and though many of the horses
taken from around Fort Arbuckle had already been recovered,
Cooper called up a force of Chickasaws and Choctaws to chase
down the Comanches. On the first day of July 1858, Cooper, along
with seventy-two members of the Chickasaw and Choctaw militia,
augmented by several Caddo, Delaware, and Cherokee volunteers
and guided by Delaware chief Black Beaver, rode into the Leased
District to make a "reconnaissance." Though the Cherokees eventually deserted, the Chickasaws, Choctaws, Delawares, and Caddos
spent sixteen days pursuing the Comanches, but to no avail. While
they found no Comanches, they did stop at Toshaquash's Wichita
village, where they recovered a horse reportedly stolen from the
Choctaws five years earlier. Still, Cooper believed the expedition
was a success in that it showed that the Chickasaws and Choctaws
were not afraid to venture out onto the plains, and a raid made
upon them would not go unpunished.[50]

While the Chickasaws' expedition may have bolstered their
confidence, it did not stop the Comanches, and by late July Comanche raiders once again struck Chickasaw corrals. On July 25 a band
of Comanches accosted Robinson Thompson, a Chickasaw man,
about two miles from Fort Arbuckle. Speaking in Caddo, the
Comanches asked him if he was an American. When Thompson
replied that he was Chickasaw, the Comanches let loose a shot. It
missed him but killed his horse. Thompson escaped into a thicket,
where he hid throughout the night, managing to make it to Fort
Arbuckle at daybreak. Soon after, other reports came in of the theft
of more than seventy horses in the area. About the same time, the
astronomer with the surveying party, Daniel G. Major, warned
by some Wichitas, Kichais, and Kickapoos that the Comanches,
Kiowas, and Cheyennes might attack his surveying party, asked

the commander at Fort Arbuckle for help. Lieutenant J. E. Powell of the First Infantry, commander of Fort Arbuckle, with all the appeals flooding in sent a scout of twenty-seven men, guided by Black Beaver, to hunt down the Comanches. Unable to send troops to aid the surveying party because he did not have enough animals available, Lieutenant Powell sent a party of trusted Kickapoos to protect them. Soon after, he reinforced the Kickapoos guarding the surveyors with twenty-four Caddos and Delawares under the command of Delaware chief Jim Ned.[51]

Chickasaws were not the only Indians to lose horses to the Comanches. No sooner had Lieutenant Powell sent out his scouting party than the Taovaya Wichita principal chief, along with three Kichais, arrived at Fort Arbuckle to make their own complaints. According to the Taovaya chief, he had been trying to keep the Comanches peaceful, but while the Comanches professed friendship, they continued stealing his horses. When he confronted them with this, they apologized but then stole more of his horses when they left his village. A few days before, the Comanches had even kidnapped a Taovaya woman. When they discovered this, some of his young men chased down the Comanches and recovered the woman, but, following the advice of Agent Cooper, they did not do any harm to the Comanches. The Taovaya chief now appealed to Lieutenant Powell, asking, "How long am I to forbear? They steal our horses and outrage our people. Must I stand quietly by and see them kill my young men, and wait till some are dead before I resist? . . . If I fight, they will overpower my people and kill us all. If I do not resist, they will steal everything we have, and we shall starve to death." The chief believed the Comanches planned to steal enough horses so they could make a truly powerful attack into Texas.[52]

Two chiefs of the Kickapoos present during the Wichita chief's speech announced that they were ready and willing to help stand against the Comanches. Lieutenant Powell advised the Kickapoos to unite with the Caddos and Delawares and send as many warriors as possible to Great Springs, about six miles west of the Taovaya village. There they should form a camp for their mutual protection and remain until he could receive instructions from his superiors.[53]

Despite Lieutenant Powell's good intentions, the army proved useless in tracking down the Comanches and protecting Chickasaw, Choctaw, and Wichita property. By early August the Comanches were still raiding Chickasaw farms and ranches. Raids became so bad that all Chickasaws living west of Fort Arbuckle again abandoned their homes and moved into the fort for protection. Once again, Agent Cooper appealed to Washington for authority to create a home defense regiment of Choctaws and Chickasaws. The surveying party again felt threatened, and a group of Chickasaws volunteered to protect it while it surveyed the Chickasaw boundary. Once the surveyors began marking the Seminole-Creek boundary, a party of fifty Creeks and fifty Seminoles was hired to guard it. But word was out that the Comanches, Kiowas, and Cheyennes were gathering in force on the Salt Plains, and the government believed a detachment of possibly two hundred men might be needed for adequate protection.[54] Jesse Chisholm, who had just met with four Comanche chiefs at the Taovaya village, returned with more bad news. According to Chisholm, the Comanches, as well as the Taovayas, Kichais, Wacos, and Kickapoos, were "deadly hostile to Texans and everything connected with Texas." Because of this, Agent Cooper felt that unless a military post was established in the Leased District and manned with cavalry or mounted riflemen, not infantry, then "we shall have a regular Indian war upon Texas, and perhaps the Choctaw and Chickasaw country."[55]

In late August 1858, just when tensions were at their highest, the commander at Fort Arbuckle received word that two Comanche chiefs, probably Penatekas, were then at the Taovaya village and wanted to hold a council with him. Lieutenant Powell of the First Infantry went to the Taovaya village, where he met with the Comanche, Taovaya, Waco, and Kichai chiefs. The Comanches expressed sorrow at all the recent problems, but they had only just become aware of the complaints made by their Taovaya friends. As soon as they had heard them, the Comanche chiefs became very angry and had seized as many horses as they could from their young men. While not supporting the attacks on the Choctaws, Chickasaws, and Wichitas, the Comanches ticked off a list of reasons why the raids had been happening. The Texas Rangers' unprovoked attack on their village had outraged the young men, who, without consent of the chiefs, had begun raiding for horses to prepare themselves for the war with the Texans. Of course they also needed horses for their buffalo hunts. And the chiefs reminded Powell that buffalo was something they could not live without. Equally as bad was that among the attacking Rangers they recognized a Kichai warrior who had once lived at the Taovaya village. This made the Comanches believe that the Taovayas had joined with the Texans to make war upon them. Powell listened to all this, then demanded that the chiefs restore the horses stolen from the Choctaws and Chickasaws. The chiefs readily agreed, saying they already had recovered many of the horses and were prepared to give them up after finding out how this council would go. They also asked Powell about being permitted to settle down and farm near the Taovayas. Powell explained to them about the Leased District and said he did not see any problem with their proposal. Taovaya Wichita chief Esauewah agreed to accompany the Comanche chiefs to Fort Arbuckle and intercede for them.[56]

All the problems over the past summer had begun when Texas Rangers invaded Indian Territory. Now, just as the fallout began settling and peace was being made with the Comanches, Texans once again invaded Indian Territory. Over the summer, the Texans fumed about the raids the Comanches had made into their state. It was no secret that the Comanches differentiated between Texans and other Americans. And the Comanches hated all Texans, especially Texas Rangers and even United States troops stationed in Texas. Texas officials firmly believed that a full-scale war with the

Comanches, Kickapoos, and other Indians was brewing. Making them cast a baleful eye on Indian Territory was their belief that various Indian peoples there supplied the Comanches, Kiowas, and Cheyennes with the guns they used to raid Texas. In late August 1858, another force of Texas Rangers, along with twenty-one Caddo, Delaware, and Shawnee warriors from the Brazos Reserve, illegally entered Indian Territory with orders to attack Indians living around the Wichita Mountains. Fortunately, this force was intercepted by the army at Fort Arbuckle and sent back to Texas before it could cause trouble.[57] The next one would not be stopped.

In late September, Comanche Kotsoteka chiefs Quohoahteme (Hair Bobbed on One Side) and Hotowokowot (Over the Buttes), and Penateka chief Potsanaquahip (Buffalo Hump), along with six hundred of their people, arrived at the Taovaya village located near present-day Rush Springs, Oklahoma. They set up their own camp on nearby Horse Creek. As they had promised Lieutenant Powell, the Comanches came to return the horses stolen from the Wichitas during the summer raids and make peace with the Chickasaws and Choctaws. From there, the chiefs were planning to go to Fort Arbuckle to make peace with the United States. Then, on the night of October 1, the U.S. Second Cavalry, then stationed in Texas under the command of Brevet Major Earl Van Dorn, rode into Indian Territory. Van Dorn's cavalry, along with 135 Tawakoni, Waco, Caddo, Tonkawa, and Delaware scouts from the Brazos Reserve under the command of Ranger Captain Sul Ross and Tawakoni Jim, attacked the Comanche village. It was a desperate battle that lasted over an hour and a half, with the Brazos Reserve Indians doing some of the hardest fighting. When the battle was over, the troops claimed they had killed fifty-six Comanche warriors, wounded an unknown number, captured three hundred horses, burned 120 lodges, and destroyed the Comanches' entire supply of ammunition, cooking utensils, clothing, dressed hides, corn, and other food stores. Van Dorn admitted that two Indian women and two Wichitas had accidentally been killed and that four of his men had been killed, one man was missing, and twelve were wounded.[58]

Once again, turmoil descended upon the Indians in the western part of Indian Territory. The Comanches believed they had been set up by the Taovaya Wichitas and vowed to exact vengeance upon them. The Taovayas and Kichais had not been involved, and the attack came as a surprise to them. Still, they knew what the Comanches would think, and, fearing reprisals, they abandoned their homes near Rush Springs and headed for the safety of Fort Arbuckle. Remembering the raids of the past summer, the Chickasaws and Choctaws prepared for the worst. Agent Cooper again appealed to the government to establish a strong Chickasaw-Choctaw mounted police, armed and paid by the government. Even Black Beaver and Jesse Chisholm, normally friends of the Comanches, now hesitated to venture too far west of Fort Arbuckle. The situation was so bad that Superintendent of Indian Affairs Elias Rector believed that unless this idea of Wichita treachery was disavowed, "we shall have prolonged border war on the Choctaw, Chickasaw, and Seminole frontier. . . . Great loss of life must necessarily result, all surveying operations in that region be suspended, and the overland mail to California cease to run, and its stations broken up." Rector advised that a commission be appointed to visit the Comanches in the spring. Accompanied by Choctaw, Chickasaw, Creek, Seminole, and Wichita delegates, and bearing plenty of presents, they could explain that the attack on the Comanche village was all a mistake. The commission should try to arrange a permanent peace and induce the Comanches to settle on reserves in the Wichita country.[59]

The Van Dorn raid and the resulting Comanche counterattacks made some Five Tribes leaders see that they might play an increasingly important role as mediators between the government and the Plains Indians in arranging peace. A Cherokee leader, I. G. Vore, saw the government's future dealings with the Plains Indians as either extermination or peace. According to Vore, a war of extermination would be immensely costly in both treasure and lives, much more so than the recent Seminole Wars and the Mormon Expedition. The Indians of the Southern Plains claimed this country as their own and did not fully understand the power and resources of the United States. "Some of them look upon the Americans as being few in numbers and protected by the Cherokees, Creeks and Choctaws, and others on our frontier, even looking upon those with contempt, feeling themselves to be the most powerful nations on the earth." A war against peoples with this mind-set would be a long and costly one.[60]

Vore and Civilized Tribes progressives recommended peace. They advised that the government appoint a peace commission to deal with the Plains Indians and that the commission should have plenty of presents to distribute. "Give them a delegation from each of the Cherokees, Creeks, and Choctaws, with a sufficient escort to the commission to command respect" and with full power to make treaties that would assign the Indians to lands with distinctly marked boundaries between the 100th and 103rd meridians.[61] Others, especially settlers in Texas, hoped for the extermination policy. Angered at the raids on their ranches and farms, and unable to get at the "northern" Comanches, their ire turned to those Indians living on the Brazos and Clear Fork Reserves.

If the government hoped to use the reserves to turn the Prairie Indians into imitations of the Civilized Tribes, meaning loyal, peaceful small farmers participating in the market economy, then by all estimates the Texas reserves, especially the Brazos Reserve, had to be considered highly successful. On the Brazos Reserve the Kadohadachos (Caddos), Anadarkos (Nadacos), Wichita Tawakonis and Kichais, Delawares, Shawnees, and even a few Choctaws all lived in and around each other and often intermarried. The Caddos and Tawakonis willingly sent their children to the reserve school, while several men, such as Delawares Jim Shaw and George Williams, held important paid staff positions. Men from all the Brazos Reserve peoples served as scouts and auxiliaries in Texas' and the United States' battles against the Comanches. The Indians also assisted the nearby settlers in finding and returning lost stock and horses and served as hunting guides, while their purchases at nearby stores added to the economy of the surrounding settlements. If living like whites counted as evidence of "civilization," then the Indians on the Brazos Reserve were civilized. This could be seen by the log cabins and panel houses they lived in, as well as the white-style clothing, tools, chairs, brass kettles, churns, spades, axes, hoes, steel traps, wagons, yokes of oxen, and head of cattle they possessed.[62]

Despite the success of the Texas reserves, white settlers in nearby Erath and Bosque Counties viewed the Indians on them with suspicion and hatred. Any crime, any loss of property, any offense committed by "northern" Comanches or Kiowas was blamed on the Indians of the Brazos and Clear Fork Reserves. Texas Indian superintendent Robert S. Neighbors, Texas Ranger Captain Rip Ford, and various army officers around Fort Belknap came to the Indians' defense. These officials tried to explain the innocence of the reserve Indians, recounted the services they rendered to the state and federal government, and tried to make the settlers see the reserve Indians' value as buffers against the "northern" Comanches. But the settlers would have none of it, and these officials came in for their share of abuse because they dared to defend the reserve Indians. Relations became so bad that white settlers did not just want just the reserves to be broken up and the Indians removed—they wanted all the Indians on them to be killed.[63]

In December 1858 the white settlers went beyond just talk when a party of whites attacked a camp of twenty-seven Caddos and Anadarkos on the Brazos Reserve, killing four men and three women and wounding all the rest. One of the women killed was the wife of Choctaw Tom, a Choctaw who had married into the Anadarko Caddos. Many of the survivors, fearing for their lives, left the reserve for the Choctaw Nation in Indian Territory, where some of their relatives lived.[64] In early May 1859 a party of whites again raided some camps of the Brazos Reserve for the sole purpose of taking plunder. They killed and scalped several Indians and took two guns, some blankets, and fifty-four Indian ponies.[65] Then in late May 1859 a party of 250 white settlers led by J. R. Baylor made a major attack on the Brazos Reserve. They intended to kill all the Indians on that reserve and then move on and do the same thing to the Penateka Comanches on the Clear Fork Reserve. Baylor's men managed to kill several reserve Indians, including Sergeant Caddo John, who had served with the Rangers and the army in its Comanche campaigns, but the Indians managed to counterattack, killing about five of Baylor's men and forcing the others to hole up in a nearby farmhouse. Only the intervention of the First Infantry prevented a massacre of either side.[66]

The attacks by the Texans on the Brazos Reserve had an impact on the Caddos, Wichitas, and Delawares living in Indian Territory. Having seen Texans raid into Indian Territory after Comanches, and not understanding why the Texans would attack their own allies who had helped them fight the Comanches, these Caddos, Wichitas, and Delawares in the Leased District now believed they might be the Texans' next target. In fear of their lives, and not having the ability to protect themselves, many left their homes in the Wichita Agency district and moved east to Chickasaw Territory. In turn, this angered the Chickasaws, who again complained about "foreign" Indians on their lands. The Chickasaws feared that such a concentration of Prairie peoples might attract the Texans and bring their wrath down on their own head.[67]

Though removing the Indians from Texas to Indian Territory had been an idea many Texas officials had supported since the beginning of the year, Baylor's attack convinced them that it had to be done immediately. Toward the end of July and the first of August 1859, Superintendent Neighbors led the Comanches of the Clear Fork Reserve and the Caddos, Anadarkos, Tonkawas, Tawakonis, Kichais, Delawares, and Shawnees of the Brazos Reserve, all totaling fourteen hundred, on their own trail of tears to Indian Territory. Two companies of the Second Cavalry escorted the exiles, while Black Beaver scouted southward from Indian Territory to assist in their arrival. The Texas Indians arrived at the Wichita Agency in the Leased District in late August, and on September 1, Samuel Blain, agent of the Wichita Agency, officially took charge of them. Though white settlers planned to attack the Indians en route, they did not, and the only action came when a party of nine Kiowas attacked a scouting party sent by Neighbors to find Agent Blain's camp.

Assigned to the Wichita Agency, these Indians received lands along the Washita, False Washita, and Canadian Rivers. The Indians from the Brazos Reserve remained somewhat together but kept themselves separate from the removed Penateka Comanches. Soon, bands of the Caddos, Kichais, Taovayas, and Delawares who had been living in the Chickasaw Nation joined their removed Texas kinspeople around Wichita Agency. All these Prairie Indians settled around the agency, and all soon came to be collectively called the Wichitas and Affiliated Bands. On October 1, 1859, the government began building Fort Cobb, about three miles west of the Wichita Agency, to protect these Indians from Comanches, Kiowas, and angry Texans, if need be. Superintendent Neighbors said good-bye to his former charges, many of whom cried on his departure and begged their old friend and protector not to leave them. Upon his return to Texas, he was gunned down—shot from behind—by a Texas citizen angry at Neighbors for letting the Indians escape.[68]

Now that they were in Indian Territory and under the good influence of the nearby Chickasaws, Seminoles, Creeks, and Choctaws, it was hoped that the "civilizing" of these Prairie Indians and Penateka Comanches might pick up where it had left off in Texas. During the 1850s the Five Civilized Tribes had influenced many bands of Caddos, Wichitas, Delawares, Shawnees, Kickapoos, and even some "southern" Comanches to emulate their life-style, making them want to settle down and take up farming. But the Chickasaws and Choctaws insisted this not be done on Chickasaw and Choctaw land. The federal government created reserves for these Prairie Indians in Texas and Indian Territory, and the "civilization" process seemed to be succeeding. As they adopted the settled life-style of the Civilized Tribes, many Prairie Indians, who had long possessed close relations with the Comanches, now began siding with the Civilized Tribes against the Plains Indians. Though the Texas reserves had been closed and the Indians removed to Indian Territory, there was no reason to think the "civilization" process would not continue among the Prairie Indians and even spread to the Comanches, Kiowas, and Southern Cheyennes. But before any progress could be made, the Civil War broke out. It virtually tore Indian Territory apart, but it added a new dynamic to relationships among the Five Tribes, the removed Indians, the Prairie Indians, and the Plains Indians.

CHAPTER SIX

CIVIL AND UNCIVIL WARS

The United States government gave the Chickasaws permission to go into the Comanche country and look for their horses. They went and found horses in large numbers, but none of their own. A few years later I went on a visit to Lawton and met a real old Comanche. I asked him why it was that we never found any of our horses. I said, "Remember anything about Comanches used to steal horses?" He said, "No, me from Texas, steal horse in Texas bring over here, steal horse over here, take him to Texas." That was the whole story. The horses that were stolen from the Chickasaws were carried to Texas, and the horses that were stolen from Texas were carried to Lawton.

OVERTON LOVE
Indian-Pioneer Histories

The dawning of the 1860s still saw the Civilized Tribes and the Plains Indians with vast cultural differences. "Northern" Comanches and their Kiowa allies continued making periodic raids into the Chickasaw Nation, while the Creeks and Seminoles still tried to exert some influence in bringing about peace and "civilization."

The Civilized Tribes could claim some success with the Prairie Indians. By 1860, just about all the Wichita, Caddo, Tonkawa, Delaware, and Shawnee bands had settled around the Wichita Agency in the Leased District and were improving their lands and building houses. These Prairie Indians had also, more or less, abandoned their close relations with the Comanches and Kiowas and turned toward the life-style advocated by the Civilized Tribes. It was hoped that the example of the Prairie Indians would influence the "northern" Comanches, but before any such "progress" could take place, the Civil War and Reconstruction interrupted the process.

By government standards, the Wichita Agency appeared on its way to a roaring success, with the Wichitas and Affiliated Bands marching steadily toward "civilization."[1] Unfortunately, the Wichita Agency Indians were not "civilized" enough for the Texans and were too "civilized" for the Comanches and Kiowas. As Comanches and Kiowas continued raiding into Texas, Texans continued blaming the Wichita Agency Indians, despite assurances from agency officials that these Prairie Indians were not involved.[2] On the other hand, although Jesse Chisholm informed agency officials that the Kiowas and Comanches wanted to make peace with the whites, these same Indians began raiding the Indians around the Wichita Agency. Several skirmishes between the Agency Indians and the Comanches and Kiowas took place in 1860, and very bad blood developed between the Kiowas and the Caddos when a Caddo warrior killed Kiowa chief Bird Appearing.[3]

Relations between the Wichita Agency Indians and the Comanches and Kiowas became so strained that once again the Creeks stepped in. Recalling their long friendship with the Plains Indians and their past services in setting up peace councils, the Creeks sent a delegation to arrange peace with the Comanches in the summer of 1861 at Council Grove, near present-day Oklahoma City. But before the peace council could ever get underway, the Civil War began, and suddenly the Creeks, themselves divided over which side to support in the war, found many other things to worry about.[4]

The Civil War proved disastrous for the Five Major Tribes. So far, in their diplomatic activities, they had usually acted in concert with each other. Now the war not only drove wedges between the various Civilized Tribes, but also split each nation as well. Among the Five Major Tribes the progressives, most of whom were slave owners and were involved in the market economy, sympathized with the Confederacy. Bolstering this sympathy was Indian Territory's geographical proximity to Confederate Texas and Arkansas. Trust funds for the Five Tribes had also been heavily invested in southern stocks and bonds. Barely had the first shot been fired when the United States withdrew its troops from the forts in Indian Territory, effectively abandoning the Civilized Tribes to the Confederates and Plains Indians. Still, most traditionalists from the Five Tribes remained loyal to the Union, insisting that they would not break the treaties they had signed with the United States.[5]

In the absence of Union forces, Confederate ambassadors Elias Rector and Albert Pike soon arrived among the Five Tribes in hopes of allying them with the South. The Choctaws and Chickasaws, virtually within the clutches of Confederate Texas and Arkansas, almost to a man went with the South. Among the Cherokees, Creeks, and Seminoles, civil wars erupted within their own nations. Situated not so close to the Confederacy, these three nations split, with some of their citizens, usually their progressive factions, allying with the Confederacy while others, often the traditionalists, stayed with the Union. Pro-Confederate Indians, under the leadership of Brigadier General Stand Watie, a Cherokee and the South's only Indian general, took the initiative and attacked first, driving most pro-Union Indians into Kansas. Later, pro-Union Indians, termed "Pins" because they used a straight pin on their collar to identify themselves, counterattacked. Over the course of the war these factions, in concert with Union and Confederate troops, savagely fought each other, devastating the Five Tribes.[6]

In the western part of Indian Territory, once the Union withdrew its troops, the Confederates moved in. By early 1862,

Confederate Chickasaw troops occupied Fort Arbuckle, while former Clear Fork Reserve Indian agent Matthew Leeper took control of Fort Cobb and the Wichita Agency for the Confederacy.[7] Just as it did among the Five Tribes, the coming of the Civil War brought confusion to the Prairie and Plains Indians in western Indian Territory. Confederate emissary Albert Pike visited the Caddos, Wichitas, and other Indians around Fort Cobb and held a council with the Comanches and Kiowas to persuade them to side with the Confederacy. Texans, who had so recently wanted to kill these same Indians, now begged them to help protect Texas from any Union advance. Several Caddo, Wichita, and Penateka Comanche chiefs, not sure of what was going on, turned to Seminole chief John Jumper for advice in their meetings with the Confederate and Texas representatives.[8]

As it had the Five Tribes, the war split the Indians living in the western part of Indian Territory. Some Caddo and Wichita bands, wanting to remain neutral, moved far out onto the plains. Others, under the influence of Albert Pike and the Texans, sided with the Confederacy. According to Sarah Ann Harlan, whose husband ran a store that supplied goods to the Plains Indians, early in the war several bands of Comanches visited the Chickasaws at Tishomingo near Fort Washita, saying they wanted to join the Confederate army.[9] Some Wichitas, such as Esauewah, signed treaties with the Confederates, while Caddo chief George Washington and Anadarko chief Iesh actually created and commanded the Caddo Frontier Guard, a Confederate home guard battalion composed of Caddos, Anadarkos, Choctaws, and Chickasaws.[10]

Other factions remained loyal to the Union. Black Beaver led his band of Delawares into Union-held Kansas, while bands of Caddos, Wichitas, Shawnees, and Kickapoos did the same.[11] To take care of these refugees, the Union created a northern Wichita Agency for the pro-Union Prairie Indians at Belmont, Kansas. By April 1862, more than seven thousand Indians from all nations had taken refuge with the Union in Kansas. These included 4,556 Creeks,

1,128 Seminoles, 636 Kickapoos, 425 Yuchees, 325 Quapaws, 270 Cherokees, 197 Delawares, 108 Chickasaws, 86 Kichais, 17 Hainais, 15 Biloxies, 5 Wichitas, and 3 Caddos. The numbers swelled as the war continued. By late 1862 the federal government had spent sixty-nine thousand dollars on provisioning these refugees.[12]

Lagging behind the Confederates, by mid-1862 the Union began recruiting Indians into the military. By late May and early June 1862 the Union army in Kansas created the "Indian Brigade," which consisted of about one thousand Creeks and Seminoles, sixty Quapaws, and sixty Cherokees as well as full companies of Delawares, Kichais, Hainais, Caddos, and Kickapoos, all totaling about fifteen hundred Indian soldiers.[13] The Indian Brigade, commanded by Union officers and supported by Union troops, soon began an advance into the eastern part of Indian Territory.

In the fall of 1862, actual fighting finally spilled over to the Indians around the Wichita Agency in Indian Territory. On the evening of October 23 a large band of Indians attacked the agency, killing Tonkawa chief Placedore and about one hundred of his people. The attackers also burned the agency and killed some of the agency's Confederate officials. The Wichitas and Affiliated Bands and other Indians served by the agency scattered. The attack was called the "Tonkawa Massacre" because the Tonkawas seemed to be the main target. The identity of the attackers and their reasons for the assault have clouded over time. Varying stories circulated and still do to this day. Some say it was an attack by Confederate-allied Wichitas, Comanches, Shawnees, and Delawares on the Tonkawas, who tended to support the Union. The Wichitas and Comanches deny this and blame the Shawnees and Delawares. Others say it was an attack by a force of Union-allied Shawnees and Delawares on the Confederate-held agency, and they just took the opportunity to kill off the Tonkawas. Others say it was merely blood revenge by either the Wichitas or the Shawnees on the Tonkawas for killing and eating some of their people. Whatever the reason, the Tonkawas had always been considered the odd people out among Texas Indians. They had been accused of cannibalism and had been allies of the Lipan Apaches, who had been enemies of the Comanches, Kiowas, Wichitas, and Caddos. Even on the Brazos Reserve the Tonkawas had kept themselves separated from the other Indians. Whatever the reason for the massacre, the Tonkawas were almost wiped out, with the few survivors retreating back into Texas. They would later get a reservation in the northern part of Indian Territory.[14]

The Civil War also provided opportunities for the Prairie and Plains Indians to make raids on the Five Major Tribes. Pro-Union bands taking refuge in Kansas often raided into Indian Territory, liberating cattle, horses, and provisions, which they took back to Kansas and sold to contractors. The contractors then resold the booty to the government, which used it to feed the Indians. Unfortunately, the fog of war meant that allies might suffer as well as enemies. In February 1863, Union officials in Kansas were distressed to learn that some bands of Union-allied Prairie Indians had raided into the Cherokee and Creek countries, but rather than attacking Confederate sympathizers, they had instead attacked pro-Union homes. In one raid, a band of Kichais and Tawakonis killed a Cherokee Unionist and captured two young Cherokee women, along with the children, twelve and two years of age, of one of them. On their way back to Kansas, the mother froze to death. Because the youngest child still needed its mother, the raiders killed it, too.[15] According to Union officials, the raid caused much bad feelings between the Cherokees and the "wild tribes." Union officials turned to Jim Ned of the Delawares to stress to the Caddos, Wichitas, and other Indians that they not attack pro-Union families. Jim Ned met with the Prairie Indians, then assured the officials that the Indians promised to make no more raids into Indian Territory. The assurances did not seem to hold, as by 1864, Union officials were again making the same complaints.[16]

By 1863, Union forces had pushed deep into Indian Territory. For the remainder of the war the Canadian River pretty much served as an unofficial boundary between Union-held Indian Territory to the north and Confederate-held land to the south. Hoping to build on this success, Union officials called a council with those Prairie and Plains Indians who still remained loyal to the South. In June 1863, E. H. Carruth, the Union's Wichita agent, met with delegates of the Hainais, Wacos, Tawakonis, Comanches, Lipan Apaches, Kiowas, Kickapoos, Sacs and Foxes, and Arapahos. Carruth found he did not have enough food and presents available for all the Indians who showed up. He also found that one of the reasons most of these Indians did not side with the Union was their long-held hostility to those Indians who did side with the Union. Carruth decided to call another council in six weeks and invited the Osages, Potawatomis, and Cheyennes. He hoped all these Indians could work out their differences. Apparently a council was held sometime in the summer of 1864 with chiefs from the Comanches, Kiowas, and Arapahos. Union officials tried to persuade the Plains Indians to make war on the South, offering them the guns to do so. But Jesse Chisholm was the interpreter, and he gave the Comanches probably the best advice they had ever received. Without the Union officers' knowing it, Chisholm told the Comanches not to get involved with this war. Listening to Chisholm, Comanche chief Ohopeyane refused to make war on the Confederate Indians, saying he had friends and brothers among them and he would not attack either the North or the South unless attacked first.[17]

By 1864 the Confederacy found it difficult to keep their Plains and Prairie allies. Some bands of Caddos, Anadarkos, Osages, Quapaws, and Penateka Comanches had sided with the Confederacy, and the South had spent thousands of dollars to supply these Indians and their families with corn, beef, salt, and sugar.[18] With Union successes in Indian Territory, many of the pro-Confederacy Indians grew nervous and began talking of surrender. The pro-Confederate Indians and their families lived in lamentable conditions, often homeless, naked, and virtually starving. Many had sought refuge in Texas, where Cherokee and Texas troops sometimes clashed. Progressive slave owners, to protect their human property from Union troops, relocated their slaves to the Brazos River. To stall talk of surrender, the Confederacy held a council with its Indian allies in March 1864 at Tishomingo in the Choctaw Nation near Fort Washita. Delegates from the Cherokees, Choctaws, Chickasaws, Creeks, Seminoles, Caddos, and Osages attended, and only with great difficulty were they persuaded to stay the course.[19]

At the same time, the Confederate Indians had to deal with the Comanches and Kiowas, who, once again, began venturing into Chickasaw Territory. With Indian Territory in turmoil, their trade networks disrupted, and most food, ammunition, and goods being funneled into the war effort, the Plains Indians found it increasingly difficult to acquire the goods they had come to rely upon. Some came peacefully to the Chickasaw Nation in search of food and manufactured goods. Reverend J. C. Robinson, who ran the Chickasaw Academy during the war, often had Comanches and Kiowas camp on the grounds of the academy, where Robinson butchered cattle to feed them. Other bands came to raid, and 1864 saw an increase in Comanche and Kiowa raids into Chickasaw territory and Texas, where the raiders took horses, captives, and plunder. The raids soon threatened the Santa Fe Trail supply line to Union-held New Mexico, and even a battle between Union Colonel Kit Carson and his New Mexico Volunteers with Kiowa warriors at Adobe Walls in the Texas Panhandle in November 1864 could not put an end to the raids.[20]

Comanche and Kiowa actions disturbed Union officials in Kansas. Some Union men, such as the Cherokee Jesse Chisholm, suggested a Comanche, Kiowa, and Apache reservation on the Arkansas River near the Kansas border.[21] Others, particularly acting Cherokee chief Lewis Downing, suggested holding another Indian peace council. According to Downing, the pro-Confederate Indians had been successful in getting the "wild tribes" to side with them during the war and had instigated the recent raids. Downing worried that with the Confederacy in its death throes, sympathetic Indians would scatter among the Plains nations, then after the formal peace and "we are off our guard, they will fall upon defenseless neighborhoods of loyal Indians, or whites, and plunder and kill unrestrained." To prevent this and keep the overland trails open, Downing suggested another council like the ones held in the 1840s. It had been a long time since a grand council had been held, he pointed out, and the leaders of the various Indian nations had forgotten the harmonious feeling and the friendships their fathers had made. Downing recommended that all the tribes of the Southwest be invited to a general convention to be held near Claremore Mound in the Cherokee Nation in order to reestablish peace and friendship. President Lincoln should send a signed speech and seals with the Great Seal of the United States, a white pipe with tobacco, a white flag, and a Bible, with all these wrapped in the United States flag.[22]

Downing may have had a good idea, as some Plains bands now made overtures to fight for the South. In January 1865 the commander of the Confederates' First Cherokee Battalion received word that the Comanches and Kiowas were prepared to join with the South and fight against the Union this coming summer.[23] About a month later, several Comanche, Kiowa, and Arapaho chiefs arrived in the Creek Confederate camp. Comanche chief Ohopeyane told the Creeks of having attended the previous year's council with Union officers, where they were urged to make war on the South. According to Ohopeyane, they were told they should "kill all the men and boys and take the women and children prisoners and drive off all the cattle and horses." When they returned from their expedition they were to "give up the white women and girls," but they could keep all the Indian women. The North would then buy all the mules, horses, the cattle from them." Taking Jesse Chisholm's advice, they refused to get involved in this plan. This angered the Union officers, so they refused to give the Plains Indians guns, ammunition, or gifts. As Tuckabatchee Micco, principal chief of the Creeks, told Cherokee brigadier general Stand Watie, "there is a perfect estrangement between those people and the North and they may now be relied on as true friends of the South." The Plains chiefs then asked the Creeks to send for Confederate delegates, but when none arrived, they went back to their camps on the plains.[24]

It would take a few months to get all the Indians together for a grand council, but by May 1865 the Confederacy was dead. All Confederate resistance had ceased east of the Mississippi River, and while General Stand Watie and a few Confederate Indians held out at Boggy Depot in the Choctaw Nation, the Civil War, for all intents and purposes, was over. Many pro-Confederate Indians still believed a grand council should be held to bring about peace and understanding among the Civilized Tribes, the Prairie Indians on the Wichita Reserve, and the Plains Indians. It was slated for late May 1865 at Council Grove, but later it was changed to Camp Napoleon near present-day Verden, Oklahoma, in the southwestern part of the state.

The Camp Napoleon council was the most comprehensive gathering of Indians since the great international councils of the 1840s. Representatives of Cherokees, Creeks, Chickasaws, Choctaws, Seminoles, Osages, reserve Caddos and Anadarkos, and reserve Comanches, all pro-Confederate, met with representatives of Kiowas, Arapahos, Cheyennes, Lipan Apaches, off-reserve Caddos, and delegates from five different Comanche divisions. Once again, these were essentially the "civilized tribes" or "timber Indians" meeting with the "wild tribes" or Plains Indians. By this time the Osages, reserve Caddos, and reserve Comanches might as well have been considered "civilized" and certainly influenced by the Five Tribes. Interestingly, no Wichitas, either reserve or "wild," were listed as attending. Still, the main object of the council was to make a permanent peace between the "civilized" Indians and the "wild" Indians. The accord, signed on May 26, 1865, called for permanent peace and friendship among these various Indian nations. It also stipulated that "the parties of this compact shall compose (as our undersigned brothers of the timbered countries have done) an Indian Confederacy, or a Band of Brothers" with peace as its object. Any future difficulty between them should be settled peacefully. In fact, the "motto or great principal [sic] of Confederate Indian tribes shall be '*An Indian shall not spill an Indian's blood*' [italics in original]."[25]

Despite the council, the peaceful intentions, and the motto, in mid-June 1865 some Comanches made a major raid into the Chickasaw Nation. Once again, the blame could be attributed to how little power a Comanche chief actually wielded. While a chief might sign a treaty and keep those people who agreed with him abiding by it, young men hungry for honor or warriors from other bands or divisions did not have to live up to it, if even they had heard of such a treaty's being made. According to Chickasaw accounts, about 350 Comanches swept into their territory, taking just about every horse, mule, and head of cattle within a fifteen-mile-wide strip that stretched almost as far east as Boggy Depot. As the Comanches began herding their spoils west, about 250 Chickasaw settlers gave chase, despite the raiders' having a couple days' head start. On its way back, the Comanche raiding party split, with the horses and livestock being taken north. The Chickasaws, wanting their stock back, followed this party, which took a month to completely circle the Wichita Mountains. Finally, in late July or early August the Chickasaws caught up with the Comanches. The Comanches, thinking they had shaken off any pursuit, did not place any guards, and during the night the Chickasaws silently surrounded the Comanche camp. At sunrise, they attacked, taking the Comanches by surprise. Finding themselves surrounded and several of their people cut down by Chickasaw fire, the Comanches parleyed and gave up all the Chickasaw stock. The Chickasaws, wanting only what was theirs, took their horses and livestock, leaving anything without their brand on it, and without the loss of a single man they headed back to Chickasaw territory.[26]

That the Chickasaws possessed horses to steal in June 1865 was rather amazing. For most peoples in Indian Territory, the Civil War had been a time of displacement, hunger, and loss. Now, with the war over, the government began relocating the Indians back onto their old lands. But these Indians, no matter whether they had fought for the North or the South or had taken refuge in Kansas, Texas, or on the plains, soon found that they were returning to nothing. The war particularly devastated Cherokee, Creek, and Seminole territories, with loyalists for both sides killed, houses and farms burned, farming implements and seed stock gone, and horses and livestock stolen and sold to Northern speculators for as little as $7.50 a head. The Indians from the Wichita Reserve found themselves in equally bad shape and dependent upon the government for food, clothing, tobacco, and farming implements.[27] Hungry and destitute of just about everything, the Indians of the Wichita Reserve, as they moved back to their former territory on the Washita River, took Chickasaw and Choctaw livestock. A sense of lawlessness gripped the western part of Indian Territory, and government officials once again decided to do something.[28]

In September 1865, Indian delegates met with representatives from the United States government at Fort Smith, Arkansas. There the Cherokees, Creeks, Choctaws, Chickasaws, Osages, Seminoles, Senecas, Shawnees, and Quapaws officially agreed to renounce any Confederate treaties and made peace with the United States. Though their signatures do not appear on the agreement, representatives from the Wichita Reserve also attended. With the war over and migration to the West picking up, the government decided to deal with the Plains Indians. The Five Civilized Tribes were to play their own role in this.[29]

In October 1865 government representatives met with various chiefs of the Comanches, Kiowas, Kiowa-Apaches, Cheyennes, and Arapahos on the Little Arkansas River. During the council the Indians returned five captives, while the government handed out quantities of blankets, tobacco, knives, and other manufactured goods. Over the course of several days they signed the Treaty of the Little Arkansas River. Essentially, the treaty provided for a large Indian reservation. The Comanches and Kiowas received sixty-two hundred square miles, which included all the Texas Panhandle and just about all of western Oklahoma and its panhandle. The Cheyennes and Arapahos got a reservation immediately to the north. Until the Indians moved to the reservation, they could roam over the unsettled portion of the lands they considered as their original homes: the Kiowas and Comanches south of the Arkansas, the Cheyenne and Arapahos between the Arkansas and the Platte. They were to refrain from raiding people friendly to the United States and allow the government to build roads and forts through their reservations. In return, they were to receive annuities for forty years, between ten and fifteen dollars per person for Comanches and Kiowas and between twenty and forty dollars for Cheyennes and Arapahos.[30]

The next year, the government renegotiated treaties with the Five Major Tribes. The federal government ignored the fact that the government virtually abandoned those nations to the Confederacy and that many citizens of the Five Tribes had fought for the Union. Now, rebel and loyalist would have to pay alike. As an indemnity for their participation in the war, the Indians ceded much of their land to the United States. The Choctaws and Chickasaws gave up all claims to the Leased District in return for $300,000—$225,000 for the Choctaws and $75,000 for the Chickasaws. The Creeks gave up the western half of their lands and the Seminoles ceded all their lands and received two hundred thousand acres between the South Canadian and North Canadian Rivers, while the Cherokees gave up all their land in Kansas and agreed to let the government settle other removed Indians on their lands. The treaties also prescribed the creation of an Indian council that would meet annually and would be composed of delegates "elected by each nation or tribe lawfully resident within Indian Territory." The government expected the Five Tribes to help "civilize" the Plains Indians and insisted that the Choctaws and Chickasaws use all their powers to "induce Indians of the plains to maintain peaceful relations with each other, with other Indians, and with the United States."[31]

With the war over and the Civilized Tribes and the Wichita Reserve Indians rebuilding their homes and farms, things began to slip back to the way they had always been. Though chiefs from most Comanche and Kiowa divisions signed the Treaty of the Little Arkansas, the Kwahadis division of Comanches had not signed and so were not bound to stop raiding Americans and their allies. Even among those divisions and bands whose chiefs had signed, young men hungry for honors and status turned again to raiding. So once again the citizens of the Chickasaw, Choctaw, and Creek Nations, as well as those of Texas, came to fear the "Comanche moon," when raiding parties swept down on them, taking horses, cattle, and captives.[32]

As they had before, the Chickasaws bore the brunt of these raids. Horse raids got so bad that Chickasaw ranchers tied up their horses inside the corrals and then stood guard over them. Chickasaw rancher Joe Colbert remembered that one night, as he and his father stood guard, two Comanches "crawled over the yard fence and were trying to steal our horses and father shot one of them. He fell in the yard and the other ran and just as he jumped the fence, father let him have it and he fell just over the fence."[33] Overton Love, a Chickasaw rancher, reported losing many horses to the Comanches and had even tried chasing them down to get his back, but with no success.[34]

Chickasaw woman Dinah Frazier also recalled the raids. "We didn't dare leave a crosscut saw outside. They like to get hold of them for arrow points. They weren't inclined to fight with us, unless we tried to catch them if they had stolen something. Then they would kill and scalp us."[35] And some Chickasaws were killed and scalped. Ida Cunnetubby's Chickasaw grandmother almost lost her hair. She and a girlfriend rode to a friend's house to do some sewing, and on their way back, a party of Comanches spotted them and gave chase. Ida Cunnetubby's grandmother dropped her cloth, jumped from the horse, and crouched in some nearby underbrush. Her girl friend tried to outrun them, but just as she got to the yard of her home, the Comanches shot and killed her, then took the cloth and both horses. From then on, whenever Ida Cunnetubby's grandmother heard noises she thought were Comanches, she and her children would run into the woods and hide.[36]

No one in the Chickasaw Nation seemed safe. Black freedmen lived in terror of the Comanches, and a black Seminole boy was taken captive in a raid made near Fort Arbuckle in January 1867.[37] Even the home of future Chickasaw governor Thomas Parker was raided. Parker, who served as the Chickasaw's governor from 1871 to 1872 and was well advanced in years, put up a spirited defense, though he lost all his cattle and horses and was seriously wounded in the thigh.[38] David Pickens, a Chickasaw member of a party chasing Comanche horse raiders, was killed by a poison arrow, and a Chickasaw woman lost her finger when a Comanche cut it off to get her ring.[39]

Government officials investigated the raids and were distressed to learn that Kansas traders and Indian agents provided revolvers, breech-loading carbines, cartridges, percussion caps, powder, and lead to the Comanches, Kiowas, Cheyennes, and Arapahos. According to Major H. Douglas at Fort Dodge, Kansas, several hundred Indians had visited his post in late 1866, and they all carried revolvers, while most had two and many carried three. Douglas reported that the Indians highly prized revolvers and often traded for one with ten or twenty times its value in horses and furs. In January 1867 the military cracked down and prohibited further sales or gifts of arms and ammunition to the Indians of the Kansas district until further orders. Despite this, revolvers and carbines still seemed to make it into Plains Indians' hands.[40]

As the raids continued, Texas governor J. W. Throckmorton demanded that the United States make another treaty with the "wild tribes" to stop them from attacking his state. He suggested a council sometime in late May or early June 1867 and recommended that the government's delegation include a few of the leading men from the Chickasaw, Choctaw, Creek, and Cherokee Nations to influence the Indians.[41] Others believed the government should try to get the Plains Indians interested in horse breeding and stock raising like the Choctaws, Cherokees, and Chickasaws. Twice-yearly fairs could be held in the Cherokee or Chickasaw country, where the government could issue breeding horses and cattle to the chiefs. Prizes could be given for the fastest horse and the fattest cattle. The best result would be that the Indians would now raise their own stock instead of raiding for it.[42] Actually, this might have worked, but these were long-term solutions, and the army, needing to stop the raids as soon as possible, once again turned to the Indians of the Wichita Reserve to serve as scouts and auxiliaries. Toshaway (Silver Brooch) and a few other Penateka Comanche chiefs as well as Caddo chiefs George Washington, Tinah, and Jim Pockmark, all met with the commanders at Fort Arbuckle in December 1866 and agreed to serve as scouts. Despite the assistance of the reserve Indians, Comanche and Kiowa raiders did not seem to suffer any reverses at the scouts' hands.[43]

Raids by bands of Kwahadi and Kotsoteka Comanches were bad enough, but with so many different peoples living in the western part of Indian Territory, relations often became strained. Grey's Store at Fort Arbuckle was just about the only place in western Indian Territory to purchase merchandise, so it attracted Caddos, Wichitas, Osages, Seminoles, Chickasaws, Comanches, Kiowas, Shawnees, and Delawares. Seminole farmers often came to the fort to sell peanuts for a dollar a bushel and then buy a yard of red calico for twenty-five cents. In fact, the Seminoles provided the fort with pecans, turkeys, and honey.[44] As all these different peoples milled and mixed together, their relations with each other often varied. When the army needed to pass a message to the Comanches and Kiowas, they often relied upon the Tawakonis and Wacos, whom they knew to be good friends of theirs.[45] Conversely, a Seminole buffalo hunting party was attacked by a band of Tonkawas, which led to several bloody incidents between the two peoples.[46]

Similarly, during the summer of 1867 the Creek police force, known as the Lighthorse, for some unknown reason attacked a party of Caddos, killed one man, wounded another, and took over $2,300 worth of horses, ponies, saddles, bridles, skins, guns, axes, and various other merchandise. The Caddos and Creeks almost went to war over this before Jesse Chisholm and the Seminoles could negotiate a peace. In a written treaty between the Caddos and the Creeks, the Creeks admitted wrong and "covered the dead" by providing cash to the wounded man and the dead man's family. According to the treaty, the Creeks paid $1,000 to Little Jim, the dead man's brother and $500 to White Bear, the wounded man, and they agreed to pay for the lost property, with $251 going to White Bear and $1,845 to Little Jim.[47]

While Caddos and Creeks might be able to work out their problems with the help of other Indians, the Comanche and Kiowa raids into Texas and the Chickasaw Nation became so bad that the government stepped in to renegotiate a treaty. In October 1867, Comanche, Kiowa, Kiowa-Apache, Cheyenne, and Arapaho chiefs met with United States' representatives at Medicine Lodge Creek in southern Kansas and signed treaties. Though the treaties made a number of stipulations, only four were the most important and would have any bearing on the Plains tribes' relations with the other Indians in Indian Territory. According to the Treaty of Medicine Lodge Creek, the Comanches, Kiowas, and Kiowa-Apaches pledged to make and keep peace with the United States and its people. They gave up all claims to lands in Texas and accepted a much smaller reservation between the Red and Washita Rivers in the southwestern part of Indian Territory. They promised to become "civilized" by sending their children to school and becoming farmers. The United States pledged to build the schools and provide teachers, blacksmiths, carpenters, instructors, clothing, farming implements, and even agricultural instruction. Finally, the Comanches, Kiowas, and Kiowa-Apaches still had the right to hunt on lands south of the Arkansas River as long as the buffalo ranged there. In return for all this, they were to receive twenty-five thousand dollars a year for thirty years. The Cheyennes and Arapahos had similar stipulations and received a reservation immediately north of the Comanche-Kiowa reservation and twenty thousand dollars a year for thirty years.[48]

While the government created the reservations for the Plains Indians, the last remaining Wichitas, Caddos, Shawnees, and Delawares of the old Wichita Reserve who had taken refuge in Kansas returned home to the reestablished Wichita Agency and joined their people already there. Confusion immediately resulted. The Treaty of Medicine Lodge Creek, which gave the Comanches and Kiowas land south of the Washita River and the Cheyennes and Arapahos lands north of the Washita, essentially violated the Fort Arbuckle Agreement of 1859, which gave these lands to the Wichitas and Caddos. And the Wichitas and Caddos adamantly continued to claim these lands. Muddying the waters was the situation in which several hundred Caddos, Wichitas, Shawnees, and Delawares had settled south of the Washita River and planted crops and now found themselves on Comanche-Kiowa land. With the new Comanche-Kiowa Agency placed just south and downstream from the Wichita Agency, these farming Indians had their lands overrun and were often intimidated by the still "wild" Comanches and Kiowas. Many abandoned their lands and moved north of the Washita, while some Shawnees settled on lands vacated by the Seminoles after the Reconstruction treaty of 1866.[49]

In reality, the treaty and the reservations did nothing to stop the raids into the Chickasaw Nation and Texas, mainly because the rations and annuities promised in the treaty arrived late, if at all. The Comanches and Kiowas, though, found weapons in sure supply, receiving them from the Comancheros out of New Mexico and

Map 3. Indian Territory, 1866–89. (Map from W. David Baird and Danney Goble, *The Story of Oklahoma* [University of Oklahoma Press, 1994])

NO MAN'S LAND
Unassigned to any State or Territory

Beaver City

1. PEORIA
2. QUAPAW
3. MODOC
4. OTTAWA
5. SHAWNEE
6. WYANDOTTE
7. SENECA
8. TONKAWA
9. PONCA
10. OTO AND MISSOURI

CHEROKEE OUTLET

CHEYENNE AND ARAPAHO

GREER COUNTY

COMANCHE KIOWA AND APACHE

Fort Sill

Fort Supply

Cantonment

Seger Colony

Darlington
Fort Reno

WICHITA AND CADDO

Santa Fe RR

Sante Fe RR

Chicago Rock Island & Pacific RR

KAW
OSAGE
Pawhuska

PAWNEE

SAC AND FOX

Iowa Village

IOWA

KICKAPOO

POTTAWATOMIE AND SHAWNEE

CHICKASAW

Tishomingo

CREEK

Okmulgee

SEMINOLE

Wewoka

Tulsa

Kansas & Arkansas Valley RR

CHEROKEE

Choteau

Tahlequah

Fort Gibson

Webbers Falls

Vinita

CHOCTAW

McAlester

St. Louis & San Francisco RR

Tuskahoma

Eagletown

Missouri Kansas and Texas Railroad

Atoka

Durant

100 miles
160 kilometers

0   50   100
0   80

from Caddo chief George Washington, who had a store near the reservation. In the Chickasaw Nation during May 1868, one Comanche-Kiowa party took seven children captive; five of them died or were killed on the journey back to the plains. Other parties took additional captives. Acting Commissioner of Indian Affairs Charles Mix hoped to call upon Chickasaw governor Cyrus Harris for assistance but did not have the rations to feed the Chickasaw militia. Hampering the efforts was the death of the Comanches' old trusted friend, Jesse Chisholm, in April 1868. Believing the raids stemmed from the government's paying ransom for captives, officials now refused payment and merely insisted that the captives be returned. Unfortunately, this showed how little the government knew of Comanche society. Once taken, the captive became the possession of the warrior, his property by his abilities as a warrior or by his purchase of the captive. Like any white American, the warrior was not about to allow his property to be taken from him without compensation. Some men, such as Colonel Jesse H. Leavenworth, agent for the Comanches and Kiowas, realized that only payments could get the captives back, and he went to great lengths to ransom the captives. So, with the Comanches and Kiowas believing that the government was not living up to its promises, whether for ransom or annuities, the raids continued. Even the creation of Fort Sill on Cache Creek near the Wichita Mountains in 1869, and the movement of the Kiowa and Comanche Agency there, could not stop them.[50]

The government now turned to the Five Civilized Tribes to help stop the raids. The Five Tribes had begun to recover since the end of the war, though deep divisions still existed among the Cherokees, Creeks, and Seminoles, particularly between those factions who had supported the Union and those who had supported the Confederacy. Adding to Cherokee problems was the United States' plan to settle other Indians, such as the Kansas Indians and Delaware and Shawnee bands from Kansas, on Cherokee lands. Cherokee lands also looked good to their old enemies, the Osages, who petitioned the government to settle there but were denied because they were still "blanket Indians" and only "civilized" could be settled east of the ninety-sixth meridian. Despite these problems, the government reminded the Five Tribes of the article in their 1866 Reconstruction treaties that called for the creation of an Indian council made up of delegates from all the Indian nations in the territory. Hoping the advances of the Five Civilized Tribes would wear off on the Plains and Prairie Indians, Congress now appropriated money for the first grand council to meet in May 1870 at Okmulgee in the Creek Nation.[51]

Not many delegates attended the May meeting, so another was set for December 1870. The grand council began on December 6 at Okmulgee, with delegates from the Cherokees, Creeks, Chickasaws, Choctaws, Seminoles, Osages, Senecas, Shawnees, Ottawas, Confederated Peorias, Wyandottes, Quapaws, and Sacs and Foxes attending. Immediately the council dealt with the subject of the Plains Indians. In a resolution, the council directed Enoch Hoag, head of the Central Superintendency, to advise the Comanches, Kiowas, Cheyennes, Arapahos, and other Plains Indians that the council's mission was to "preserve peace and friendship, among themselves, with all other Red Men, and with the people of the United States; to promote the general welfare of all Indians and to establish friendly relations with them." The council offered to help the Plains Indians in establishing permanent friendly relations with the United States. After dealing with the Plains Indians, the council wanted to impress upon the American people that the attending nations were different from the Plains Indians. The delegates pointed out that despite the belief held by many Americans that all Indians lived by hunting, fishing, and trapping, the nations attending this council were agricultural peoples and relied upon farming and stock raising for their livelihood. With this, the council adjourned and planned to meet again in June 1871.[52]

As the Comanche and Kiowa raids in the Chickasaw Nation and Texas continued into 1871, many people placed hope in the scheduled June grand council. The editor of *The Frontiersman*, a newspaper in Gatesville, Texas, appealed to the *Cherokee Advocate*, since it was an Indian newspaper, to try to get the Comanches and other Plains Indians to stop their raiding and show these peoples a better way of life.[53] Superintendent Enoch Hoag directed Wichita agent Jonathan Richards and Comanche-Kiowa agent Lawrie Tatum to meet with the Comanches, Kiowas, and Apaches and urge them to attend the June grand council. "The great object of this will be to induce the roving, hunting and raiding tribes to change their customs and habits and enter into friendly and permanent relations with the civilized tribes and with the people of the U.S."[54] Even the *Cherokee Advocate* came out in favor of the council, certain it would have a good influence on the "wild" Indians because, the *Advocate* said, the Plains Indians had never been mistreated by the Choctaws, Cherokees, or Creeks. "We stand in relation to them as elder brothers of the same family, as natural allies, with a future alike in trouble, perplexity and danger to us all."[55]

Before the June council could get underway, General William T. Sherman, commander of the Division of the Missouri, under whose jurisdiction the Comanche-Kiowa reservation fell, arrested Kiowa chiefs Satank, Satanta, and Big Tree for recent raids and killings in Texas. Sent to stand trial in Texas, Satank was killed en route trying to escape. In Texas, Satanta and Big Tree were tried and sentenced to death. Now the Civilized Tribes came to their defense. Rather than hanging them, as General Sherman wanted, the *Cherokee Advocate* advocated keeping them alive but in prison. Hanging was "scarcely prudent. . . . There is no more efficient check upon a man's friends than to have him in your power to treat him as you like if *they* don't please you" [italics in original]. The idea seemed valid, so Satanta and Big Tree were imprisoned at the Texas State Penitentiary at Huntsville in hopes this would stop the raids. And the *Advocate* proved correct; raiding into Texas diminished.[56]

Despite the arrest of the Kiowa chiefs, some Kiowa, Apache, and Caddo representatives showed up for the June council. It could not be considered a success. The Plains Indians were on unfamiliar ground geographically and kept themselves separate from the other Indians by camping several miles west of Okmulgee. Though the Civilized Tribes provided a huge feast and smoked the pipe with them, the Plains Indians remained suspicious, fearing some retaliation because of past raids. Once again, the delegates proposed to meet the following year.[57]

While the imprisonment of Satanta and Big Tree checked Kiowa raids, it did not stop the Comanches. In February 1872 a large Comanche party raided into the Chickasaw Nation and Texas, killing several people and taking dozens of horses. Chickasaw settlers chased down the Comanches, fought a brief battle, and managed to recover many of their horses. Now the Chickasaws changed their tactics and showed just how far down the road of American "civilization" they had traveled. Rather than fight the Comanches with just bullets, the Chickasaws brought suit against the Comanches for their losses. With Comanches receiving a government annuity, the Chickasaws hoped to tap into the payments as an indemnity for the raids against them. Though the suit marked a legalistic turn in Chickasaw-Comanche relations, nothing came of it. Now, more than ever, it seemed the Plains Indians needed to be brought into council with the Civilized Tribes.[58]

From June 3 to June 18, 1872, the grand council met again at Okmulgee, this time with better attendance, if not results. While the Chickasaws, still angry over the recent raid into their territory, did not send a delegation, Choctaw, Creek, Cherokee, Seminole, Wyandotte, Ottawa, Seneca, Eastern Shawnee, Quapaw, and Sac and Fox delegates represented the "civilized," agricultural nations. Black Beaver represented the Absentee Delawares, and Joseph Ellis and John Sparnee represented the Absentee Shawnees, as these bands living in the western part of Indian Territory were called.

Chief George Washington of the more progressive Whitebead band, along with Caddo Jake, Guadeloupe, and Little Captain, spoke for the Caddos, while Kernoostie was representatives for the Ionies (Hainais). The Wichitas sent Otsquitsto, probably Utstutskins, while Toshaway, principal chief of the Penateka Comanches, and Ten Bears, principal chief of the Yamparika Comanches, also attended.[59]

After the handshaking, the pipe smoking, and the presentation of credentials, Toshaway of the Penatekas and Otsquitsto of the Wichitas expressed their desire for peace and friendship with white people and with all Indians. They said they had heard the good talk of their "elder brothers" of the council and would not forget them. One thing they especially wanted from the council was to have their lands in the western part of Indian Territory guaranteed to them, and then their people "would feel ready for improvement in the habits of civilized life." The council agreed and motioned that Superintendent Enoch Hoag urge the government to secure permanent homes for the Wichitas, Caddos, Wacos, Tawakonis, Kichais, Absentee Delawares, and other members of the Affiliated Bands on the lands they now occupied. The council also suggested that the best way to get the Plains Indians and the Wichitas and Affiliated Bands involved in farming and stock raising would be to organize permanent agricultural societies. These would create competition and "a spirit of emulation among the various tribes inhabiting the same."[60]

The council then turned its attention to the recent raids. Superintendent Enoch Hoag, president of the council, believed the influence of the Civilized Tribes would be most helpful here. The Indian delegates also regretted the raids committed by the Plains Indians and stressed that it was their earnest desire that all nations live in peace. Not satisfied with mere lip service, the Council then proposed to send a delegation to meet in July near the Wichita Agency with the Kiowas and other Plains Indians who were not at the June council. There they would be assured "of the continued friendship of the nations and tribes confederated in the General Council, of their readiness to aid them in establishing friendly relations with the government of the United States, [and] to urge upon them the necessity of abstaining from further hostilities." Penateka chief Toshaway, Caddo chief Guadeloupe, and Delaware chief Black Beaver volunteered to deliver the message to the Kiowas. Other members of the delegation included Coleman Cole and J. P. Folsom of the Choctaws; Eli Smith, D. H. Ross, and James Vann of the Cherokees; Chilly McIntosh, D. M. Hodge, and Micco Hutkey of the Creeks; and John Jumper and Fushutchee Harjo of the Seminoles.[61]

Toshaway, Guadeloupe, and Black Beaver did their jobs well, spending sixteen days among the Kiowas, Comanches, Kiowa-Apaches, Cheyennes, and Arapahos, which ensured a huge turnout. The council convened at Fort Cobb, near the Wichita Agency, and ran from July 22 to August 4, 1872. It was a veritable *Who's Who* of Indians of the Southern Plains. Besides representatives of the United States and the leaders from the Five Civilized Tribes, the Fort Cobb council included Delaware chief Black Beaver; Caddo chiefs Guadeloupe and George Washington; Toshaway, Esahabbe, Asatoyet, Piyou, and Straight Feather of the Penateka Comanches; White Wolf, Horse Back, Red Food, and Little Crow of the Noconi Comanches; Ten Bears, Iron Mountain, Quirtsquip, and Tabananaka of the Yamparika Comanches; Lone Wolf, Fast Bear, Woman's Heart, Kicking Bird, Sun Boy, Hossing, and White Horse of the Kiowas; Pacer and Shaking of the Kiowa-Apaches; Little Raven, Big Mouth, and Spotted Wolf of the Arapahos; and Little Robe, Spotted Mouth, White Shield, and Little Black Kettle of the Cheyennes. Also there were Taovaya chief Isadowa, Waco chief Buffalo Good, Tawakoni chief Tawakoni Dave, and Kichai chief Kauwiddyhuntis. Significantly absent were chiefs of the Kwahadi and Kotsoteka Comanches.[62]

According to the United States representatives, the main object of the council was to encourage these chiefs, particularly the Kiowas, to keep the peace. Cherokee chief James Vann, Creek chief

Chilly McIntosh, Seminole chief John Jumper, and Delaware chief
Black Beaver all made speeches urging the Plains Indians to end
their raids and make peace with the United States. John Jumper,
who had fought the United States in the Seminole Wars, told of his
own experiences and the folly of fighting the overwhelming force
of the United States. James Vann went even further and suggested
they settle down, become farmers, and raise corn. Holding the
Civilized Tribes up as an example, Vann told them that "a great
many of your brothers in this country have built houses. . . . We
have cows, horses, hogs, chickens, &c., they are our meat, and if
you adopt this road you can have them too." He warned them that
"the buffalo will soon be gone, and you will be destitute. If you
built houses and raise these things for yourselves, you will have
homes and subsistence when the buffalo are gone." Completing
the imagery, Vann rhapsodized, "This road is like a clear sky without a cloud, and these houses the proper place for your old men
and women and helpless children, of whom you have many."[63]

With the backing of these chiefs, the United States representatives proposed a five-point plan: the Plains Indians would uncon-
ditionally surrender their white captives; they would cease all their
raiding; they would appoint a delegation to visit Washington; they
would return to their agency and there receive their rations and
remain under the protection of their agent until their delegation
returned from Washington; and Kiowa chief Satanta's release from
prison would be left to the discretion of Washington. John Jumper,
Chilly McIntosh, Black Beaver, and George Washington all urged
the Kiowas and Comanches to accept this proposal.[64]

If the United States and the Civilized Tribes thought the Plains
Indians would jump at this, they were sadly mistaken. In the first
place, the Comanches and Kiowas were not all that impressed with
the delegates from the Five Tribes. Yamparika Comanches commented on them, saying, "They are an old dirty inefficient looking
set, hardly capable of managing their own affairs, we don't take
much stock in them."[65] As if to highlight their indifference to the

Five Civilized Tribes, while the council was in session a party of six Noconi Comanches stole about twenty head of stock from Chickasaw farms near the mouth of the Washita River. These Chickasaws declared they were going to go to the council and sue Comanche and Kiowa agent Lawrie Tatum and the Comanches chiefs as well. Making matters worse was that while the council was in session, some of Toshaway's own Penatekas made off with horses belonging the Chickasaw delegation.[66]

While the horse raids enraged the delegates from the Civilized Tribes, the delayed release of Satanta angered the Kiowas. Kiowa chief Lone Wolf told the council that he was ready to abide by the plan and even go further than that if need be, but "we were once, twice promised the release of Satanta. Let us see his face and we will surrender the captives, all the government property—everything, and pledge ourselves to white and red jointly in a peace which shall never be broken by us." Yamparika chief Ten Bears seconded this. Even Caddo chief Guadeloupe agreed with Lone Wolf, saying, "Let the government of the United States fulfill its promise as to Satanta, and every other demand will be promptly met."[67]

The Fort Cobb council ended on August 4 without any promises being made. Still, to show their good faith the Comanches returned most of the horses they had taken from the Chickasaws, while a few days later, the Kiowas brought in two captives and agreed to send a delegation to Washington and to return additional stolen stock. Kiowa chief Kicking Bird also told the agent that the Kiowa chiefs had held a council and instructed their young men not to raid into Texas anymore. The Kiowas also asked that their agency be moved away from Fort Sill and back to Black Beaver's area along the Washita, as they did not like to receive their rations where there were so many soldiers. The *Cherokee Advocate* came to the defense of the Kiowas and recommended that the Kiowas' agency be returned to its old location, as its present site was demoralizing and menacing to the Kiowas and Comanches. Agent

Tatum refused. He also refused to give the Kiowas the presents they asked for, saying that Washington told him he could not give presents to Indians who were killing people and stealing stock.[68]

Over the next few months the Kiowas and Comanches sent a delegation to meet with President Grant, most Comanche bands reported to the reservation, and raids into the Chickasaw Nation and Texas decreased. At their Fourth Annual General Council held in May 1873 at Okmulgee, the Civilized Tribes took credit for these successes, saying it was the work of their peace council at Fort Cobb that brought all these good things to fruition. The general council then passed a resolution congratulating the Kiowas, Cheyennes, and other Plains Indians on their recent good conduct and friendly relations. Building on this, the council proposed sending another delegation of one Choctaw, one Creek, one Cherokee, and any others appointed by the council president to visit the Kiowas, Cheyennes, and other Plains Indians to help maintain the peace. They also offered to send two members of the general council with any Southern Plains Indian delegation that wanted to go to Washington in order to help establish good relations between them and the United States and bring permanent peace to the frontier. While the workings of the peace council and the general council may have had some effect on the actions of the Kiowas and Comanches, that could also have been a result of Colonel Ranald Mackenzie's attack on a large Comanche village in the Texas Panhandle on September 29, 1872. Though the village was considered at the time to be a Kwahadi Comanche village of 292 lodges, it was actually a mixed camp of Kwahadis, Kotsotekas, Yamparikas, Noconis, and Penatekas. Mackenzie killed 24 Indians, and captured 124 women and children, who were held captive at Fort Sill. Having their women and children taken captive and Satanta and Big Tree still in prison probably had a much greater effect on Comanche and Kiowa raiding than did the words of the Civilized Tribes' peace council.[69]

The May 1873 general council, though, was not well attended. While the usual "civilized" nations were represented, the Caddos,

Wichitas, Cheyennes, Arapahos, Comanches, and Kiowas did not send delegates. Still, the general council was willing to support the Kiowas concerning the release of Satanta and Big Tree. The two Kiowa chiefs had been scheduled for release in April 1873, but Kintpuash, chief of the California Modocs, killed several American negotiators during a peace conference, which turned public opinion against leniency toward Indians and so delayed the Kiowa chiefs' release. The council members, led by D. H. Ross of the Cherokees, pointed out that the Kiowas had lived up to their part of the bargain and met all the conditions imposed upon them by the United States. Now it was time for the government to live up to its part and release Satanta and Big Tree. Ross's resolution reminded the government that its delay in releasing the two chiefs was "destroying the confidence of the 'Plains Indians' in the promises of the government." It also placed the Civilized Tribes in a "false position . . . as *friends* and *advisors* of their brothers of the plains" [italics in the original].[70]

Despite the general council's resolution, complications surrounded the release of Satanta and Big Tree. Many officials, including General William T. Sherman and Texas governor E. J. Davis, spoke against it. No matter what the government promised, they believed that keeping the Kiowa chiefs in jail was the only way to keep the Kiowas from raiding. Making matters worse, the government now tried to tie the good behavior of the Comanches to the release of the Kiowa chiefs. The Comanches were not so willing to comply, especially as their women and children taken captive in the Mackenzie raid were released in June 1873. Though most Kiowas and Comanches remained peaceful, there were several reports of Comanche raids into Texas during the summer. The government now said they would not release Satanta and Big Tree unless these raiders were turned in. Commissioner of Indian Affairs Edward P. Smith demanded that at least five Comanche raiders be turned over for punishment or not only would the Kiowa chiefs not be released, but the government would also cut off the Comanches' rations and annuities promised them in the Medicine Lodge Treaty. How much influence the general council of Civilized Tribes had is not known, but the two Kiowa chiefs were finally released in October 1873 without the five Comanche warriors' being turned in. This did not assuage the government, and in November the commissioner of Indian affairs cut off the Comanches' annuities until they turned over the five raiders.[71]

In its December 1873 meeting at Okmulgee, the general council took the government to task over this. Now with the Caddos, Wacos, Kichais, and Tawakonis attending, the council sent word to the Comanches and Kiowas that the council stood with them, would continue to make appeals to Washington on their behalf, and urged them to remain at peace and be patient. At the same time, the council expressed its conviction that the government was being unreasonable in cutting off the Comanches' rations. As the delegates pointed out, most Comanche chiefs were trying to comply with the government on everything else, including the returning of captives and stolen stock, and even serving as auxiliaries in chasing down raiders. The council also believed the government was holding the Comanches to a standard that even whites could not rise to; after all, the Comanche chiefs could not control all their people from "evil practice," but "the same failure exists with the authorities in the adjoining states under well organized governments. Then can it be just to distress the weaker therein and excuse the stronger?" The council had a point, as thieves from the Chickasaw Nation and Texas were decimating Comanche horse herds. The council went on to remind the government that depriving the Comanches of clothing and food, particularly during the winter, would "seriously embarrass the work of civilization so happily progressing among the tribes of the southwest, and the evils arising therefrom would be extended to all the Indians of this confederacy." In a side issue, the council addressed the Kickapoos, who had gone to Mexico during the Civil War and now wanted to come back. The council welcomed them to return and settle on the Arkansas River west of the Osages.[72]

All the good words of the general council came to naught when in June 1874 most Comanches, Kiowas, Cheyennes, and Arapahos left their reservations and went on the attack in what is usually called the Red River War. Virtual starvation on the reservations from the lack of rations and annuities; the overkilling of buffalo by white hunters south of the Arkansas River; the need to avenge two attacks by U.S. troops led by Seminole and Tonkawa guides; and a spiritual resurgence stemming from a May Sun Dance have all been seen as causes of the war.[73] The Red River War was the last major conflict fought by the Indians of the Southern Plains, and while it is usually viewed as a war between the United States and the Southern Plains Indians, it also pitted removed and Prairie Indians against the Plains Indians.

In late July–early August, the army dispatched troops to fight the Indians. Among the many scouts employed by the army were twenty Eastern Delawares from the Cherokee area. In a battle on August 13, a party of nearly seventy-five Cheyennes ambushed the scouts, led by Lieutenant Frank D. Baldwin. Only hard fighting by the Delawares avoided disaster and gave General Nelson Miles a sorely needed victory. Unfortunately, Miles virtually ignored the Delawares' efforts in his reports.[74]

Just over a week later, a large party of Comanches and Kiowas attacked the Wichita Agency on the Washita River, where the Caddos, Wichitas, Delawares, and Penateka Comanches lived. Though a contingent of troops defended the agency, some Kiowa warriors crossed the river and raided the farm of Delaware chief Black Beaver. The Kiowas also bullied some Caddos into helping them. A Caddo man, Huwahnee, considered by the agent to be peaceful and respected, killed Black Beaver's son-in-law, E. B. Osborne. Not far down the Washita, four civilian hay cutters were killed. The Kiowas denied involvement in this, blaming it instead on the Caddos and Wichitas. The next day, the army got the upper hand and drove off the Kiowas and Comanches. But the damage had been done, with most agency buildings burned; several whites,

Caddos, and Penateka Comanches killed or wounded; and most of the Indians' fields destroyed. Many Indians abandoned the agency and took refuge along the Canadian River or with kinspeople in different nations or bands. A few months after the Wichita Agency battle, an official investigation implicated the Caddos, Wichitas, Kiowas, Comanches, and even a Pawnee in the hay cutters' deaths.[75]

The Wichita Agency battle angered the Affiliated Bands, and many young men joined with the army to serve as scouts and auxiliaries. Future Wichita principal chief Kiowa earned his name during the Red River War, not only because he could speak some Kiowa but also because he captured several Kiowa warriors. Other scouts from the Wichitas and Affiliated Bands included Billie Wilson, John Whitebread, Tawakoni Jim, Yellow Bird, and George Washington. It would take almost another year and several more battles before these auxiliaries and the United States Army compelled the surrender of all the Comanches, Kiowas, Cheyennes, and Arapahos. The last band of Kwahadi Comanches surrendered at Signal Mountain near Fort Sill on June 2, 1875. Satanta was returned to his penitentiary cell in Texas, but in 1878 he found freedom when he committed suicide by jumping from the upper floor of the prison. To teach the Indians a lesson, the United States packed off over threescore Kiowa, Comanche, Cheyenne, Caddo, and Arapaho warriors, some of them not even involved in the fighting, to Fort Marion, Florida, where they remained incarcerated for three years.[76]

When the American Civil War began fourteen years earlier, Indian Territory had been divided among Civilized Tribes, Prairie Indians who were gradually adopting the "civilization" life-style, and Plains Indians who still roamed free. The war brought devastation and turmoil to the all Indians of Indian Territory and had given free rein to the Plains peoples. But by the summer of 1875 the Southern Plains Indians found themselves defeated, broken, and confined to their reservation. Now their "civilization" process began in earnest. The Plains Indians would need the advice of the Five Tribes to help them with this transition. The question was, Could these very different peoples work together?

CHAPTER SEVEN

ONE RED FAMILY?

When the Great Spirit created the white and red man, he made a road for the white and the red man to go. I have seen the white man's road, and the way they live, but am afraid we cannot live in it. We want to do as the white man does, but are afraid we will not be able to find the road. . . . When I see so many other chiefs going the white man's road, I want to try it also.

CHEEVERS
Yamparika Comanche chief, 1875

The end of the Red River War in 1875 should have initiated a new era in the relations between the Southern Plains Indians and the "civilized" Indian nations. Militarily defeated and confined to reservations, the Southern Plains Indians now received intensive doses of Christianity, education, farming instruction, and detribalization. Essentially, the Civilized Tribes had carried the day, and their agrarian way of life had been validated, so close relations among all these peoples should have developed. With the Southern Plains and Prairie Indians now forced to adopt this life-style, one would imagine them turning to the Civilized Tribes for help in making the transition into this new age. While the Five Tribes did provide some assistance, for the most part the Southern Plains and Prairie Indians walked this new road on their own.

Things did not start out to be this way. The Red River War was a watershed in Plains Indian–removed Indian relations, but few Indians realized it at the time. Hoping to pick up where they had left off when the war started, the Civilized Tribes called for the sixth annual general council to meet at Okmulgee. With most of the fighting in the Red River War done and only a few bands of Comanches left to surrender, the General Council of Indian Territory met from May 3 to 15, 1875. This council had more delegates from more nations than ever before. Attending nations included the Creeks, Cherokees, Choctaws, Seminoles, Pawnees, Confederated Peorias, Eastern Shawnees, Absentee Shawnees, Ottawas, Sacs and Foxes, Mexican Kickapoos, Kaws, Osages, Potawatomis, Wyandots, Delawares, Wichitas, Wacos, Tawakonis, Kichais, Caddos, Anadarkos, Ionies, Penateka Comanches, Cheyennes, Arapahos, and even a contingent of California Modocs sent to Indian Territory after their disastrous war of 1872–73. Again, conspicuously absent were the Chickasaws, the Kiowas, and the other bands of Comanches.[1]

If the Civilized Tribes ever doubted their effect on the Prairie and Plains Indians, this council should have dispelled it, and they probably swelled with pride as delegate after delegate from the Prairie and Plains nations acknowledged their desire to become like them. "I was a camper and a hunter. When I saw the Cherokee, Creek, Choctaw working the fields, I took hold of the plow handle," announced George Washington of the Caddos. "I now have sixty-eight acres of corn, one acre of wheat, and two acres of orchard." Pawnee chief Running Chief admitted that "the buffalo are most all gone; war has ceased some time ago to be an occupation with us. Right here, my brothers of the Cherokees and Choctaws and Muscogees [Creeks] and Seminoles, whom I see at a great distance above me, show me the way." Big Mouth of the Arapahos admitted that "when I sleep or am awake, I am always thinking about my new farming operations, and what good corn I will raise. . . . My people and myself are trying to live like white men, and have thrown away our buckskin clothes. Everything I have on is white men's manufacture."[2]

Besides these good words, the general council tried to take some important actions. In deference to appeals by Left Hand of the Arapahos and White Shield of the Cheyennes, who complained that many innocent men had been arrested and incarcerated by the government during the recent Red River War, the council requested that the President of the United States hold fair trials for all those jailed and return to their nations those found not guilty. A hot debate also erupted over whether the council should accept a committee report about creating a constitution for all the nations of Indian Territory. Some, such as Stephen Tehee of the Cherokees, were against it, feeling it opened the door for the United States to violate treaties made with the Cherokees. He pointed out that many of the rank and file of the nations would not understand the powers of the new constitution. Keokuk of the Sacs and Foxes favored it, saying that at the present, a person or person injured by other Indians could get no redress, "but if we had this constitution and laws to help us we could be protected in both our lives and our property." The council voted to adopt the report, 54 to 29, and the move toward a single Indian Territory government took a step forward.[3] While it is not known how the Plains and Prairie Indians voted on the proposal, they later came out against an Indian Territory constitution, believing their people needed to become a little more educated before they would be ready for it.[4]

The grand council met again in September 1875 with many of the same delegates, but, more importantly, this time chiefs from the Miamis, Quapaws, Kiowas, Yamparika Comanches, Kiowa-Apaches, and Apaches attended. The Yamparika Comanches and Kiowas hoped to enlist the aid of the council in getting their Red River War prisoners released from Fort Marion, Florida. In speech after speech they pointed out that most of the blame for the war could be laid on white outlaws who had stolen their horses and committed depredations on them. While they admitted that some of their people had done wrong and should be punished, none of the whites had been punished, nor had the Indians been reimbursed by the government for their losses as the Treaty of Medicine Lodge Creek prescribed. With this in mind, their prisoners, many of whom were not involved in the fighting in the first place, should be released. The general council concurred and reaffirmed its appeal to the President made during its May session. If delegates hoped that Indian unity could be forged out of the war and the council sessions, Tabananaka, a Yamparika Comanche chief who had three sons imprisoned at Fort Marion, may have made them think again. As for his participation in the war and why his people should be returned, Tabananaka bitterly complained that "the Wichitas have made me poor. When [off the reservation] they compelled me to stay there, and they took my clothes and everything from me." He then scolded the Caddos, Wichitas, and Penateka Comanches, saying, "My people being on friendly terms, not only with the whites but with all other Indians, object to [them] furnishing scouts for the commanding officer at Fort Sill, which causes much bad feeling among my people and the other tribes."[5]

The September council briefly addressed a topic that would later consume all the Indians of Indian Territory—the breakup of the reservations and the allotment of Indian lands. The general council unanimously repudiated a scheme proposed by Cherokee businessman Elias Cornelius Boudinot. In concert with the white business interests then growing in Indian Territory, Boudinot proposed opening all the lands in Indian Territory to white settlement.[6] While general councils continued to be held every year, attendance of Plains and Prairie Indians tailed off for a few years—at least until Boudinot's plan caught on with the government and the breakup of the reservations and the allotment of lands to individual Indian families became a major concern for all Indians in Indian Territory.

If the general councils brought together chiefs and leading men from the various nations, the advent of Indian International Fairs during the 1870s brought together the average citizens. The first Indian International Fair was held in September 1875 at Muskogee, Creek Nation, and continued to be held for several years to come. Originally, the fair was to show the progress of the Civilized Tribes, but as interest in the fair grew, the organizers invited the Plains and Prairie Indians to participate. Many did, including Sacs and Foxes, Delawares, Shawnees, Osages, Comanches, Arapahos, and Cheyennes. There were exhibits, horse races, and riding contests for both men and women. But the fair showed just how different the Civilized Tribes and the Plains Indians still were. The citizens of the Civilized Tribes seemed both shocked and charmed by "wild" Indians. One Cherokee woman remembered that "we saw a tribe of wild Indians, dressed in breech-clout and they were terrible looking. They danced Indian dances and ate raw meat!"[7] The Plains Indians' blankets, tepees, headdresses, silver ornaments, and colorful clothing fascinated Ella Robinson, a little girl at the time. She most remembered a big Osage chief dressed in a beaded shirt, black broadcloth trousers, and a linen duster, wearing an eagle-feather headdress that almost touched the ground, but walking through the mud barefoot with his trouser legs rolled up.[8] Plains Indian women riding astride their horses astounded Joe Martin, and when one took first place in a riding contest, she refused the woman's sidesaddle and insisted instead on a man's saddle. Martin recalled that at the 1879 fair, several horses of Plains Indians were stolen, and Comanche chief Toshaway had to borrow a saddle horse from Cherokee leader Joshua Ross, secretary of the fair, to get home. Although Ross asked for help in locating the horses, saying, "It will be a credit to the civilized Indians to find the horses and deliver them to our brothers of the west," the horses were never recovered, and Joshua Ross never got his horse back from Toshaway.[9]

Still, the fairs and the general councils gave every appearance of breaking down national and cultural barriers and seemed to portend a future when all Indians of Indian Territory might form into one great mass. As early as 1874, the Absentee Delawares merged with the Caddos and placed themselves under the leadership of a Caddo chief, something the main body of Delawares had done a few years earlier with the Cherokees. About thirty Delawares, though, lived with the Comanches and Kiowas on their reservation.[10] The Wichitas began to consolidate even more. Though the Wichitas had once been divided into such groups as Taovayas, Wacos, Tawakonis, and Kichais, the term *Wichita*, originally applied to the Taovayas and an Osage word meaning "scattered camps," was now given to all the people of these groups.[11] In 1878 the government consolidated the Comanche, Kiowa, and Wichita agencies. This single agency eventually administered over four thousand Comanches, Kiowas, Kiowa-Apaches, Taovayas, Wacos, Tawa-konis, Kichais, Delawares, and Caddos. The Comanches, Kiowas, and Apaches lived south of the Washita River, while the Taovayas, Wacos, Tawakonis, Kichais, Delawares, and Caddos—the Wichitas and Affiliated Bands—lived north it. Most remaining Tonkawas and Lipan Apaches at that time lived in Texas, near Fort Griffin.[12]

Reservation life and official activities also brought the various Indians peoples into close contact. The times when the federal government distributed annuities, rations, and cattle to be slaughtered brought people together in an almost circus atmosphere. Caddo and Wichita farmers often visited the Kiowas and Comanches on ration day to exchange watermelons and pumpkins for fresh meat, sugar, and coffee. Horses, blankets, and other items might be traded, dances held, and smokes made, and it would not be long before playing cards would be broken out and the gambling commenced. Jenny Horse, a Kiowa woman, remembered that during the ration issues, Indian people from all over would get together to gamble. All the "tribes gambled a lot—all tribes did—Chickasaws, Caddos, Comanches, Apaches, and Kiowas."[13]

The reservations and the government's introduction of American-style "civilization," farming, and Christianity among the Plains and Prairie Indians brought these people into closer contact with some citizens of the Civilized Tribes. Religious denominations, with government support, created schools for the Prairie and Plains Indians, such as the Quaker-built Riverside Indian School at the Wichita Agency. Citizens of the Five Tribes held some of the service positions, while some Civilized Tribes children attended the school. John Wolf, a Seminole who married the daughter of Wichita chief Tawakoni Jim, worked as a laborer at the school.[14] Cherokee Polly Keyes served as the school's cook.[15] As the Prairie and Plains Indians took up farming and ranching, they hired citizens of the Five Tribes as farm hands and cowboys.[16] The government also used Chickasaw teamsters to haul freight and Chickasaw and Cherokee cowboys to drive cattle to the western reservations.[17]

As the chiefs pointed out during the 1875 general council, the Prairie and Plains Indians often turned to the Five Civilized Tribes for farming instruction and advice concerning their lands.[18] During the early 1880s, with the cattle drives in full swing, ranchers in Texas approached the Comanches, Kiowas, Cheyennes, Arapahos, Wichitas, and Caddos about leasing some of their reservation lands as grazing pasturage. In 1882 the Cheyennes and Arapahos leased 3 million acres for sixty thousand dollars a year, while in 1884 the Comanches and Kiowas leased 1.5 million acres of their reservation for fifty thousand dollars a year. In 1889 the Wichitas asked George Washington Grayson, a Creek businessman and a representative at the general councils, to arrange a leasing agreement for them. Grayson and another Creek, Joseph M. Perryman, visited the Wichitas, where they "were received with genuine aboriginal hospitality."[19] Within a couple of days, and much to the anger of the Wichitas' agent, Grayson and Perryman signed a contract with the Wichitas to lease several hundred thousand acres of their reservation. About the same time, former Texas governor James W. Throckmorton approached the Caddos and asked to be named as their attorney of record. The Caddos, unfamiliar with the former governor, whom they called "Frogmountain or Jackmarten," turned to Grayson for advice. Grayson in turn had high praise for the former governor.[20]

While some citizens of the Five Civilized Tribes, such as Grayson, provided advice and instruction to the Prairie and Plains Indians, others hoped to reap a crop of souls for Christ. The Five Tribes had been exposed to Christianity while they still lived in the East. Many progressives had become Christians, and the impetus remained strong after they moved to Indian Territory.[21] Although most traditionalists still followed the ancient religions, and many citizens of the Five Tribes combined both Christianity and the old ways in their spiritual lives, it was the adoption of Christianity by the political leaders of the Five Tribes that made these tribes "civilized" in American eyes. Following the dictates of Christ to "go ye into the highways and byways and compel them come in," and to bring "civilization" to their more "savage" brothers, missionaries from the Five Civilized Tribes joined their white colleagues in opening churches among the Prairie and Plains Indians.

As early as 1874 the Baptist Convention of Texas sent Creek missionary John McIntosh, son of Chief Chilly McIntosh, to the Wichita Agency. At the agency Reverend McIntosh persuaded Black Beaver to interpret for him, and soon he began preaching to the Indians. McIntosh quickly found that differences existed between Creek Indians and Prairie Indians. As McIntosh visited those he wanted to save, he found he was expected to eat. Black Beaver told him it was the Indian way, and he had to eat. "But I soon found that I had to only mince, I did not know what kind of food I was eating much of the time, meals peculiar to this tribe."[22] This being right before the Red River War broke out, not many of the Plains and Prairie Indians were interested in hearing what he had to say. Many considered him just another government official come to dictate to them. McIntosh persevered. He soon had several converts; formed the Baptist Muskogee, Wichita, and Seminole

Association; and eventually founded the Rock Springs Baptist Church just north of present-day Anadarko, Oklahoma. When McIntosh died, his son, Jobe, continued his missionary work, and well into the twentieth century the Creek Association sent missionaries to the Rock Springs church.[23]

Building on the success of John McIntosh, the Dutch Reformed Church sent Dr. Frank H. Wright, a Choctaw born at Boggy Creek, to the Southern Plains in the 1890s. Like McIntosh, Wright also gained impressive results, eventually counting Apache leaders Geronimo and Naiche as members of his flock.[24] The spread of Christianity among the Prairie and Plains Indians brought them into further contact with the Civilized Tribes. Camp meetings held in the Seminole Nation might be attended by nearby Wichitas and Caddos.[25] Some went even further. About 1900, approximately forty Wichita Methodists took the train into eastern Choctaw territory for a revival meeting. Mary Cole, a Choctaw freedwoman, remembered calling "them wild Indians, or the 'wild bunch,' and they really were pretty uncivilized." The revival included preaching, singing, and testifying. Cole also recalled that an old Wichita man spoke, saying "'We have not come to rob or steal, but to extend you the right hand of fellowship.' He was a wild looking figure. He had on leather leggings and moccasins, a calico shirt and a vest, but no trousers. And his hair was long, down to his shoulders." The revival seemed to go very well.[26]

Not all Prairie and Plains Indians accepted the Christianity offered. In 1890 the Ghost Dance swept through Indian Territory and then peacefully passed without causing the bloodshed it brought to the Lakotas at the Battle of Wounded Knee. Ironically, the "Peyote Road," or Native American Church, became one of the most pervasive religious movement in Indian Territory. It began among the Plains and Prairie Indians and spread to the removed Indians and Five Tribes. Using peyote, but mixing both ancient and Christian spiritual beliefs and teachings, the Native American Church began during the 1880s among the Indians on the reservations of the Comanches and Kiowas and the Wichitas and Affiliated Bands. While agents and white churchmen condemned the religion because they felt the use of peyote was a throwback to tribal days, the adherents advocated a peaceful, harmonious, industrious life, and their ceremonies were always marked by quiet dignity. The church rapidly spread to the other Indian peoples in Indian Territory and soon gained converts among Indians throughout the United States. As the 1944 charter of the Native American Church proclaimed, some of its purposes were to "promote morality, sobriety, industry, charity and right living and cultivate a spirit of brotherly love and union among the members of the several tribes of Indians throughout the United States."[27]

Despite all these interactions, the Indians were not melded into one intertribal mass; national differences continued to divide them. Though the Wichitas were quickly merging, each Wichita division still recognized its own chief, though it was the Taovaya chief, such as Isadowa, who was considered the Wichita principal chief.[28] In 1878, when the Wichita and Comanche-Kiowa Agencies consolidated, the Wichitas protested, not wanting their people in such close contact with the Comanches and Kiowas. Wichita leaders complained that the government wanted to make them one big tribe, something their people were opposed to.[29] Problems also arose between the Wichitas and the Caddos. Wichitas and Caddos had been Prairie Indians with much in common, but they insisted upon their differences, and while the Taovayas, Tawakonis, Wacos, and Kichais might coalesce into one nation, the Caddos refused to join them. Even though the Wichitas and the Caddos spoke Caddoan dialects, there was such a significant difference between them that the two peoples could not readily understand each other's language. Wichitas complained that whenever the Wichitas received annuities from the government, the Caddos demanded a share as one of the Affiliated Bands, but when the Caddos won a lawsuit over lands they gave up in Louisiana, they refused to share the proceeds with the Wichitas.[30]

The biggest problem the Wichitas had was over the land they felt the government promised them. In the 1850s Wichita chief Toshaquash complained about the government's giving lands claimed by the Wichitas to the Chickasaws without Wichita permission. Now the Wichitas, Caddos, and Chickasaws as well complained about the government's giving their land away to make the Comanche-Kiowa and Cheyenne-Arapaho reservations. The Chickasaws claimed that their treaty with the United States in 1855 gave them the right to settle on the Comanche-Kiowa reservation. Their agent quickly disabused them of this, reminding them of their 1866 treaty, in which they had given up all claims to the Leased District.[31] The Wichitas' and Caddos' complaint may have been stronger, claiming that lands promised to them by treaty in August 1859 had been taken from them by executive order in August 1869 to make the Cheyenne-Arapaho reservation and parts of the Comanche-Kiowa reservation.[32] Special Agent E. B. Townsend, sent to investigate Wichita claims, had little sympathy for them. Though Townsend conceded that the land was originally held by the Wichitas, he felt this was not enough to rule in their favor. He ignored their 1859 treaty claims, not on legal ground, but because he believed it was wrong for the Wichitas to claim so much land, as it was more than they needed. This country, he asserted, was intended for use by all men, so it "is not consistent with the 'divine plan' that a few—the denizens of the forest—shall monopolize and absorb vast tracts of land to be held in idleness to the exclusion of others needing and standing ready to cultivate and improve them."[33] With this, Townsend ruled against the Wichitas and in favor of the Cheyennes and Arapahos, who were leasing the land to white cattlemen.[34]

The words of Toshaquash must have come back to haunt the Wichitas when the government told them the main reason they were continually overlooked when it came to land was that their land legally belonged to the Choctaws and Chickasaws. In the removal treaties made with the Choctaws and Chickasaws during the 1830s, without ever consulting the Wichitas the government assigned the land in western Indian Territory to the Choctaws and Chickasaws. So to make the Cheyenne-Arapaho reservations, the government treated with the Choctaws and Chickasaws to get them to cede the Leased District and ignored Wichita claims. Even Townsend pointed out the unfairness of this, as the removal treaties of the 1830s stipulated that the rights of Indians who occupied that country before the treaties would be respected.[35]

As the Wichitas argued for their reservation boundaries, other Indian nations tried to protect their own lands and prerogatives. Congress created the Pawnee reservation out of lands taken from the Cherokees in 1866, and now the Cherokees wanted Congress to pay them for it. The commissioner of Indian affairs refused.[36] A few years later, the Cherokees again complained about the government's locating the Pawnees, Poncas, Nez Percés, Otos, Missouris, and Osages on land west of the Arkansas River claimed by the Cherokees. They demanded fair market value as well as reparations for the timber these Indians cut.[37]

For many Cherokees, settling these Indians on Cherokee lands was more than just loss of land; it was more of an invasion of civilized people by wild Indians. Cook McCracken, a Cherokee progressive, may have explained the Cherokee attitude best in an interview he gave during the late 1930s:

> Then they brought down them crazy wild Indians called the Osages and put them on the land. They were too lazy to work and lived around in wigwams and painted all up and wore feather head-gear and go on a crazy war dance and then come over to our part what we did have left and wanted to take all of our game away from us and that made us pretty mad. We had instinct enough to find out when they were going to band up and come over and take our little neighborhood and we were usually ready for them. . . . I have seen some of the Cherokees ride up by the side of an Osage on his

pony and hit him in the head with an ax and the feathers
would fly out of his head-gear like picking a turkey.[38]

Conversely, the "wild" Indians had their complaints about their
"civilized" neighbors. The Pawnees griped about a scam the Five
Tribes, particularly the Creeks, perpetrated on them. According to
the Pawnees, Creek horse traders would come to their territory,
and Pawnee citizens would buy a few horses. A few days later, the
Creeks would report the horses stolen, then send a Creek search
party to Pawnee country to round up the "stolen" horses.[39]

Though most Indians in Indian Territory now lived on reservations and were subject to the government's civilization program,
the Five Civilized Tribes still viewed the Prairie and Plains Indians
as savages and their reservations as a wilderness on the western
edge of civilization. The Chickasaws, remembering years of Comanche raids, when they rewrote their constitution in 1876 provided
for their militia to be called out by the governor or even a militia
company commander "whenever there is sufficient evidence that
marauding or hostile Indians are in the Chickasaw Nation."[40] Ten
years later, the Chickasaws realized just how civilized the Comanches and Kiowas had become when these Plains Indians proposed
levying a tax of one dollar on each head of Chickasaw cattle found
on the Comanche-Kiowa reservation. Chickasaw governor W. M.
Guy howled in protest, claiming that the Chickasaws never taxed
Comanche-Kiowa cattle on Chickasaw land. With a little arrogance,
Governor Guy demanded that the Comanches and Kiowas should
allow the Chickasaws to get their cattle because the Chickasaws
were civilized and the Comanches and Kiowas were not. Guy
claimed it was "the policy of those who are *considered civilized*, to
extend to those less fortunate, all aid within their power to promote their welfare and lead them to a higher state of civilization"
[italics in the original].[41]

Like the Chickasaws, other members of the Five Tribes also
considered the western reservations uncivilized and wild—and so

perfect places to take refuge. In 1882–83 the "Green Peach War" broke out among the Creeks. In it the Creek government split between a traditionalist, formerly Union, faction led by Isparhecher (Green Peach) and a progressive, formerly Confederate, faction led by Chief Samuel Checote. Violence broke out between the factions, and in February 1883 Isparhecher and three hundred of his followers took refuge among the Comanches until federal troops rounded them up and sent them back to Creek country.[42]

The Green Peach Creeks were just one example of Indians from one nation taking up residence on another reservation. This mixture of peoples on various reservations seemed normal during the 1890s. A band of Shawnees tried to take up residence at the Kiowa Agency until the Kiowa agent complained and refused to allow them.[43] Joe Northfork, a Sac and Fox, lived among the Caddos and even received his annuity checks there.[44] Cherokee George Butler and his family came to the Anadarko area in 1890s when he was hired to work as a cowboy for a Texas cattle outfit. He eventually settled down, cleared about four acres of bottomland, planted corn, and got along very well with his Wichita neighbors, though he found their customs very strange and somewhat frightening. He seemed a welcome neighbor, as the Wichitas even shot one of their own horses that continually got into Butler's corn.[45]

The Seminoles were the Civilized Tribe living closest to the Prairie and Plains Indians, but their progressive leaders went to great extremes to keep them separate. During the early 1870s several Seminole families settled among the Caddos at the Wichita Agency, where they rented land. In April 1874, Seminole chief John Jumper wrote Caddo chief Guadeloupe asking that he send these Seminoles back to Seminole territory. According to Jumper, these Seminoles' stay among the Caddos had made them regress in terms of civilization. "They are no better than the painted Indians of the Staked Plains, without an even reputation or character. Seminoles like those living among you & yet citizens of this nation, making it responsible for their actions, places the matter in a complicated shape." Jumper encouraged the Caddos to continue their progress down the road to "civilization" but to send these Seminoles back home, as they would only hinder the Caddos and not help them.[46]

While it is not known how Guadeloupe took Jumper's letter, John Chupco, the leader of the Seminoles living among the Caddos, may have felt insulted. In reality, those Seminoles living around the Wichita Agency had been an inspiration to all. They rented their land, improved it by building cabins, cultivated crops, and erected fences. Their Caddo landlords certainly enjoyed having such prosperous tenants. But Jumper's request made an impression, and most of the Seminole families left their holdings and returned to Seminole territory. They asked for and apparently received remuneration for the improvements as well as the flourishing crops they left behind.[47] Not all left, though, and ten years later fourteen Seminoles still lived at the Wichita Agency. While there, a few Seminole men married Caddo and Wichita women and began raising children, but this did not stop the Seminole chief from trying to persuade them and their children to return to Seminole territory.[48] This bad blood with the Seminole government carried on for several years, as in the 1890s the Kichais complained that the Seminoles were stealing money from Kichai orphans placed in their care.[49]

As always, kinship continued to play an important role among all Indians peoples. After the end of the Red River War, increasing numbers of Civilized Tribes Indians migrated to western Indian Territory in search of opportunities. Many found jobs on the reservations of the Comanches and Kiowas and the Wichitas and Affiliated Bands. The Plains and Prairie Indians sometimes adopted these migrants into their families.[50] Adoption was one thing, but intermarriage was something else. With more and more citizens of the Five Tribes working on the western reservations, intermarriage between citizens of the Five Tribes and the Prairie and Plains Indians should have become common. Ironically, despite the government's promotion of an agrarian life-style and these Indian peoples' tradition of incorporating outsiders into their families, this did not happen. Though Plains and Prairie Indians often intermarried, little intermarriage took place between them and the Five Civilized Tribes. As previously mentioned, a few Seminoles married Caddo women. A Comanche woman named Tomaso married Joseph Chandler, who was part Creek or Cherokee and who was eventually adopted by the Penateka Comanches.[51] In the early 1900s, a Potawatomi woman and an Oneida woman married Comanche men. Most intermarriages took place among the members of the Wichitas and Affiliated Bands—Delawares, Caddos, Wichitas, Wacos, Tawakonis, and Kichais. There was a little intermarriage between the Wichitas and Affiliated Bands and the Comanches, Kiowas, and Kiowa-Apaches. The twentieth century saw more intermarriages, particularly among those Indian peoples living in proximity to each other and among Indians who went to live in cities. But other than those mentioned, intermarriage between any of the Indians in western Oklahoma and the Five Civilized Tribes during the nineteenth and early twentieth centuries was minimal.[52]

Conversely, many whites intermarried with Indian people from all nations. Many of these whites played both sides of the ball, on the one hand demanding the same rights concerning land and money that the government promised the Indians, and on the other, demanding the same opportunities and privileges of American citizens, such as the protection of American, rather than Indian, laws and courts. Many of these intermarried whites felt that Indian nations' holding their tribal lands in common restricted whites' profits, and they urged the government to break up the reservations. Others whites, termed *Boomers*, felt that the Indians controlled more land than they needed and that the "excess" land in Indian Territory should be opened to white settlement. They often invaded Indian lands and remained on them until removed by the army. Similarly, eastern friends of the Indians believed the reservations and tribal lands held in common hindered the civilization process and the assimilation of the Indians into American society. They also called for the allotment of the tribal lands to individual Indians. By the 1880s, these white factions had the government's ear, and the allotment process, which would break up the reservations and give each Indian a tract of land of his or her own, gained momentum.[53]

Just about every Indian in Indian Territory came out against land allotment and correctly saw it as a threat to their national sovereignty, lands, and way of life. Initially, this temporarily brought the Plains, Prairie, removed, and "civilized" Indians together. As early as 1879, many Indians became worried at the influx of whites into their lands. They had also heard rumors that the government planned to establish federal courts among the Indian nations and make Indian Territory into a full-fledged territory, complete with a territorial governor. To fight this, delegates from the Five Tribes and the Sacs and Foxes met at Eufaula, Creek Nation, on May 27, 1879, to make their opposition known.[54]

In 1881, the nations of the Comanche, Kiowas, and Wichitas and Affiliated Bands met to voice similar opposition. A few years earlier, the government had consolidated the Comanche-Kiowa reservation and the reservation of the Wichitas and Affiliated Bands with the agency headquarters at Anadarko. The conference held on June 10 at Anadarko was attended by delegates from the Comanches, Kiowas, Kiowa-Apaches, Wichitas, Wacos, Caddos, Tawakonis, Kichais, and Delawares. Tinah, a Caddo orator and speaking for all the delegates, addressed the agent, saying, "We know this is our country. Our Father gave us this land to live on. . . . At that time we thought we had a large country, but since then our country has become smaller. But we still remember the talk and ask our Father to have mercy and not cut up our country. Now white men are talking of running a railroad into our country. We don't want this."[55]

While Tinah's plea probably fell on deaf ears, Agent P. B. Hunt took the opportunity the council afforded to point out just how different the Wichitas and Affiliated Bands were from the Comanches, Kiowas, and Kiowa-Apaches. Over the decades, these Prairie Indians had shifted away from their Comanche and Kiowa allies and life-style to that of the Five Civilized Tribes. Hunt now pointed out that the Wichitas and Affiliated Bands had "advanced much farther in the ways of civilization than the [Comanches and Kiowas]. . . . Much [of] the larger portion dress in citizen's dress, live in houses, and are cultivating the soil. . . . Of these bands the Wichitas are making the greatest improvement, and the Caddoes the least. I think the order from [the Commissioner of Indian Affairs] to stop the rations, except beef to the Caddos and Delawares was a proper one."[56]

Agent Hunt may have been surprised at just how "civilized" his charges actually were, as they all grasped just what the allotment process meant. In March 1886, delegates from the Cherokees, Creeks, Choctaws, Chickasaws, Seminoles, Delawares, Comanches, Kiowas, Caddos, Hainais (Ionies), Kichais, Tawakonis, and Wichitas met in Eufaula, Creek Nation. There they signed a compact opposing the Dawes General Allotment Act, then making its way through Congress. Ironically, the Dawes Act may have achieved what the government had tried to bring about decades earlier: a unified Indian confederacy. The compact's purpose was not only to promote the general welfare of all Indians, but also "to preserve our lands and rights intact." In all, the compact outlawed revenge and retaliation among the signatory nations, set up ways to deal with crimes committed by citizens of one nation upon citizens of another, and detailed trade and immigration regulations between nations. Above all it stated in Section 4 that in order to "prevent any future removal and to transmit to our posterity any unimpaired title to the lands guaranteed to our respective nations by the United States . . . no Nation party to this compact shall without consent of all the other parties 'cede' or in any manner alienate to the United States any part of their present territory."[57]

It made no difference what the Indians said or how many of them protested, the breakup of the reservations and the allotment of Indian lands was a fait accompli. On February 8, 1887, the Dawes General Allotment Act became law, authorizing the president to survey those reservations with adequate farming and grazing land and then allot the lands to individual Indians. Indian heads of families were to receive 160 acres; unmarried Indians over eighteen years of age and Indian orphans under eighteen were to receive 80 acres; other Indians under eighteen were to receive 40 acres. The government later did away with these graduated allotments and eventually gave every Indian man, woman, and child an 80-acre allotment. The allotments would be doubled for individuals on reservations with lands only suitable for grazing. The allotments were then held in trust for the Indians for twenty-five years and so could not be sold during that period. After twenty-five years, the Indians received the land in fee simple. After all the allotments had been made, the government would negotiate for the purchase of the surplus reservation lands. These would then be sold, with the money held by the government and slated for "civilizing" and educating the Indians. In Indian Territory the Dawes Act did not initially apply to the Five Civilized Tribes, Osages, Miamis, Peorias, and Sacs and Foxes.[58]

The Indians of the territory came out solidly against the act.[59] Despite their protests, not long after the act's passage, the president ordered the allotment process to begin. Although the Five Civilized Tribes had been excluded from the Dawes Act, the government hoped to acquire additional land for white settlers by persuading the Cherokees to sell the Cherokee Outlet. In March 1889 the Cherokee Commission, which eventually consisted of David H. Jerome, Alfred M. Wilson, and Warren G. Sayre, began negotiating with the Cherokees and other nations over the sale of their lands west of the ninety-sixth meridian. In 1890 the commission bought the Cherokee Outlet—six million acres—for $8.5 million.[60]

With that work done, the commission, now called the Jerome Commission, turned its attention to the reservations in the western part of Indian Territory. Despite the protests of the Indians, the Jerome Commission negotiated the allotment and purchase of the Cheyenne-Arapaho reservation in October 1890 for $1.5 million, the reservation of the Wichitas and Affiliated Bands in June 1891 for $715,000, and the Comanche-Kiowa reservation in October 1892 for $2 million.[61] Almost immediately, the Chickasaws and Choctaws protested the government's agreements concerning these reservations. The Chickasaws and Choctaws insisted that any money stemming from the government's purchase of the surplus lands of these reservations should be paid to them, as they had never fully given up their claim to the Leased District. To expedite the allotment process at the behest of settlers who wanted the reservations opened to them, the government paid the Chickasaws and Choctaws over $3 million for their claims to the Cheyenne-Arapaho reservation, more than what the Cheyenne and Arapahos received for giving up their lands. In 1900 the Supreme Court voided Chickasaw-Choctaw claims to the payments for the reservations of the Wichitas and Affiliated Bands and the Comanches and Kiowas.[62]

Virtually every other Indian people in Indian Territory underwent the same process. Ironically, the Quapaws, whom the Five Tribes had often characterized as the one of the most uncivilized, seemed to be the most far-sighted. In 1887, when the government proposed allotting their land into eighty-acre tracts, the Quapaws protested, and the government delayed. This gave the Quapaws time to act. In 1893 the Quapaw council allotted their own land, giving each Quapaw a two-hundred-acre tract. In 1895, Congress approved the Quapaw allotment, and so the Quapaws, who were the only Indians to handle their own allotment, managed to triple their individual allotments in comparison to other Indians of the Territory.[63]

If the Five Civilized Tribes expected to escape the allotment process, they were sadly mistaken. In 1894 the Dawes Commission, headed by former senator Henry L. Dawes, the author of the allotment act, began negotiating with the Five Tribes over the allotment of their lands. Like the Plains and Prairie Indians before them, the Five Tribes did everything possible to stop the allotment process, but to no avail. Finally, in April 1897 the Chickasaws and Choctaws signed the Atoka Agreement, which created a formula for allotment and surplus land purchases. The Seminoles signed the agreement in 1898, the Creeks in 1901, and the Cherokees in 1902. At the same time the Five Tribes were losing their lands, they were also losing their national authority. In 1895, Congress created two new United States courts in Indian Territory, and Congress later stipulated that beginning in 1898 all criminal and civil cases in Indian Territory would be tried in these courts. The last blow came in June 1898, when Congress passed the Curtis Act, which essentially abolished the national governments of the Five Tribes, outlawing their national courts and voiding all their national laws. In 1901, Congress declared every Indian in Indian Territory to be a citizen of the United States.[64]

While the Cheyennes and Arapahos had their reservation thrown open to white settlement in 1892, only two years after negotiating their agreement, most Indians experienced a lag between the signing of their agreements, the ratification of the agreements by Congress, and then the opening of their reservations. This gave them time to try to avoid the allotment process. Some Kickapoos wanted to refuse their allotments and be allowed to go live with the Caddos.[65] Some Cherokees considered moving to Mexico. After word of this got out, a few Kiowas, Comanches, and members of the Wichitas and Affiliated Bands asked if they could accompany them. The International Irrigation and Improvement Company of Hermosillo, Mexico, informed the Cherokees it would be happy to sell them land south of the border. Apparently nothing came of this.[66] Others decided to continue the fight for their lands. Quickly learning the new ways, Kiowa chief Lone Wolf filed suit to prevent the allotment of the

Kiowa-Comanche reservation. In *Lone Wolf* v. *Hitchcock*, attorneys for the Kiowas pointed out that the Treaty of Medicine Lodge Creek of 1867 stipulated that no reservation lands could ever be ceded without three-fourths of the adult males approving it. In January 1903 the Supreme Court rejected Lone Wolf's arguments, ruling that Congress could make law for the Indians and was not bound by previous Indian treaties.[67]

While Lone Wolf's case was making its way through the court system, the government was already breaking up his reservation. In July 1901 the government allotted then opened to white settlement the reservations of the Comanches and Kiowas and the Wichitas and Affiliated Bands.[68] Soon after signing the Atoka Agreement, the lands belonging to the Five Tribes were allotted in varying amounts. The Choctaws and Chickasaws received 320 acres per person, the Creeks 160 acres, the Seminoles 120 acres, and the Cherokees 110 acres. After the Five Tribes' allotment, there was not much surplus land remaining to be thrown open to white settlement, as most was reserved for townsites, schools, or was coal, oil, and mineral land designated for the benefits of the tribes.[69] Still, many citizens of the Five Tribes, especially traditionalists, found themselves swindled out of their allotments by white entrepreneurs, "guardians," and people who loudly proclaimed themselves to be their friends.

The Indians of Indian Territory were united in their opposition to the allotment process, but this "mighty pulverizing engine for breaking up the tribal mass" made them realize it was every nation for itself.[70] Government officials hoped that land allotment and the civilization process would mold the Indians into a single homogeneous people who could then quickly be assimilated into mainstream American society. With their own governments and lands under attack, the Five Tribes had little time or inclination to nurture relations with Plains and Prairie Indians. Now court decisions, not treaties, shaped Indian life, and lawyers, instead of Indian intermediaries, interceded with the government.

With most Indian peoples trying to make a living off their allotment or just trying to hang on to it, there was little reason for the
various Indian peoples to come together. In some ways the government precipitated this continued division. Indians had long had a
tradition of visiting one another. But even here the divisions among
the Indians could be seen. A. Sharpe, Indian agent for the Poncas,
noticed that Plains and Prairie Indians, such as the Kiowas and
Wichitas, tended to visit Indians similar to them, such as the
Osages, Poncas, Apaches, and Cheyennes. None of these, though,
visited the Chickasaws, Creeks, or other Civilized Tribes unless it
was to trade.[71] Hoping to speed along the civilization process, the
government now discouraged these visitations. In the government's mind, when Indians visited other Indians, it meant a dance
would take place, with the hosts giving away large quantities of
gifts, such as ponies and blankets. Rather than seeing this as "buf-
fering exchange" that ensured access to goods when hard times
came, officials saw these giveaways as the way Indians impov-
erished themselves and as an uncivilized relic of the past.[72] Similarly,
Texas prohibited Indians of Indian Territory from entering that state,
which prevented many Apaches and Comanches from visiting any
relatives there or in Mexico. At the same time, the Chickasaws
required Comanches and Kiowas to have a pass from a federal
marshal to venture onto Chickasaw land.[73]

The final blows for any Indian unity came, ironically, when the
United States government actually began trying to smash the individual Indian nations into one great red mass of individuals. In
May 1890 the desires of Cherokee Elias Cornelius Boudinot began
to come to fruition as the government split Indian Territory down
the center. All the lands in Indian Territory west of those occupied
by the Five Tribes were designated as Oklahoma Territory. Into
this fell the reservations belonging to the Wichitas and Affiliated
Bands, the Kiowas and Comanches, and the Cheyennes and
Arapahos. The lands of the Five Tribes now constituted Indian
Territory. In 1898 the Curtis Act abolished the Indian national

governments and their court system and nullified their laws. With this, the Indian general councils fell by the wayside, and there was less and less contact between Indians in the eastern and western parts of the territory.

By the turn of the century every Indian nation in the two territories was much more concerned with keeping its own head above water than helping out the others. It was every nation for itself as Sooners, Boomers, and the government carved up Indian lands. By 1905 the Five Tribes were more than willing to abandon the Plains Indians to the whites in hopes of saving themselves. As white citizens in both territories pressed for statehood, the Five Tribes petitioned Congress to have their own lands in Indian Territory combined into a separate state, which would enter the Union with the name "Sequoyah." The Plains Indians living in the west would be left to the white-dominated territory of "Oklahoma." Congress ignored their plan. Two years later, Congress joined Oklahoma Territory in the west and Indian Territory in the east, and in 1907 the state of Oklahoma entered the union.[74]

After statehood there was less need, inclination, or time for the Five Civilized Tribes in the eastern part of Oklahoma to have a relationship with the Plains and Prairie Indians of western Oklahoma, and vice versa. Now Indian peoples throughout Oklahoma, under pressure from the various layers of government, white settlers, ranchers, farmers, oil companies, and unscrupulous entrepreneurs, spent most of their time trying to hang on to their lands and resources. Factionalism within the nations, always a problem, became even more severe as progressives tried to take advantage of the economic exploitation going on in their nations, while traditionalists tried to stop it or merely ignored it. After statehood, most interactions among the different groups of Indians, when they took place, did so on an individual basis. Comanches, Caddos, Shawnees, and Cherokees might meet at boarding schools, at church conventions, or just as neighbors who held lands close to each other.[75]

Finally, after centuries of differences, the dawning of the twentieth century showed the removed Indians and the Plains Indians
to have much in common: defeat, governments abolished, lands
allotted, traditional ways under attack, and poverty. But these very
situations caused them to remain separate. All Indians were
swimming for their lives and so could not help anyone else. It
would not be until the second half of the twentieth century, as the
intertribal movement touched all the Indian people in the United
States, that removed Indians and Plains Indians would once again
begin working together.

CHAPTER EIGHT

CONCLUSION

Not the Five Civilized Tribes. They're content with what they've got now. And most of them are white people. . . . They're mixed so much with the white society that they have no inclination towards the Indian thinking, Indian views, Indian ways. . . . They go to stomp dances, [and] they're lost. . . . Maybe they've never been Indian inclined.

WALLACE COFFEE
Comanche, 1969

Not until the Europeans arrived did "Indians" exist. There were millions of people in North America in 1492, but the concept of all the indigenous people of North America being lumped together as a racial category was inconceivable. Like the peoples of Europe, Asia, and Africa, North Americans were divided into ethnic groups. And such a tremendous diversity of peoples and ethnicities it was. There were sophisticated agriculturalists surrounded by enormous fields of maize, small bands of hunter-gatherers on the move toward greener pastures, and villages that used some of both. For any given individual, some of these peoples might be very much like those of his own village, his own band, his own peoples, similar in geography, beliefs, and mode of production. Others would appear frighteningly different, with little in common and alien in every way.

The gulf between certain types of peoples expanded tremendously after about A.D. 700 with the coming of large-scale corn horticulture and the rise of the Mississippian cultural tradition. Before that, most peopled lived a hunting-gathering existence; some peoples were almost entirely nomadic, while others lived for longer times in one place, but both scoured a territory for what they needed. But the coming of maize horticulture to the American Southeast and Mississippi River valley about that time was truly a revolution. It totally changed the way people in these areas thought and lived. As their mode of production changed from hunting-gathering to horticulture, their religion, social organization, and way of life changed along with it. Now peoples like the Choctaws, Cherokees, Creeks, and Chickasaws saw themselves as very different from the hunting-gathering peoples around them.

The next revolution for the peoples of North America came in the 1600s and 1700s with the arrival of the horse. These animals proved a boon to hunting-gathering peoples on both sides of the prairie-plains. Soon newly mounted peoples flooded out onto the Great Plains, now even better hunter-gatherers, which only reinforced their mode of production, which in turn influenced their religion and social organization. The Comanches, Kiowas, Kiowa-Apaches, and Plains Apaches, and to some degree the Wichitas, came to dominate the Southern Plains. So by the early 1800s two wholly different peoples populated much of the lower half of North America. In the Southeast lived the populous settled agriculturalists, and on the Southern Plains the powerful horse-mounted hunter-gatherers. Adding to the differences, about the same time, the Southeastern Indians were already being influenced by a European culture that only solidified their agrarian beliefs.

It would have been fascinating to see how they would have developed if they had been left in isolation. With the technology then available, the Southeastern Indians probably would not have ventured onto the plains and the Southern Plains Indians would not have gone far into the eastern woodlands. But this was not to be. During the 1830s these two different peoples were forced into contact with each other as the United States government moved the Southeastern agricultural Indians to Indian Territory and onto lands the Southern Plains Indians claimed as their own. As they faced off, each saw the other as different and inferior, certain of their own cultural superiority. This did not make for the best of relations.

Compounding the problems was that a sense of "Indianness"—Indian as a racial category—had developed since the arrival of Columbus. The Europeans brought it. To them, it was a strange world they had "discovered"—a strange land with strange animals and even stranger peoples. Wherever they turned, much of what they saw baffled them. And so to make sense of it all, they shaved down the differences among these North American peoples and lumped them all together as "Indians." That one people might live in grass huts and plant corn and another might live in skin houses and hunt buffalo was just different aspects of the same strangeness. So for Europeans, "Indians" were not members of different ethnic groups but were peoples belonging to a "red" race. And this race the whites equated with "savagery."

Initially, most native peoples of North American probably found it incongruous that they were considered all one people, and savage as well. But they found themselves caught in a paradox. On one hand they recognized that there were many different peoples that made up native North America, while on the other they found themselves bound together under the classification of "Indian." Eventually, some Indians found they had to accommodate this European view. If Europeans were going to insist on seeing white and red, the native peoples were more than willing to do the same. They insisted that there were red people and white people, a red road and a white road, and that the Creator had placed red people in this hemisphere and white ones in the other. After all, there did seem to be major differences between the way most native peoples, even those with differing modes of production, saw the world and the way Europeans saw it. Differences over land, religion, kinship, hospitality, and law were just some of the big issues.

Over time, as Indians and whites came into close contact, particularly in the Southeast, the edges blurred between what was Indian and what was white. Some Southeastern Indians began to adopt characteristics associated with Europeans: classical education, rule of written law, Christianity, and capitalism—things vastly different from "traditional" Indian ways. To be sure, these progressives, as they came to be called, insisted that they had not ceased to be "Indian" but were changing in order to protect that very "Indianness." This caused a schism among their own peoples as many traditionalists demanded that their society remain true to the ancient ways. Still, the progressives were encouraged by American leaders, educated during the Enlightenment, who firmly believed that Indians could progress up to "civilization" if they continued to adopt Euroamerican characteristics. Given enough time, these educated Euroamericans believed Indians could become "white."

As Southeastern farmers and Plains Indian hunter-gathers came into contact with each other in Indian Territory, it did not take long for the question to arise over what constituted an Indian. Progressives, who held the reins of power among the Southeastern nations, took a modern political view. Indians were the indigenous peoples of this hemisphere and as such were members of any one of many different Indian nations or peoples. They were different from whites by virtue of their citizenship in one of these Indian nations. The progressives believed that for Indians to survive, they must not provoke the powerful United States. Additionally, whether it was through realism or opportunism, they insisted that Indians become civilized, which essentially meant giving up hunting-gathering, becoming farmers, and accepting most of these Euroamerican characteristics. As the progressives of the Southeastern Indians saw it, their own people were quickly becoming civilized, and the Plains Indians, whom they saw as savages, should follow their example as quickly as possible. Not all Southeastern Indians would have agreed with this, and traditionalists disavowed the progressives' vision. Many Plains Indians also had a differing view of "Indianness." If there was a red road and a white road, then going too far down the white road meant become white. Could an Indian cease to be an Indian if he or she took on too many white characteristics?

So in Indian Territory, Plains peoples and Southeastern peoples found themselves divided three ways. First, it was a clash between modes of production, between agriculturalists and hunter-gathers and their wholly different way of seeing the world. Second, it was H. G. Wells's age-old battle between nomads and settled folk, between invader and defender. Third, it was a clash between the progressive ideas pushed by Indians who held power among the Southeastern nations and the traditionalism of the Plains Indians, between "civilization" as Peter Pitchlynn saw it and "savagery." Or as the Plains peoples saw it, it was between artificial Indians and real Indians. It was these differences, often exacerbated by the United States government, that kept these two Indian peoples apart, often breeding suspicion, hatred, and contempt. Though the twentieth century has seen amazing pan-Indian and intertribal alliances, national identities have prevailed. Over the years Indian peoples have often joined together to win significant victories, but beneath the label "Indian," or "Native American," glorious histories, old suspicions, and remembered outrages bubble and ferment.

NOTES

ABBREVIATIONS

CHNR Cherokee National Records, Indian Archives, Oklahoma Historical Society, Oklahoma City

CKNR Chickasaw National Records, Chickasaw Nation Headquarters, Ada, Oklahoma

CRHC C. Ross Hume Collection, Western History Collections, University of Oklahoma, Norman

CRNR Creek National Records, Indian Archives, Oklahoma Historical Society, Oklahoma City

CSS Congressional Serial Set

DD Doris Duke American Indian Oral History Collection, Western History Collections, University of Oklahoma, Norman

IPH Indian-Pioneer Histories, Oklahoma Historical Society, Oklahoma City

IC International Councils, Indian Archives, Oklahoma Historical Society, Oklahoma City

JRC James Reagle, Jr., Collection, Western History Collections, University of Oklahoma, Norman

KA Kiowa Agency Records, Indian Archives, Oklahoma Historical Society, Oklahoma City

LCC Lewis Cass Collection, Western History Collections, University of Oklahoma, Norman

LR-OIA:CHA Letters Received, Office of Indian Affairs, Cherokee
Agency, National Archives, RG 75
LR-OIA:CKA Letters Received, Office of Indian Affairs, Chickasaw
Agency, National Archives, RG 75
LR-OIA:CTA Letters Received, Office of Indian Affairs, Choctaw
Agency, National Archives, RG 75
LR-OIA:CRA Letters Received, Office of Indian Affairs, Creek Agency,
National Archives, RG 75
LR-OIA:SA Letters Received, Office of Indian Affairs, Seminole Agency,
National Archives, RG 75
LR-OIA:SS Letters Received, Office of Indian Affairs, Southern Super-
intendency, National Archives, RG 75
LR-OIA:WA Letters Received, Office of Indian Affairs, Wichita Agency,
National Archives, RG 75
LR-OIA:WS Letters Received, Office of Indian Affairs, Western Super-
intendency, National Archives, RG 75
PPPC Peter P. Pitchlynn Collection, Western History Collections,
University of Oklahoma, Norman

CHAPTER 1

1. Quote in W. David Baird, *Peter Pitchlynn: Chief of the Choctaws*, 203.

2. Theda Perdue and Michael D. Green, *The Cherokee Removal: A Brief History with Documents*, 10.

3. Morris W. Foster, *Being Comanche: A Social History of an American Indian Community*, 31–35; Ernest Wallace and E. Adamson Hoebel, *The Comanches: Lords of the Southern Plains*, 5–11, 34–36; Thomas W. Kavanagh, *Comanche Political History: An Ethnohistorical Perspective, 1708–1875*, 57–62.

4. Mildred P. Mayhall, *The Kiowas*, 1–15, 135–36.

5. Preston Holder, *The Hoe and the Horse on the Plains*, 89–90.

6. Willard H. Rollings, *The Osages: An Ethnohistorical Study of Hege-mony on the Prairie Plains*, 5–12.

7. David La Vere, *The Caddo Chiefdoms: Caddo Economics and Politics, 700–1835*, 90–105.

8. Bernard W. Sheehan, *Seeds of Extinction: Jeffersonian Philanthropy and the American Indian*, 3–12, 130–35, 166–74.

9. Ibid., 3–4, 148–91.

10. Ibid., 128, 141–42; Joel W. Martin, *Sacred Revolt: The Muskogees' Struggle for a New World*, 92–113; Francis Paul Prucha, *The Great Father: The United States Government and the American Indians*, 135–58.

11. Perdue and Green, *The Cherokee Removal*, 11–14.

12. Ibid.

13. Dianna Everett, *The Texas Cherokees: A People between Two Fires, 1819–1840*, 6–17; Martin, Sacred Revolt, 1–3.

14. John Fowler to John Jamison, April 16, 1819, in Clarence E. Carter, ed., *The Territorial Papers of the United States: Arkansas Territory* 19:70–71.

15. Sheehan, *Seeds of Extinction*, 10–11, 166–74, 180–81.

16. Ibid., 243–45; Baird, *Peter Pitchlynn*, 32–33.

17. Prucha, *The Great Father*, 192–95, 206, 215–19.

18. Ibid., 243–48; Carl Waldman, *Atlas of the North American Indian*, 117–18.

19. Many excellent works on the removal of the Southeastern Indians have been written, including Michael D. Green, *The Politics of Indian Removal: Creek Government and Society in Crisis*, and Perdue and Green, *The Cherokee Removal*, while the classic work is Grant Foreman, *Indian Removal: The Emigration of the Five Civilized Tribes of Indians*.

20. Grant Foreman's *The Five Civilized Tribes: Cherokee, Chickasaw, Choctaw, Creek, Seminole* remains one of the standards on the removed Southeastern Indians' renaissance in Indian Territory.

21. Robert F. Berkhofer, Jr., *The White Man's Indian: Images of the American Indian from Columbus to the Present*, 88–97.

22. E. P. Thompson, *The Making of the English Working Class*, 9–10.

CHAPTER 2

1. W. David Baird, *The Quapaw Indians: A History of the Downstream People*, 3–8; Daniel Richter, *The Ordeal of the Longhouse: The Peoples of the Iroquois League in the Era of European Colonization*, 50–74.

2. Baird, *The Quapaw Indians*, 6–7, 10, 14–15.

3. Jean-Baptiste Bénard de La Harpe, *The Historical Journal of the Establishment of the French in Louisiana*, 179; Dan Flores, ed., *Journal of an Indian Trader: Anthony Glass and the Texas Trading Frontier, 1790–1810*, 8.

4. La Harpe, *Historical Journal*, 148.

5. Rollings, *The Osage*, 101–102.

6. Frank Raymond Secoy, *Changing Military Patterns of the Great Plains Indians*, 6–14, 20–32.

7. Richebourge Gaillaird McWilliams, trans. and ed., *Fleur de Lys and Calumet: Being the Pénicaut Narrative of French Adventure in Louisiana*, 112.

8. Several books deal with the effect of European manufactured goods on Indian societies. Two of the best are Daniel K. Richter's *The Ordeal of the Longhouse* and Richard White's *The Roots of Dependency: Subsistence, Environment, and Social Change among the Choctaws, Pawnees, and Navajos*.

9. Theda Perdue, *Slavery and the Evolution of Cherokee Society, 1540–1886*, 23–35; John Lawson, *A New Voyage to Carolina*, 208–209.

10. Elizabeth A. H. John, *Storms Brewed in Other Men's Worlds: The Confrontation of Indians, Spanish, and French in the Southwest, 1540–1795*, 223, 265–66, 306–307, 317–18.

11. La Harpe, *Historical Journal*, 137.

12. Ibid., 142–43.

13. Périer to Maurepas, April 1730, in *Mississippi Provincial Archives: French Dominion* 4:33–34.

14. Letter of Laforest Leaumon, May 27, 1754, in Germaine Portre-Bobinski, ed. and trans., *Natchitoches: Translation of Old French and Spanish Documents*, 88–91.

15. Rollings, *The Osage*, 130–35.

16. De Blanc to Miró, September 30, 1789, in Lawrence Kinnaird, ed., *Spain in the Mississippi Valley, 1765–1794: Post War Decade, 1782–1792* 2:281, hereafter cited as *SMV*; De Blanc to Miró, March 27, 1790, *SMV* 2:316; De Blanc to Carondelet, February 18, 1792, SMV 3:9–11. For more information on the Caddo-Osage warfare, see David La Vere, *The Caddo Chiefdoms*, 90–100.

17. Mary A. O'Callaghan, "An Indian Removal Policy in Spanish Louisiana," *Greater America: Essays in Honor of Eugene Herbert Bolton*, 281; Location of Indians around Natchitoches, Estevan Miró, December 12, 1785, *SMV* 2:160; De Blanc to Carondelet, April 16, 1792, *SMV* 3:25–27.

18. Baird, *The Quapaw Indians*, 30; Grant Foreman, ed., *Adventure on Red River: Report on the Exploration of the Headwaters of the Red River by Captain Randolph B. Marcy and Captain G. B. McClellan*, 153–54; J. Leitch Wright, *The Only Land They Knew: The Tragic Story of the American Indians in the Old South*, 137–45; Ralph A. Smith, ed. and trans., "Account of the Journey of Bénard de la Harpe: Discovery Made by Him of Several Nations Situated in the West," *Southwestern Historical Quarterly* 62 (October 1958): 251.

19. See White, *The Roots of Dependency*, particularly the section dealing with the Choctaws, 1–146.

20. Charles Hudson, *The Southeastern Indians*, 442; Fred B. Kniffen, Hiram F. Gregory, and George A. Stokes, *The Historic Indians Tribes of Louisiana: From 1542 to the Present*, 83–85; David K. Bjork, ed. and trans., "Documents Regarding Indian Affairs in the Lower Mississippi Valley, 1771–1772," *Mississippi Valley Historical Review* 13 (June 1926–March 1927): 398–410.

21. De Blanc to Carondelet, December 1, 1792, *SMV* 3:99–100.

22. De Blanc to Gayoso, May 20, 1794, Legajo 47, Papeles Procedentes de Cuba, Archivo General de Indias, Seville, Spain; De Blanc to Miró, March 27, 1790, *SMV* 2:316; De Blanc to Carondelet, April 16, 1792, *SMV* 3:25–27; De Blanc to Christobal Cordova, June 27, 1792, Reel 22, Béxar Archives, Microfilm, Microtext Department, Sterling Evans Library, Texas A&M University, College Station; Carondelet to De Blanc, October 18, 1792, *SMV* 3:92; Sotechaux to Bernardo Fernández, August 25, 1796, Reel 26, and Nava to Elquezabal, November 10, 1800, Reel 29, Bexar Archives; "Cadoquias, called by . . . ," Daniel Clark to James Madison, September 29, 1803, *Territorial Papers* 9:63.

23. Emmet Starr, ed. and pub., *Cherokees "West": 1794–1839*, 129; Everett, *The Texas Cherokees*, 9–10.

24. Thurman Wilkins, *Cherokee Tragedy: The Ridge Family and the Decimation of a People*, 25–27.

25. Everett, *The Texas Cherokees*, 9; Martin, *Sacred Revolt*, 150–68.

26. John Sibley, "A Report from Natchitoches in 1807," 16, 39, 51; Everett, *The Texas Cherokees*, 10.

27. Ibid., 11–13.

28. Starr, *Cherokees "West,"* 22; Everett, *The Texas Cherokees*, 10–11, 14; George E. Lankford, "The Cherokee Sojourn in North Arkansas," *Independence County [Arkansas] Chronicle* 18 (January 1977): 6; Daniel F. Littlefield, Jr., and Lonnie E. Underhill, "The Cherokee Agency Reserve, 1828–1886," *Arkansas Historical Quarterly* 31 (Summer 1972): 166–67.

29. Stephen H. Long to Thomas A. Smith, January 30, 1818, *Territorial Papers, Arkansas Territory* 19:4–5; U.S. Senate, 24th Cong., 1st sess., S. Doc. 247, March 15, 1836, CSS, vol. 281; Baird, *The Quapaw Indians*, 54–56; Christopher C. Dean, *Letters on the Chickasaw and Osage Missions*, 36.

30. Starr, *Cherokees "West,"* 41.

31. Rollings, *The Osage*, 237.

32. Ibid., 239–46.

33. Everett, *The Texas Cherokees*, 14–16.

34. *Arkansas Gazette* (Little Rock), December 30, 1820, p. 3, col. 1.

35. Grant Foreman, *Advancing the Frontier: 1830–1860*, 35; Rollings, *The Osages*, 247–51; Dean, *Letters on the Chickasaw and Osage Missions*, 49–51, 78–81.

36. Rollings, *The Osage*, 247–51; Statement of Samuel Perry, Shawnee, IPH, 8:182–86; Dean, *Letters on the Chickasaw and Osage Missions*, 85.

37. Rollings, *The Osage*, 260–61; Dean, *Letters on the Chickasaw and Osage Missions*, 46, 72, "entreated him," 104–105.

38. Rollings, *The Osage*, 252–53; Foreman, *Advancing the Frontier*, 35.

39. Charles J. Kappler, ed., *Indian Treaties*, 217–21.

40. Rollings, *The Osage*, 254–58; *Arkansas Gazette*, March 14, 1826, p. 1., cols. 1–3, and p. 2, col. 1; Dean, *Letters on the Chickasaw and Osage Missions*, 116–18, 120–23; William Clark to James Barbour, January 4, 1827, LR-OIA:CHA, Roll 77, no. 243; William Clark to E. W. Duval, January 20, 1827, LR-OIA:CHA, Roll 77, no. 255; Col. M. Arbuckle to E. Butler, March 26, 1827, LR-OIA:CHA, Roll 77, no. 290; Gen. Thomas James, *Three Years among the Indians and Mexicans*, 254.

41. W. David Baird, "Arkansas's Choctaw Boundary: A Study of Justice Denied," *Arkansas Historical Quarterly* 28 (Autumn 1969): 203–204; Memorial of John Jolly, October 27, 1824, LR-OIA:CHA, Roll 77, no. 63.

42. Spring Frog et al. to John C. Calhoun, February 27, 1825, LR-OIA:CHA, Roll 77, no. 74.

43. U.S. House, 20th Cong., 1st sess., H. Doc. 233, March 26, 1828, CSS, vol. 174.

44. U.S. Senate, 18th Cong., 2nd sess., S. Doc. 21, January 27, 1825, CSS, vol. 109; Barbour's quotes in U.S. House, 19th Cong., 1st sess., H. Doc. 102, February 3, 1826, CSS, vol. 135; Waldman, *Atlas of the North American Indian*, 181–82.

45. Littlefield and Underhill, "The Cherokee Agency Reserve," 167.

46. *Cherokee Phoenix*, October 29, 1828, p. 2, cols. 3–4.

47. Ibid.; U.S. Senate, 23rd Cong., 1st sess., S. Doc. 512, vol. 2, December 21, 1831, CSS, vol. 244.

48. *Cherokee Phoenix*, May 14, 1828, p. 3, col. 3.

49. *Cherokee Phoenix*, October 22, 1828, p. 4, col. 5.

50. See "How many honest," in the *Cherokee Phoenix*, September 17, 1828, p. 3, cols. 2–4; October 8, 1828, p. 2, col. 5–p. 3, col. 1; February 25, 1829, p. 1, col. 5–p. 2, col. 1; March 3, 1829, p. 2, col. 5–p. 3, cols. 1–2.

51. Diary of Peter Pitchlynn, September 26, 1828, Folder 2, Box 5, PPRC, Western History Collections, University of Oklahoma, Norman.

52. Pitchlynn diary, November 2, 1828, Folder 2, Box 5, PPPC.

53. Pitchlynn to his father, November 27, 1828, Folder 2, Box 6, PPPC.

54. Speech to the Osages by Pitchlynn, November 1828, Folder 2, Box 6, PPPC.

55. Pitchlynn to his father, November 27, 1828, Folder 2, Box 6, PPPC.

56. *Cherokee Advocate*, February 28, 1877, in Folder 13, Box 6, PPPC.

57. Pitchlynn to his father, November 28, 1828, Folder 2, Box 6, PPPC; Pitchlynn diary, December 2, 1928, Folder 2, Box 5, PPPC; *Cherokee Advocate*, March 7, 1877, in Folder 13, Box 6, PPPC; William McClellan to P. B. Porter, December 14, 1828, LR-OIA:CHA, Roll 184, no. 46; Baird, *Peter Pitchlynn*, 32.

58. Nehah Micco et al. to the Secretary of War, April 8, 1831, U.S. Senate, 23rd Cong., 1st sess., S. Doc. 512, vol. 2, CSS, vol. 244.

CHAPTER 3

1. Kappler, *Indian Treaties*, 1035–40; Lewis Cass to William Carroll, Montfort Stokes, and Robert Vaux, July 14, 1832, U.S. Senate, 23rd Cong., 1st sess., S. Doc. 512, CSS 244:870–75.

2. John W. Morris, Charles R. Goins, and Edwin C. McReynolds, eds., *Historical Atlas of Oklahoma*, maps 24 and 25; *Arkansas Intelligencer* (Van Buren), January 11, 1845, p. 2, col. 2; Report of Col. James Logan, August 20, 1844, *Arkansas Intelligencer*, March 15, 1845, p. 1, col. 4; quote from Ida Cunnetubby, IPH 21:352.

3. Lewis Cass to the President of the United States, February 16, 1832, U.S. Senate, 23rd Cong., 1st sess., S. Doc. 512, CSS, vol. 244.

4. Creek Chiefs to the President, October 21, 1831, LR-OIA:CRA, roll 236, no. 240.

5. Creek Chiefs to the President of the United States, October 29, 1831, LR-OIA:CRA, Roll 236, no. 233.

6. John Campbell to Lewis Cass, November 5, 1831, LR-OIA:CRA, Roll 236, no. 231.

7. Issac McCoy and John Donelson, Jr., to Lewis Cass, September 12, 1832, U.S. Senate, 23rd Cong., 1st sess., S. Doc. 512, CSS 245:449.

8. M. Stokes to Lewis Cass, October 27, 1833, ibid., CSS 246:623–24.

9. To-Shuh-Quash to Thomas Drew, July 19, 1854, LR-OIA:SS, Roll 833, no. 282; Memorial of A. H. Jones and H. M. C. Brown, May 18, 1860, U.S. House, 36th Cong., 1st sess., 1860, H. Rep. 532, CSS 1070:6–7. For more information on Indians warring for territory, see Richard White,

"The Winning of the West: The Expansion of the Western Sioux in the Eighteenth and Nineteenth Centuries," *Journal of American History* 65 (September 1978): 319–43.

10. Hudson, *Southeastern Indians*, 186.

11. Foster, *Being Comanche*, 63; Mayhall, *The Kiowas*, 129.

12. Hudson, *Southeastern Indians*, 196–201; Wallace and Hoebel, *The Comanches*, 132, 138–41; Mayhall, *The Kiowas*, 130.

13. Mayhall, *The Kiowas*, 130.

14. Elsie Clews Parsons, *Notes on the Caddo*, 28.

15. Francis Jennings, "American Frontiers," in *America in 1492: The World of the Indian Peoples before the Arrival of Columbus*, 353; Henri Joutel, "Joutel's Historical Journal of Monsieur de la Salle's Last Voyage to Discover the River Mississippi," *Historical Collections of Louisiana, Embracing Many Rare and Valuable Documents Relating to the Natural, Civil and Political History of that State*, 1:146–48, 171–72.

16. Parsons, *Notes on the Caddos*, 28; Wallace and Hoebel, *The Comanches*, 132, 138–41; Marcel Mauss, *The Gift: Forms and Functions of Exchange in Archaic Societies*, 193–99.

17. Diary of James Reagle, 27–29, JRC, R-45, 1240.

18. Marvin Harris, *Cultural Materialism: The Struggle for a Science of Culture*, 90–92; Patricia C. Albers, "Symbiosis, Merger, and War: Contrasting Forms of Intertribal Relationship among Historic Plains Indians," in *The Political Economy of North American Indians*, 106–10.

19. Issac McMcoy to Lewis Cass, March 6, 1832, U.S. Senate, 23rd Cong., 1st sess., S. Doc. 512, CSS 245:289.

20. Chiefs of the Choctaws to Lewis Cass, March 20, 1832, LR-OIA: CTA, Roll 184, no. 202; John Rogers, Roley McIntosh, et al. to the Secretary of War, May 14, 1834, LR-OIA:CRA, Roll 236, no. 456.

21. Baird, *Peter Pitchlynn*, 56; E-Yaar-Ho-Kar-Tubbe to John H. Eaton, January 16, 1831, U.S. Senate, 23rd Cong., 1st sess., S. Doc. 512, CSS 244:392–93.

22. Report made by R. M. Johnson, Committee of Military Affairs, December 28, 1832, U.S. House, 22nd Cong., 2nd sess., H. Rep. 17, vol. 1, CSS, vol. 236.

23. John Campbell to Lewis Cass, September 27, 1832, LR-OIA:CRA, Roll 236, no. 277.

24. Lewis Cass to William Carroll, Montfort Stokes, and Roberts Vaux, July 14, 1832, U.S. Senate, 23rd Cong., 1st sess., S. Doc. 512, CSS 244: 870–75.

25. Natuckiche to Capt. McLellan, May 26, 1833, LR-OIA:CTA, Roll 184, no. 322; Maurice Boyd, *Kiowa Voices: Myths, Legends and Folktales*, 2:49–50, 137–38.

26. Cherokee and Creek treaties with the Osages, June 28, 1831, U.S. Senate, 23rd Cong., 1st sess., S. Doc. 512, CSS 244:499–506; Richard W. Cummins to Gen. William Clark, March 1, 1832, ibid., CSS 245:306–307; Pawhuska and Clermont to Andrew Jackson, January 1832, ibid., CSS 245:354–56.

27. Journal of the Proceedings of a Council Held by the United States' Commissioners with the Osage Indians, 25 February 1833, ibid., CSS 246:207–30.

28. Stokes to Cass, October 27, 1833, ibid., CSS 246:625; Ellsworth to E. Herring, November 14, 1833, ibid., CSS 246:702–703; Moosh-O-La-Tub-Bee et al. to Capt. David McClellan, April 3, 1834, LR-OIA:CTA, Roll 184, no. 260; F. W. Armstrong to Herring, November 20, 1834, LR-OIA:CHA, Roll 79, no. 23.

29. May 20, 1834, U.S. House, 23rd Cong., 1st sess., H. Rep. 474, CSS 263:22, 34–38; Major Thomas Hunt to Cass, January 8, 1836, U.S. Senate, 24th Cong., 1st sess., S. Doc. 77, vol. 2, CSS, vol. 280; S. W. Kearney et al. to the Secretary of War, December 11, 1836, U.S. House, 25th Cong., 2nd sess., H. Doc. 278, CSS, vol. 328.

30. Stokes to Cass, October 27, 1833, U.S. Senate, 23rd Cong., 1st sess., S. Doc. 512, CSS 246:623–26.

31. Stokes to Cass, November 26, 1833, ibid., CSS 246:735–36.

32. A Journal of the Campaign of the Regiment of Dragoons for the Summer of 1834, T. B. Wheelock, August 27, 1834, U.S. Senate, 23rd Cong., 2nd sess., S. Doc. 1, CSS 226:73–93; George H. Shirk, "Peace on the Plains," *Chronicles of Oklahoma* 28 (Spring 1950): 2–8.

33. Journal of the Campaign, T. B. Wheelock, August 27, 1834, U.S. Senate, 23rd Cong., 2nd sess., S. Doc. 1, CSS 226:81.

34. Ibid., 83–86.

35. Ibid.

36. Ibid., 87–93; Grant Foreman, "The Journal of the Proceedings of Our First Treaty with the Wild Indians, 1835," *Chronicles of Oklahoma* 14 (December 1936): 394; Foreman, *Advancing the Frontier*, 131–37.

37. Stokes to Cass, May 14, 1835, Letter 2, Box C-32, Minor Archives, LCC.

38. Stokes to Cass, May 19, 1835, Letter 3, Box C-32, LCC; Foreman, "Journal of the Proceedings of Our First Treaty," 396.

39. Speech given by Musha-La-Tubbe, Box A-46, Minor Archives, Musha-La-Tubbe Collection, Western History Collections, University of Oklahoma, Norman.

40. Speech of Roley McIntosh, FF1, Box M-45, Minor Archives, Rolly McIntosh Collection, Western History Collections, University of Oklahoma, Norman.

41. Foreman, "Journal of the Proceedings of Our First Treaty," 413–16.

42. Stokes to Cass, September 15, 1835, Letter 5, Box C-32, LCC; Foreman, "Journal of the Proceedings of Our First Treaty," 409–11; Kappler, *Indian Treaties*, 435–39, 489–91.

43. Quote in Foreman, "Journal of the Proceedings of Our First Treaty," 411–12; C. C. Rister, "A Federal Experiment in Southern Plains Indian Relations, 1835–1845," *Chronicles of Oklahoma* 14 (December 1956): 450; P. L. Choteau [Chouteau] to Stokes, April 26, 1836, Letter 11, Box C-32, LCC.

44. Stokes to Cass, December 29, 1935, Letter 8, Box C-32, LCC.

45. Prucha, *The Great Father*, 243–48; James H. Howard, *Shawnee! The Ceremonialism of a Native Indian Tribe and Its Cultural Background*, 15–20; Everett, *The Texas Cherokees*, 36–40.

46. P. L. Choteau [Chouteau] to Stokes, April 19, 1836, Letter 10, Box C-32, LCC; Choteau [Chouteau] to Stokes, April 26, 1836, Letter 11, Box C-32, LCC.

47. Choteau [Chouteau] to Major William Armstrong, February 1, 1837, Letter 18, Box C-32, LCC.

48. John Dougherty to Gen. William Clark, November 9, 1831, U.S. Senate, 23rd Cong., 1st sess., S. Doc. 512, CSS 244:721–22.

49. William Armstrong to C. A. Harris, February 13, 1837, Letter 21, Box C-32, LCC.

50. Quotes from Armstrong to Harris, ibid.; Armstrong to Choteau [Chouteau], Letter 20, Box C-32, LCC; J. R. Poinsett to A. P. Choteau [Chouteau], April 7, 1837, Letter 22, Box C-32, LCC.

51. Kingsberry to Armstrong, May 8, 1839, LR-OIA:CKA, Roll 137, no. 493.

52. W. W. Newcomb, Jr., *The Indians of Texas*, 346–48; Everett, *The Texas Cherokees*, 99–100; F. Todd Smith, *The Caddo Indians: Tribes at the Convergence of Empires, 1542–1854*, 141–42.

53. A. M. M. Upshaw to Arbuckle, February 5, 1841, LR-OIA:WS, Roll 923, no. 287.

54. Kingsberry to Armstrong, May 8, 1839, LR-OIA:CKA, Roll 137, no. 493; Gen. M. Arbuckle to Brigadier General R. Jones, February 24, 1841, LR-OIA:WS, Roll 923, no. 274; U.S. Consul at Matamoros to the Department of State, January 1, 1840, Foreman Transcripts, Commissioner of

Indian Affairs, 1:285–86, Indian Archives Division, Oklahoma Historical Society, Oklahoma City; Nathaniel Amory to Daniel Webster, May 19, 1841, LR-OIA:WS, Roll 923, no. 429; Upshaw to Armstrong, September 13, 1841, LR-OIA:WS, Roll 923, no. 360.

55. Kingsberry to Armstrong, May 8, 1839, LR-OIA:CKA, Roll 137, no. 493.

56. Ibid.; Armstrong to Crawford, May 16, 1839, LR-OIA:CKA, Roll 137, no. 491.

57. A. P. Sheldon et al., to A. M. M. Upshaw, February 13, 1841, LR-OIA:WS, Roll 923, no. 278; Assistant Surgeon J. Sloan to Surgeon H. L. Heiskell, March 4, 1841, LR-OIA:WS, Roll 923, no. 424.

58. Armstrong to T. Hartley Crawford, March 30, 1841, LR-OIA:WS, Roll 923, no. 272.

59. Thomas Wall to P. P. Pitchlynn, April 1, 1841, Box 1, Folder 62, PPPC.

60. Arbuckle to Upshaw, February 24, 1841, LR-OIA:WS, Roll 923, no. 281.

61. Armstrong to Crawford, May 26, 1841, LR-OIA:WS, Roll 923, no. 294.

62. Ibid.

63. Report of Capt. B. D. Moore, June 20, 1841, LR-OIA:WS, Roll 923, no. 302.

64. Armstrong to Elbert Herring, April 29, 1836, Letter 13, Box C-32, LCC.

65. Choteau [Chouteau] to Armstrong, May 22, 1837, Letter 26, Box C-32, LCC; A. P. Choteau [Chouteau] to C. A. Harris, December 16, 1837, Letter 36, Box C-32, LCC; Armstrong to Harris, April 23, 1838, Roll 225, no. 471, LR-OIA:CRA; G. P. Kingsberry to Armstrong, May 8, 1839, LR-OIA:CKA, Roll 137, no. 493.

66. A. P. Choteau [Chouteau] to Harris, December 16, 1837, Letter 36, Box C-32, LCC.

67. Foster, *Being Comanche*, 57–63; Wallace and Hoebel, *The Comanches*, 210–16; Kavanagh, *Comanche Political History*, 36–56. Though it concentrates on the Lakota Sioux, one of the best explanations of band societies and the role of the chief is in Robert M. Utley, *The Lance and the Shield: The Life and Times of Sitting Bull*, 8–13.

CHAPTER 4

1. William Medill to Chester Ashley, July 21, 1846, U.S. Senate, 29th Cong., 1st sess., S. Doc. 461, CSS 478:1–6.

2. Armstrong to Crawford, September 10, 1842, LR-OIA:WS, Roll 923, no. 556.

3. Kingsberry to Lewis F. Linn, September 10, 1837, U.S. House, 25th Cong., 2nd sess., H. Doc. 276, CSS, vol. 328.

4. A. P. Choteau [Chouteau] to C. A. Harris, November 25, 1837, Letter 34, Box C32, LCC; William S. Coodey to John Ross, November 26, 1837, in *The Papers of Chief John Ross*, 1:551–52.

5. John Rogers to Arbuckle, May 3, 1839, Letter 40, Box C-32, LCC.

6. Armstrong to Crawford, June 8, 1839, Letter 43, Box C-32, LCC.

7. Ethan Allen Hitchcock, *A Traveler in Indian Territory: The Journal of Ethan Allen Hitchcock, Late Major-General in the United States Army*, 69–70; Angie Debo, *The Road to Disappearance: A History of the Creek Indians*, 134.

8. Hitchcock, *A Traveler in Indian Territory*, 104–105, 159, 168–69, 181, 256–57.

9. Upshaw to Crawford, July 2, 1842, LR-OIA:CKA, Roll 138, no. 1011.

10. Upshaw to Armstrong, August 15, 1842, U.S. Senate, 27th Cong., 3rd sess., S. Exec. Doc. 1, 1842–43, CSS 413:459–61.

11. Stanley Noyes, *Los Comanches: The Horse People*, 280–84, 288–89; Newcomb, *The Indians of Texas*, 350; Wallace and Hoebel, *The Comanches*, 294.

12. Maj. James R. Oneal to Chiefs and Principal Officer of Choctaw and Chickasaw Nations, ca. July 1, 1842, LR-OIA:CKA, Roll 138, no. 1007; Hitchcock, *A Traveler in Indian Territory*, 168–69, 184, 257–58.

13. Upshaw to Chief Isaac Albertson, July 5, 1842, LR-OIA:CKA, Roll 138, no. 1008.

14. Armstrong to Crawford, May 24, 1842, LR-OIA:WS, Roll 923, no. 528; James Logan to Crawford, May 30, 1842, LR-OIA:CRA, Roll 226, no. 570; Armstrong to Crawford, September 10, 1842, Report of the Commissioner of Indian Affairs for 1842, U.S. Senate, 27th Cong., 3rd sess., S. Exec. Doc. 1, CSS 413:453; Foreman, *Advancing the Frontier*, 201–204.

15. Armstrong to Crawford, May 24, 1842, LR-OIA:WS, Roll 923, no. 528; Foreman, *Advancing the Frontier*, 202–204.

16. Logan to Crawford, May 30, 1842, LR-OIA:CRA, Roll 226, no. 570; Armstrong to Crawford, August 14, 1842, LR-0IA:WS, Roll 923, no. 535; Foreman, *Advancing the Frontier*, 204.

17. Armstrong to Crawford, May 24, 1842, LR-OIA:WS, Roll 923, no. 528.

18. Foreman, *Advancing the Frontier*, 202; John Fowler to John Jamison, April 16, 1819, in Carter, *The Territorial Papers of the United States, Arkansas Territory* 19:70–71.

19. Quotes from Creek Chiefs to Caddo Chiefs, July 20, 1842, FF3, Box 2A, CRHC; Report of the Indian Commissioners, September 4, 1842, FF6, Box 2A, CRHC; Hitchcock, *A Traveler in Indian Territory*, 258.

20. Armstrong to Crawford, September 10, 1842, LR-OIA:WS, Roll 923, no. 556.

21. J. Dawson to Crawford, May 25, 1843, LR-OIA:CRA, Roll 227, no. 80; Quote from "Letter from Rolly McIntosh," *Arkansas Intelligencer*, July 6, 1844, p. 1, cols. 2–4.

22. Report of the General Superintendent of Indian Affairs for the Republic of Texas, December 4, 1843, FF5, Box A, CRHC.

23. J. Logan, Creek Agent, to the *Arkansas Intelligencer*, March 15, 1845, p. 2, col. 4; A-Poak-Oak-Yoh-Ola, Creek Chief, to the *Arkansas Intelligencer*, March 8, 1845, p. 2, col. 3.

24. Logan to the *Arkansas Intelligencer*, March 15, 1845, p. 2, col. 5.

25. *Arkansas Intelligencer*, February 22, 1845, p. 2, col. 2; March 1, 1845, p. 2, col. 2; P. M. Butler to Crawford, February 26, 1845, LR-OIA:CRA, Roll 227, no. 428.

26. Logan to Armstrong, September 20, 1845, U.S. Senate, 29th Cong., 1st sess., S. Doc. 1, CSS 470:517–18.

27. Ibid.

28. Logan to the *Arkansas Intelligencer*, March 15, 1845, p. 2, col. 4.

29. J. B. Suce to Armstrong, March 2, 1845, LR-OIA:CRA, Roll 227, no. 440.

30. Logan to Crawford, March 3, 1845, LR-OIA:CRA, Roll 227, no. 451.

31. P. M. Butler to Armstrong, May 18, 1845, LR-OIA:WS, Roll 923, no. 785; A. M. Gibson, "An Indian Territory United Nations: TheCreek Council of 1845," *Chronicles of Oklahoma* 39 (Winter 1961–62): 404–405.

32. *Arkansas Intelligencer*, May 31, 1845, p. 2, col. 3; Gibson, "An Indian Territory United Nations," 405, 412; Armstrong to Crawford, September 30, 1845, U.S. Senate, 29th Cong., 1st Sess., S. Doc. 1, CSS 470:507.

33. Notes Taken at the Grand Council, P. M. Butler, May 21, 1845, LR-OIA:WS, Roll 923, no. 791.

34. Gibson, "An Indian Territory United Nations," 404; *Arkansas Intelligencer*, May 24, 1845, p. 2., col. 3.

35. Notes Taken at the Grand Council, P. M. Butler, May 21, 1845, LR-OIA:WS, Roll 923, no. 791; Gibson, "An Indian Territory United Nations," 404–405.

36. Quotes from Notes Taken at the Grand Council, P. M. Butler, May 21, 1845, LR-OIA:WS, Roll 923, no. 791; Gibson, "An Indian Territory

United Nations," 408–409; Fixico to the Editors, *Arkansas Intelligencer*, June 19, 1845, p. 2, col. 3.

37. *Arkansas Intelligencer*, May 31, 1845, p. 2, col. 3.

38. Richard W. Cummins to Major T. H. Harvey, September 15, 1845, U.S. Senate, 29th Cong., 1st sess., S. Doc. 1, CSS 470:540; *Arkansas Intelligencer*, March 15, 1845, p. 1, col. 1.

39. *Arkansas Intelligencer*, August 30, 1845, p. 2, col. 1.

40. Thomas H. Harvey to Crawford, September 10, 1845, U.S. Senate, 29th Cong., 1st sess., S. Doc. 1, CSS 470:537; Armstrong to Crawford, September 30, 1845, ibid., CSS 470:507.

41. Thomas Harvey to Crawford, September 10, 1845, ibid., CSS 470:536–37.

42. Armstrong to Crawford, June 10, 1845, LR-OIA:WS, Roll 923, no. 803; Journal of Lieutenant J. W. Abert, August 8, 1845, U.S. Senate, 29th Cong., 1st sess., S. Doc. 438, CSS, vol. 477.

43. Harvey to Crawford, September 10, 1845, U.S. Senate, 29th Cong., 1st sess., S. Doc. 1, CSS 470:537; Logan to Armstrong, September 20, 1845, ibid., CSS 470:518.

44. Butler and Lewis to William Medill, August 8, 1846, U.S. House, 29th Cong., 2nd sess., H. Doc. 76, CSS 500:2–9.

45. Ibid.

46. Grant Foreman, ed., "The Journal of Elijah Hicks," *Chronicles of Oklahoma* 13 (March 1935): 75–76.

47. Foreman, "Journal of Elijah Hicks," 80–81.

48. Butler and Lewis to William Medill, August 8, 1846, 29th Cong., 2nd sess., H. Doc. 76, CSS 500:2–9; Foreman, "Journal of Elijah Hicks," 86–89.

49. Butler and Lewis to William Medill, August 8, 1846, 29th Cong., 2nd sess., H. Doc. 76, CSS 500:5.

50. Foreman, "Journal of Elijah Hicks," 82–99; *Cherokee Advocate*, October 29, 1846, p. 3, col. 2.

51. Ibid., quote on 82, 92–93.

52. Ibid., 91.

53. Kappler, *Indian Treaties*, 554–57.

54. Report Relative to the Comanches and Other Indians of Texas and the Southwestern Prairies, October 8, 1846, U.S. House, 29th Cong., 2nd sess., H. Doc. 100, CSS 500:2–5.

55. Foreman, ed., *Adventure on Red River*, 174.

56. Report Relative to the Comanches and Other Indians of Texas and the Southwestern Prairies, October 8, 1846, 29th Cong., 2nd sess., H. Doc. 100, CSS 500:2–5.

57. Ibid.

58. Stan Hoig, "Jesse Chisholm: Peace-maker, Trader, Forgotten Frontiersman," *Chronicles of Oklahoma* 66 (Winter 1988–89): 350–56.

59. Ibid., 356–61; Hitchcock, *A Traveler in Indian Territory*, 156, 182.

60. Hitchcock, *A Traveler in Indian Territory*, 182; M. Duval to Medill, October 15, 1846, U.S. Senate, 29th Cong., 2nd sess., S. Doc. 1, CSS 493:279; Hoig, "Jesse Chisholm," 362.

61. Armstrong to Crawford, September 30, 1845, U.S. Senate, 29th Cong., 1st sess., S. Doc. 1, CSS 470:508.

62. Duval to Medill, October 15, 1846, ibid., CSS 493:279–80.

63. R. S. Neighbors to Medill, January 6, 1847, U.S. House, 29th Cong., 2nd sess., H. Doc. 100, CSS 500:4.

64. Armstrong to Crawford, March 12, 1842, LR-OIA:WS, Roll 923, no. 501; Armstrong to Crawford, September 30, 1845, U.S. Senate, 29th Cong., 1st sess., S. Doc. 1, CSS 470:507–508; Upshaw to Col. S. M. Rutherford, September 21, 1847, U.S. Senate, 30th Cong., 1st sess., S. Doc. 1, CSS 503:885; Thomas Harvey to Medill, October 29, 1847, 30th Cong., 1st sess., S. Doc. 1, CSS 503:835.

65. Report of Captain R. B. Marcy, October 20, 1849, U.S. Senate, 31st Cong., 1st sess., S. Exec. Doc. 64, 1849–59, CSS 562:214–15.

66. Duvall to William L. Marcy, May 20, 1847, LR-OIA:SA, Roll 81, no frame number.

67. Hitchcock, *A Traveler in Indian Territory*, 256; Foreman, *Adventure on Red River*, 173.

68. R. S. Neighbors to Medill, January 6, 1847, U.S. House, 29th Cong., 2nd sess., H. Doc. 100, CSS 500:4; Upshaw to Rutherford, September 21, 1846, U.S. Senate, 30th Cong., 1st sess., S. Doc. 1, CSS 503:885; Rutherford to Medill, October 20, 1847, U.S. Senate, 30th Cong., 1st sess., S. Doc. 1, CSS 503:879.

69. Duval to Marcy, May 31, 1847, LR-OIA:SA, Roll 801, no number given; John M. Richardson to Samuel M. Rutherford, September 1, 1848, U.S. House, 30th Cong., 2nd sess., H. Exec. Doc. 1, CSS 537:541–42.

70. Perdue, *Slavery and the Evolution of Cherokee Society*, 3–18.

71. Ibid., 19–35, 50–72.

72. Kniffen, Gregory, and Stokes, *The Historic Indian Tribes of Louisiana*, 65; Lyle N. McAlister, *Spain and Portugal in the New World, 1492–1700*, 154–55; John, *Storms Brewed in Other Men's Worlds*, 70–71, 383–84.

73. John C. Ewers, "The Influence of Epidemics on the Indian Populations and Cultures of Texas," *Plains Anthropologist* 18 (May 1973): 104–15.

74. Wallace and Hoebel, *The Comanches*, 15, 241–42, 259; Mayhall, *The Kiowas*, 127, 138; Kavanagh, *Comanche Political History*, 102–103, 237–38; George Catlin, *North American Indians*, illustration 39 on p. 334.

75. Wallace and Hoebel, *The Comanches*, 39.

76. Foreman, "Journal of Elijah Hicks," 93.

77. Dan Flores, "Bison Ecology and Bison Diplomacy: The Southern Plains from 1800 to 1850," *Journal of American History* 78 (September 1991): 471; Wallace and Hoebel, *The Comanches*, 264; Interview with Nathan J. McElroy, IPH 35:110–15.

78. Flores, "Bison Ecology," 471, 479, 483; Alan M. Klein, "Political Economy of the Buffalo Hide Trade: Race and Class on the Plains" in *The Political Economy of North American Indians*, 142–43; Rachel Plummer, "Narrative of the Capture and Subsequent Sufferings of Mrs. Rachel Plummer," *The Rachel Plummer Narrative*, 97.

79. A. P. Choteau [Chouteau] to J. R. Poinsett, September 18, 1837, Letter 31, Box C-32, LCC; Foreman, "Journal of Elijah Hicks," 95; A Journal of the Campaign of the Regiment of Dragoons for the Summer of 1834, T. B. Wheelock, August 27, 1834, U.S. Senate, 23rd Cong., 2nd sess., S. Doc. 1, CSS 226:73–93.

80. Peter Pitchlynn's Journal, September 23, 1837, Folder 3, Box 6, PPPC; Plummer, *Rachel Plummer Narrative*, 92–118; Wallace and Hoebel, *The Comanches*, 261–63, 271; David Roberts, *Once They Moved Like the Wind: Cochise, Geronimo, and the Apache Wars*, 41–42.

81. See Thomas B. Marquis, *Keep the Last Bullet for Yourself: The True Story of Custer's Last Stand*.

82. Peter Pitchlynn's Journal, September 23, 1837, Folder 3, Box 6, PPPC.

83. Zachary Taylor to Adjutant General of the Army, September 13, 1842, U.S. House, 27th Cong., 1st sess., H. Doc. 99, CSS 420:4–5.

84. Interview with John Johnson, IPH 31:261–63; Interview with Nathan J. McElroy, IPH 35:110–15.

85. Duvall to Marcy, May 20, 1847, LR-OIA:SA, roll 801, no frame number.

86. Deposition of Charles Cohea, November 6, 1857, LR-OIA:CKA, Roll 142, no. 444.

87. Thomas H. Harvey to Crawford, September 10, 1845, 29th Cong., 1st sess., S. Doc. 1, CSS 470:537–38.

88. Interview with Nathan J. McElroy, white captive of the Comanches, IPH 35:110–15; Duvall to Marcy, May 20, 1847, LR-OIA:SA, Roll 801, no number provided.

89. *Arkansas Intelligencer*, July 12, 1845, p. 1, col. 5.

90. G. W. Long to Luke Lea, March 18, 1850, LR-OIA:CKA, Roll 140, no. 382.

91. Grant Foreman, ed., *A Pathfinder in the Southwest: The Itinerary of Lieutenant A. W. Whipple during His Explorations for a Railway Route from Fort Smith to Los Angeles in the Years 1853 & 1854*, 60, 64; Baldwin Mollhausen, *Diary of a Journey from the Mississippi to the Coasts of the Pacific with a United States Government Expedition* 1:95–97; Interview with Elizabeth Ross and E. Jan Ross, IPH 107:504–507.

92. Upshaw to Armstrong, September 13, 1841, LR-OIA:WS, Roll 923, no. 360; Upshaw to Crawford, September 4, 1843, U.S. Senate, 28th Cong., 1st sess., S. Exec. Doc. 2, CSS 431:419; Statement of Jesse Chisholm, September 14, 1845, LR-OIA:CRA, Roll 227, no. 408; Hoig, "Jesse Chisholm," 356–57.

93. J. C. Eldredge to Sam Houston, May 29, 1843, FF5, Box 2A, CRHC; Duval to Medill, July 13, 1846, LR-OIA:SA, Roll 801, no number given; Neighbors to Medill, March 2, 1848, U.S. Senate, 30th Cong., 1st sess., S. Doc. 171, CSS 512.

CHAPTER 5

1. Foreman, *A Pathfinder in the Southwest*, 58, 68; Mollhausen, *Journey from the Mississippi*, 1:73–74.

2. Neighbors to Medill, March 2, 1848, U.S. Senate, 30th Cong., 1st sess., S. Doc. 171, CSS 512; *Fort Smith Herald*, May 2, 1849, p. 2, cols. 2–3; Duvall to Medill, June 4, 1849, LR-OIA:SA, Roll 801, no frame number; Diary of Mrs. John B. Lilley, 28–29, 36–37, Mrs. John B. Lilley Collection, Box L-5, Minor Archives, Western History Collections, University of Oklahoma, Norman; Foreman, *Adventure on Red River*, xi, 166; Kenneth W. Porter, "Wild Cat's Death and Burial," *Chronicles of Oklahoma* 21 (March 1943): 41–43.

3. Remonstrance of Colonel Peter Pitchlynn, February 3, 1849, 30th Cong., 2nd sess., H. Misc. Doc. 35, CSS 544:1–4.

4. Memorial to the President, September 6, 1850, Constitution, Acts and Laws, Constitution of the Chickasaws, Third Session, November 4, 1848, Section 8, pp. 27–28, CKNR, Microfilm, Reel 4, Vol. 64; quote from Winchester Colbert et al. to Col. L. Lea, April 29, 1851, LR-OIA:CKA, Roll 140, no. 233; Puckshanubbe to *Fort Smith Herald*, January 24, 1851, p. 2, col. 5; Foreman, *The Five Civilized Tribes*, 135–37; Foreman, *Adventure on Red River*, 112, 119–20.

5. Foreman, *Adventure on Red River*, 119–20.

6. Mollhausen, *Journey from the Mississippi*, 1:218.

7. Kenton Harper to L. Lea, September 22, 1851, LR-OIA:CKA, Roll 140, no. 278.

8. To-Shuh-Quash to Thomas Drew, July 19, 1854, LR-OIA:SS, Roll 833, no. 282.

9. Puckshanubbe to *Fort Smith Herald*, January 24, 1851, p. 2, col. 5; William T. Hagan, *United States–Comanche Relations: The Reservation Years*, 10–12.

10. Hagan, *United States–Comanche Relations*, 12.

11. Foster, *Being Comanche*, 48–49.

12. Flores, "Bison Ecology," 481–83; Mollhausen, *Journey from the Mississippi*, 1:133–34.

13. Report of Captain R. B. Marcy, October 24, 1849, U.S. Senate, 31st Cong., 1st sess., S. Exec. Doc. 64, CSS 562:217–18; Foreman, *Adventure of Red River*, 112.

14. Duval to Medill, June 4, 1849, LR-OIA:SA, Roll 1801, no frame number; quote from D. Atchison, Chairman, Committee on Indian Affairs, March 18, 1850, U.S. Senate, 31st Cong., 1st sess., S. Misc. Doc. 70, CSS 563:1.

15. Duvall to Medill, June 4, 1849, LR-OIA:SA, Roll 801, no number given; Foreman, *Adventure on Red River*, 166; William T. Hagan, *The Sac and Fox Indians*, 226–29, quote on 229.

16. Report of Captain R. B. Marcy, April 30, 1849, U.S. Senate, 31st Cong., 1st sess., S. Exec. Doc. 64, CSS 562:173; Percival G. Lowe, *Five Years a Dragoon, ('49 to '54): And Other Adventures on the Great Plains*, 28–29.

17. Report of Captain R. B. Marcy, April 30, 1849, U.S. Senate, 31st Cong., 1st sess., S. Exec. Doc. 64, CSS 562:173, 219; Foreman, *Adventure on Red River*, 163–64; Carolyn Thomas Foreman, "Black Beaver," *Chronicles of Oklahoma* 24 (Autumn 1946): 270–74.

18. Deposition of Charley Kohee, January 19, 1853, LR-OIA:CKA, Roll 142, no. 77; Deposition of R. J. Humprheys, January 19, 1853, LR-OIA:CKA, Roll 142, no. 103; Statement of Jesse Chisholm, June 20, 1856, LR-OIA:CKA, Roll 142, no. 72; Report of Andrew Done, September 20, 1856, LR-OIA:CKA, Roll 142, no. 99.

19. Constitution of the Chickasaws, Fifth Session, October 14, 1852, CNR, p. 23; Constitution of the Chickasaws, Called Session, December 15, 1853, CKNR, 156; Foreman, *A Pathfinder in the Southwest*, 58, 81; Kappler, *Indian Treaties*, 600–602; Hagan, *United States–Comanche Relations*, 15–16.

20. Charles E. Mix to J. Thompson, August 11, 1853, LR-OIA:SS, Roll 834, no. 347.

21. Foreman, *A Pathfinder in the Southwest*, 59.

22. Thomas S. Drew to B. H. Smithson, January 15, 1853, Records of the Southern Superintendency, 1832–70, and Western Superintendency, 1832–51, Letters Sent, National Archives, RG 75, Microfilm 640, Roll 17, no. 30.

23. A. H. Rutherford to Manypenny, January 9, 1854, LR-OIA:SS, Roll 833, no. 205; Drew to Manypenny, LR-OIA:SS, Roll 833, no. 216.

24. Kappler, *Indian Treaties*, 614–18, 634–36; Drew to Manypenny, June 3, 1854, LR-OIA:SS, Roll 833, no. 270; Mollhausen, *Journey from the Mississippi*, 1:90–92; Foreman, *Adventure on Red River*, 131.

25. F. Todd Smith, *The Caddos, the Wichitas, and the United States, 1846–1901*, 39–45.

26. A. J. Smith to Manypenny, May 5, 1854, LR-OIA:CKA, Roll 141, no. 240.

27. Drew to Manypenny, March 24, 1855, LR-OIA:SS, Roll 833, no. 435.

28. Drew to Manypenny, October 20, 1854, LR-OIA:SS, Roll 833, no. 294.

29. Memorial of the Wichita Indians to the President of the United States, September 1, 1855, LR-OIA:SS, Roll 833, no. 382.

30. Maj. Geo. Andrews to Manypenny, September 6, 1855, LR-OIA:SS, Roll 833, no. 379.

31. Foreman, *The Five Civilized Tribes*, 130–31; Smith, *The Caddos, the Wichitas, and the United States*, 43.

32. A. H. McKisick to Elias Rector, October 21, 1857, LR-OIA:WA, Roll 928, no. 20.

33. McKisick to Rector, October 21, 1857, LR-OIA:WA, Roll 928, no. 20; Foreman, *The Five Civilized Tribes*, 143; Onis Gaines Jones, "Chickasaw Governors and Their Administrations, 1856–1895," 52–54.

34. Neighbors to Major General D. E. Twiggs, July 17, 1857, U.S. Senate, 35th Cong., 1st sess., S. Exec. Doc. 11, CSS 919:553–58; McKisick to Rector, October 21, 1857, LR-OIA:WA, Roll 928, no. 20; Smith, *The Caddos, the Wichitas, and the United States*, 43.

35. Sam Houston to J. Thompson, March 15, 1857, LR-OIA:SS, Roll 834, no. 80; S. P. Ross to Robert S. Neighbors, September 11, 1857, U.S. Senate, 35th Cong., 1st sess., S. Doc. 11, CSS 919:557–58.

36. Neighbors to Twiggs, July 17, 1857, U.S. Senate, 35th Cong., 1st sess., S. Exec. Doc. 11, CSS 919:553–55.

37. Capt. W. G. Evans to Capt. Jno. Withers, January 14, 1858, LR-OIA:WA, Roll 928, no. 817; Neighbors to Charles E. Mix, January 17, 1858, U.S. House, 35th Cong., 2nd sess., H. Exec. Doc. 27, CSS 1004:9–12.

38. Captain A. Montgomery to Colonel Samuel Cooper, March 13, 1858, U.S. House, 35th Cong., 2nd sess., H. Exec. Doc. 2, vol. 2, CSS 998:415–16.

39. Douglas Cooper to Mix, April 5, 1858, LR-OIA:SS, Roll 834, no. 281.

40. Ibid., nos. 278, 281, 284.

41. McKisick to Col. R. P. Pulliam, April 15, 1858, LR-OIA:WA, Roll 923, no. 59.

42. Cooper to Rector, May 26, 1858, LR-OIA:SS, Roll 834, no. 422.

43. Neighbors to Capt. N. N. B. Marlin, August 9, 1858, U.S. House, 35th Cong., 2nd sess., H. Exec. Doc. 2, CSS 998:424.

44. Jno. R. Baylor to Neighbors, March 21, 1857, LR-OIA:WA, Roll 928, no. 822.

45. John S. Ford to H. R. Runnels, May 22, 1858, U.S. House, 35th Cong., 2nd sess., H. Exec. Doc. 27, CSS 1004:17–21.

46. Lieutenant J. E. Powell to Second Lieutenant Offley, August 27, 1858, U.S. House, 35th Cong., 2nd sess., H. Exec. Doc. 2, CSS 998:422.

47. Cooper to Rector, June 7, 1858, LR-OIA:SS, Roll 834, no. 428.

48. For oral histories about Comanche raids on the Chickasaws and Choctaws, see the Indian-Pioneer Histories. Interview with I. M. Lawson, IPH 109:107–108; Interview with Mrs. E. F. Robinson, IPH 82:72–80; Interview with Fred Watkins, IPH 6:278.

49. A. H. Jones and H. M. C. Brown to Mix, June 25, 1858, LR-OIA:SS, Roll 834, no. 333; A. C. Love to *Dallas Herald*, July 20, 1858, U.S. House, 35th Cong., 2nd sess., H. Exec. Doc. 27, CSS 1004:32-33; Jones and Brown to Mix, September 14, 1853, LR-OIA:SS, Roll 834, no. 360; Memorial of H. H. Jones and H. M. C. Brown, May 18, 1860, U.S. House, 36th Cong., 1st sess., H. Rep. 532, CSS 1070:6–7.

50. Cooper to Rector, July 21, 1858, LR-OIA:SS, Roll 834, no. 435; Cooper to Rector, October 14, 1858, U.S. Senate, 35th Cong., 2nd sess., S. Exec. Doc. 1, CSS 974:509; Jones, "Chickasaw Governors," 54; Grant Foreman, ed., "A Journal Kept by Douglas Cooper of an Expedition by a Company of Chickasaws in Quest of Comanche Indians," *Chronicles of Oklahoma* 5 (December 1927): 381–90.

51. Lt. J. E. Powell to the Assistant Adjutant General, July 27, 1858, U.S. House, 35th Cong., 2nd sess., H. Exec. Doc. 2, CSS 998:417; Daniel G. Major to Powell, July 27, 1858, LR-OIA:SS, Roll 834, no. 386; Certification of Captain W. E. Prince, August 5, 1858, LR-OIA:WA, Roll 928, no. 100; Captain W. E. Prince to Lieutenant George D. Ruggles, August 9, 1858, U.S. House, 35th Cong., 2nd sess., H. Exec. Doc. 2, CSS 998:419.

52. Lt. J. E. Powell to the Assistant Adjutant General, July 27, 1858, U.S. House, 35th Cong., 2nd sess., H. Exec. Doc. 2, CSS 998:418.

53. Ibid.

54. Cooper to Rector, August 1, 1858, LR-OIA:SS, Roll 834, no. 453; Cooper to Rector, August 5, 1858, LR-OIA:SS, Roll 834, no. 459; Samuel M. Rutherford to Rector, August 18, 1858, U.S. Senate, 35th Cong., 2nd sess., S. Exec. Doc. 1, CSS 974:505; Majors to Mix, August 14, 1858, LR-OIA:SS, Roll 834, no. 389; Cooper to Mix, August 19, 1858, LR-OIA:SS, Roll 834, no. 291.

55. Cooper to Mix, August 19, 1858, LR-OIA:SS, Roll 834, no. 291.

56. Prince to Major D. C. Buell, August 26, 1858, and Powell to Second Lieutenant Offley, August 26, 1858, U.S. House, 35th Cong., 2nd sess., H. Exec. Doc. 2, CSS 998:420–23.

57. Ford to Runnels, July 5, 1858, U.S. House, 35th Cong., 2nd sess., H. Exec. Doc. 27, CSS 1004:29–31; Prince to Buell, August 27, 1858, U.S. House, 35th Cong., 2nd sess., H. Exec. Doc. 2, CSS 998:423–24; Twiggs to Lt. Col. L. Thomas, September 17, 1858, U.S. House, 35th Cong., 2nd sess., H. Exec. Doc. 27, CSS 1004:36; Prince to Capt. Charles J. Whiting, October 2, 1858, U.S. House, 35th Cong., 2nd sess., H. Exec. Doc. 27, CSS 1004:51; Runnels to Col. James Bourland, October 8, 1858, U.S. House, 35th Cong., 2nd sess., H. Exec. Doc. 27, CSS 1004:41–42.

58. Report of Brevet Major Earl Van Dorn, October 5, 1858, U.S. House, 35th Cong., 2nd sess., H. Exec. Doc. 27, CSS 1004:53; William Y. Chalfant, *Without Quarter: The Wichita Expedition and the Fight on Crooked Creek*, 38, 40; Smith, *The Caddos, the Wichitas, and the United States*, 58–59.

59. Cooper to Rector, October 14, 1858, U.S. House, 35th Cong., 2nd sess., H. Exec. Doc. 2, CSS 997:509; quote from Rector to Mix, October 23, 1858, U.S. Senate, 36th Cong., 1st sess., S. Exec. Doc. 2, CSS 1023:585–86; Rector to Mix, October 26, 1858, U.S. House, 35th Cong., 2nd sess., H. Exec. Doc. 2, CSS 997:484; Report of Mr. E. F. Beale, October 28, 1858, U.S. House, 36th Cong., 1st sess., H. Exec. Doc. 42, CSS 1048:8.

60. I. G. Vore to Col. R. L. Armistead, January 19, 1859, LR-OIA:SS, Roll 834, no. 530.

61. Ibid.; Edward Hale to Jacob Thompson, March 5, 1859, LR-OIA:SS, Roll 834, no. 536.

62. S. P. Ross to Neighbors, September 6, 1858, U.S. House, 35th Cong., 2nd sess., H. Exec. Doc. 2, CSS 997:534; Z. E. Combes to Ross, September 7, 1858, U.S. House, 35th Cong., 2nd sess., H. Exec. Doc. 2, CSS 997:535; Ross to Neighbors, January 26, 1859, U.S. Senate, 36th Cong., 1st sess., S. Exec. Doc. 2, CSS 1023:596–98; General Statement of the Houses Formerly

Occupied by Each of the Several Tribes at Brazos Agency, July 30, 1859, LR-OIA:WA, Roll 928, no. 218; Invoice of Indian Property Belonging to the Caddo Tribe, Anahdahko [*sic*] Tribe, September 1, 1859, LR-OIA:WA, Roll 928, no. 228; Chalfant, *Without Quarter*, 51.

63. John A. Goodlet et al. to Jacob Thompson, October 29, 1858, LR-OIA:WA, Roll 928, no. 1083; Ford to Col. J. A. Wilcox, April 12, 1859, LR-OIA:WA, Roll 928, no. 801; E. J. Gurley to Neighbors, May 5, 1859, LR-OIA:WA, Roll 928, no. 796; S. H. McHenry to John H. Reagan, November 28, 1859, LR-OIA:WA, Roll 928, no. 1440.

64. J. J. Sturm to Ross, December 28, 1858, U.S. Senate, 35th Cong., 1st sess., S. Exec. Doc. 2, CSS 1023:588–89; Sturm to Ross, January 15, 1859, U.S. Senate, 35th Cong., 1st sess., S. Exec. Doc. 2, CSS 1023:598–99.

65. Ross to Neighbors, May 9, 1859, LR-OIA:WA, Roll 928, no. 790.

66. Captain J. B. Plummer to Assistant Adjutant General, May 23, 1859, LR-OIA:WA, Roll 928, no. 784; Ross to Neighbors, May 24, 1859, LR-OIA:WA, Roll 928, no. 787; Ross to Neighbors, May 30, 1859, Roll 928, no. 874.

67. Blain to Rector, May 14, 1859, LR-OIA:WA, Roll 928, no. 309; Rector to A. B. Greenwood, June 15, 1859, LR-OIA:SS, Roll 834, no. 629.

68. Governor H. B. Runnels to Allison Nelson et al., June 6, 1859, LR-OIA:WA, Roll 928, no. 888; S. A. Blain to Neighbors, August 12, 1859, LR-OIA:WA, Roll 928, no. 1031; Neighbors to Greenwood, August 18, 1859, LR-OIA:WA, Roll 928, no. 187; Letterbook on Indian Removal from Texas, September 1, 1959, LR-OIA:WA, Roll 928, no. 243; Statement of Persons Who Died Enroute, Robert S. Neighbors, September 1, 1859, LR-OIA:WA, Roll 928, no. 1132; Explanation of Estimates for the Indian Service, Elias Rector, September 20, 1859, U.S. House, 36th Cong., 1st sess., H. Misc. Doc. 24, CSS, vol. 1067; Rector to Greenwood, September 20, 1859, U.S. Senate, 36th Cong., 1st sess., S. Exec. Doc. 2, CSS 1023:533; Deposition of Kiowa, Wichita Indian, September 15, 1937, IPH 109:22–23; Jones, "Chickasaw Governors," 55–56; Raymond Estep, "Lieutenant Wm. E. Burnett: Notes on Removal of Indians from Texas to Indian Territory," *Chronicles of Oklahoma* 38 (Autumn 1960): 274–79; Smith, *The Caddos, the Wichitas, and the United States*, 77–79.

CHAPTER 6

1. Blain to Greenwood, January 25, 1860, LR-OIA:WA, Roll 928, no. 363.

2. M. Leeper to Greenwood, May 2, 1860, ibid., no. 1378.

3. Rector to Greenwood, May 3,1860; John Shirley to the Colonel, December 28, 1860, LR-OIA:WA, Roll 928, nos. 1452, 1582; W. S. Nye, *Carbine and Lance: The Story of Old Fort Sill*, 28.

4. Coweta Micco et al. to the Council of the Muskogee Nation, November 2, 1876, and Letter from Henry Clay, no date, Roll 37, nos. 30782, 30798, CRNR.

5. Prucha, *The Great Father*, 415–18; Charles B. Keith to Col. H. B. Branch, August 24, 1861, LR-OIA:SS, Roll 834, no. 898.

6. Prucha, *The Great Father*, 418–29.

7. W. B. Morrison, "Fort Arbuckle," *Chronicles of Oklahoma* 6 (March 1928): 32; Jeanne V. Harrison, "Matthew Leeper, Confederate Agent at the Wichita Agency, Indian Territory," *Chronicles of Oklahoma* 47 (Autumn 1969): 249.

8. Report of E. H. Carruth, 11 July 1861, LR-OIA:SS, Roll 834, no. 950; W. E. Woodruff, *With the Light Guns in '61-'65: Reminiscences of Eleven Arkansas, Missouri, and Texas Light Batteries in the Civil War*, 69–70; Annie Heloise Abel, *The Indian as Participant in the Civil War*, 64n141(b), 112–13; Colonel Charles DeMorse, "Indians for the Confederacy," *Chronicles of Oklahoma* 50 (Winter 1972–73): 474–78.

9. Interview with Sarah Ann Harlan, IPH 28:54–56.

10. Interview with Kiowa, IPH 109:26; Interview with Zach Gardner, IPH 8:335–36; Robert L. Ream, "A Nearly Forgotten Fragment of Local History," *Chronicles of Oklahoma* 4 (March 1926): 35.

11. Keith to Branch, August 14, 1861, LR-OIA:SS, Roll 834, no. 898; Interview with Mary Inkanish, August 29, 1929, FF23, Box 2A, CRHC; Interviews of Old Indians of the Wichita and Affiliated Bands, September 24, 1927, FF24, Box 4, CRCH; C. Ross Hume to Grant Foreman, January 15, 1944, FF28, Box 4, CRHC; Interview with Jack Thomas, IPH 46:333; Foreman, "Black Beaver," 279–80.

12. Report of W. G. Coffin, April 1, 1862, LR-OIA:SS, Roll 834, no. 1560; Caleb Smith to Mix, September 20, 1862, LR-OIA:SS, Roll 834, no. 1505; Census of Southern Refugee Indians Belonging to the Southern Superintendency, December 13, 1862, LR-OIA:SS, Roll 834, no. 1414.

13. Coffin to W. P. Dole, June 15, 1862, LR-OIA:SS, Roll 834, no. 1234.

14. Speech to the President of the United States by Whitebread, Chief of the Caddos, February 3, 1888, FF7, Box 2A, CRHC; Diary of James Reagle, JRC; J. W. Throckmorton to the Commissioner of Indian Affairs, September 20, 1866, LR-OIA:SS, Roll 837, no. 922; Interview with Lizzie Little Bear, IPH 3:374; Interview with John Clark, IPH 65:132–34; Interview with Bertha Plummer Brewer, IPH 93:353–62; C. Ross Hume, "Historic

Sites around Anadarko," *Chronicles of Oklahoma* 16 (December 1938): 415; Harrison, "Matthew Leeper," 242; Newcomb, *The Indians of Texas*, 359.

15. Coffin to Dole, February 7, 1863, LR-OIA:SS, Roll 835, no. 107.

16. Coffin to Dole, February 24, 1863, LR-OIA:SS, Roll 835, no. 112; Milo Gookin to Coffin, November 14, 1864, LR-OIA:SS, Roll 835, no. 868.

17. Carruth to Coffin, June 14, 1863, LR-OIA:SS, Roll 835, no. 248; H. W. Martin to Coffin, June 18, 1863, LR-OIA:SS, Roll 835, no. 252; Coffin to Dole, June 25, 1863, LR-OIA:SS, Roll 835, no. 246; Prucha, *The Great Father*, 426; Tuckabatche Micco to Stand Watie, February 21, 1865, *Cherokee Cavaliers: Forty Years of Cherokee History as told in the Correspondence of the Ridge-Watie-Boudinot Family*, 213–15.

18. Documents 39, 40, 41, 43, 44, Confederate States of America— Indian Affairs Collection, M-2135, Box C-6B, Location: 1036 (Minor Collections), Western History Collections, University of Oklahoma, Norman.

19. John Cox to Coffin, March 16, 1864, LR-OIA:SS, Roll 835, no. 714; W. A. Phillips to Major General S. R. Curtis, March 17, 1864, LR-OIA:SS, Roll 835, no. 975.

20. Interview with John Johnson, IPH 5:469–71, 31:262–63; Interview with Mrs. Raymond Gordon, IPH 4:101–11; Interview with Andy Addington, IPH 1:59–62; Interview with Ella Coody Robinson, IPH 107:451–84; Robert Utley, *The Indian Frontier of the American West, 1846-1890*, 95; Wallace and Hoebel, *The Comanches*, 303–306.

21. Letter from the Secretary of the Interior, April 12, 1864, U.S. House, 38th Cong., 1st sess., H. Exec. Doc. 73, 1863–64, CSS, vol. 1193; Gookins to Coffin, November 25, 1864, LR-OIA:SS, Roll 835, no. 866.

22. Lewis Downing to Abraham Lincoln, December 20, 1864, LR-OIA:SS, Roll 836, no. 84.

23. L. P. Chouteau to James M. Bell, January 21, 1865, *Cherokee Cavaliers*, 209–10.

24. Tuckabatche Micco to Stand Watie, February 21, 1865, ibid., 213–15.

25. Anna Lewis, "Camp Napoleon," *Chronicles of Oklahoma* 9 (December 1931): 359–64.

26. Ream, "A Nearly Forgotten Fragment of Local History," 36–44.

27. Coffin to Dole, February 14, 1865, LR-OIA:SS, Roll 836, no. 101; John Field to Elijah Sells, December 8, 1865, LR-OIA:SS, Roll 837, no. 578; Field to Sells, December 15, 1865, LR-OIA:SS, Roll 837, no. 590; Lt. Col. George H. Keogh to Lt. J. A. Cramer, January 24, 1866, LR-OIA:SS, Roll 837, no. 76.

28. Field to Sells, December 8, 1865, LR-OIA:SS, Roll 387, no. 578; Field to Sells, April 26, 1866, LR-OIA:WA, Roll 928, no. 1929; Census of the

Wichita Agency and Partial List of Their Property Taken in June 1866, LR-
OIA:WA, Roll 928, no. 1857.

29. James Harlan to D. N. Coody, August 24, 1865, LR-OIA:SS, Roll
836, no. 385; Field to Sells, May 17, 1866, LR-OIA:SS, Roll 837, no. 822; V.
K. Hart to O. D. Green, December 19, 1866, LR-OIA:SS, Roll 837, no. 1231;
Kappler, *Indian Treaties*, 1050–52.

30. Kappler, Indian Treaties, 887–95; Hagan, *United States–Comanche
Relations*, 21–23.

31. Quotes from Treaty with Choctaw and Chickasaw, 1866, in
Kappler, *Indian Treaties*, 918–31; Kappler, *Indian Treaties*, 931–37, 942–50;
Charles J. Kappler, *Indian Affairs: Laws and Treaties*, 2:910–18.

32. J. W. Throckmorton to the Commissioner of Indian Affairs,
September 20, 1866, LR-OIA:SS, Roll 837, no. 922; Col. Eli Parker to Gen.
U. S. Grant, October 15, 1866, LR-OIA:SS, Roll 837, no. 1031; Throck-
morton to the Commissioner of Indian Affairs, November 5, 1866, LR-
OIA:SS, Roll 837, no. 931; David Burnet et al. to the Commissioner of
Indian Affairs, December 10, 1866, LR-OIA:SS, Roll 837, no. 1081; Inter-
view with Bianca Babb Bell, August 20, 1946, Folder FF15, Box 28, CRHC;
Interview with T. D. Moore, IPH 71:415–19; Interview with Barney
Leader, IPH 33:132.

33. Interview with Joe Colbert, IPH 20:177.

34. Interview with Overton Love, IPH 6:319.

35. Interview with Dinah Lewis Frazier, IPH 3:582–85.

36. Interview with Mrs. Ida Cunnetubby, IPH 21:348–52.

37. Interview with Amanda Kimball, IPH 53:232–38; Diary of James
Reagle, 17, JRC.

38. Typed copy of *The Daily Oklahoman* article, August 26, 1928, in
Thomas Parker Collection, F1, P-10 (1208), Western History Collections,
University of Oklahoma, Norman.

39. Interview with Overton Love, IPH 6:319; Interview of John Criner,
IPH 2:323–25.

40. Report by a citizen of Denton, Texas, October 22, 1866, LR-OIA:SS,
Roll 837, no. 935; Letter from the Secretary of War, January 13, 1867, U.S.
House, 39th Cong,, 2nd sess., H. Misc. Doc. 41, CSS, vol. 1302; Report of
Brevet Major General A. J. Smith, January 26, 1867, U.S. Senate, 40th Cong.,
2nd sess., S. Exec. Doc. 13, CSS, vol. 1380.

41. Extract of a letter from Governor Throckmorton, December 23,
1866, LR-OIA:SS, Roll 837, no. 1170.

42. E. O. D. Ord to O. H. Browning, January 8, 1867, LR-OIA:SS, Roll
837, no. 1236.

43. Diary of James Reagle, p. 14, JRC; Capt. E. L. Smith to Col. O. D. Greene, February 16, 1867, LR-OIA:SS, Roll 837, no. 1183.

44. Diary of James Reagle, pp. 12–14, JRC; James Reagle to Mother, November 19, 1866, JRC.

45. Report of J. H. Leavenworth, May 22, 1867, U.S. Senate, 40th Cong., 1st sess., S. Exec. Doc. 13, CSS, vol. 1380.

46. Interview with Loney Hardridge, IPH 4:317–18.

47. Caddo-Creek Articles of Agreement, July 11, 1867, Roll 37, no. 30783, CRNR.

48. Kappler, *Indian Treaties*, 977–89; Alfred A. Taylor, "The Medicine Lodge Peace Council," *Chronicles of Oklahoma* 2 (June 1924): 89–118; Hagan, *United States–Comanche Relations*, 27–43.

49. Smith, *The Wichitas, the Caddos, and the United States*, 93–98; Partial letter, author unknown, June 6, 1868, FF13, Box 4, CRHC.

50. Letter of the Secretary of War, May 23, 1868, U.S. Senate, 40th Cong., 2nd sess., S. Exec. Doc. 60, CSS, vol. 1317; Interview with Mary Alice Gibson Arendell, IPH 1:155–63; Hoig, "Jesse Chisholm," 370; Hagan, *United States–Comanche Relations*, 44–49; Nye, *Carbine and Lance*, 115; William E. Unrau, "Investigations or Probity? Investigations into the Affairs of the Kiowa-Comanche Indian Agency, 1867," *Chronicles of Oklahoma* 42 (Autumn 1964): 301, 316.

51. John Ross et al., to James Steele, June 8, 1864, *Papers of Chief John Ross*, 2:585–88; Memorial of Lewis Downing, March 22, 1869, U.S. Senate, 41st Cong., 1st sess., S. Misc. Doc. 16, CSS 1399:1–3; An Act in Reference to Negotiating with the Osages and Kansas Tribes of Indians, December 1, 1870, Microfilm, Roll 81, no. 62, Foreign Relations, CHNR; *Cherokee Advocate*, April 1, 1871, p. 2, cols. 4–5; C. A. Weslager, *The Delaware Indians: A History*, 423–27; Clarence W. Turner, "Events among the Muskogees," *Chronicles of Oklahoma* 10 (March 1932): 25.

52. Quote from Proceedings of the General Council of the Indian Territory Assembled December 6, 1870, at Okmulgee, Muskogee Nation, IC, Section X, Federal Relations; "Journal of the Adjourned Session of First General Council of Indian Territory," *Chronicles of Oklahoma* 3 (April 1924): 120–40.

53. *Cherokee Advocate*, January 14, 1871, p. 2, cols. 2–3.

54. Enoch Hoag to Jonathan Richards, February 20, 1871, Roll 48, no. 45, Council and Courts, KA, Microfilm.

55. *Cherokee Advocate*, March 18, 1871, p. 2, cols. 2–3.

56. Ibid., October 14, 1871, p. 3, col. 1; Nye, *Carbine and Lance*, 143–46; Hagan, *United States–Comanche Relations*, 75–77; Utley, *The Indian Frontier*, 141–48.

57. *Cherokee Advocate*, September 30, 1871, typed copy found in FF2, Box M-45, Minor Archives, Rolly McIntosh Collection, Western History Collections, University of Oklahoma, Norman; Interview with Charles E. Gurnsey, IPH 4:200–207.

58. Cyrus Beede to Richards, May 18, 1872, Roll 39, no number, Foreign Relations, KA; Message of Chickasaw Governor Thomas Parker, no date, Thomas Parker Collection, F2, Western History Collections, University of Oklahoma, Norman; Interview with Clayburn Pickens, IPH 40:56–58; Interview with Will Brown, IPH 1:380–86.

59. Journal of the Third Annual Session of the General Council of the Indian Territory held at Okmulgee, I.T., from the 3d to the 18th of June 1872, IC.

60. Journal of the Third Annual Session, June 1872, IC.

61. Ibid.

62. *Cherokee Advocate*, August 31, 1872, p. 2, cols. 3–4.

63. Ibid., February 22, 1873, p. 1, cols. 1–4; typed copy in IPH 95:85–99.

64. Ibid., August 31, 1872, p. 2, cols. 3–4.

65. Quote in Hagan, *United States–Comanche Relations*, 86.

66. Major C. Schofield to Lawrie Tatum, July 26, 1872, Councils and Courts, Roll 48, no. 68, KA; *Cherokee Advocate*, August 31, 1872, p. 2, cols. 6–7.

67. *Cherokee Advocate*, August 31, 1872, p. 2, cols. 3–4.

68. Ibid.; Hagan, *United States–Comanche Relations*, 86.

69. Journal of the Fourth Annual Session of the General Council of Indian Territory held at Okmulgee, Indian Territory, from the 5th to the 15th of May 1873, IC; Resolution Relating to the Kiowas, Cheyennes, and Other Tribes of the Plains, May 1873, FF10, Box 2, CRHC; Hagan, *United States–Comanche Relations*, 87–91.

70. Journal of the Fourth Annual Session, May 1873, IC.

71. Hagan, *United States–Comanche Relations*, 93–102.

72. Journal of the Fourth Annual Session of the General Council of the Indian Territory, composed of delegates duly elected from the Indian Tribes legally assembled in Council, at Okmulgee, Indian Territory, December 1, 1873, IC.

73. Hagan, *United States–Comanche Relations*, 103–109; James L. Haley, *The Buffalo War: The History of the Red River Indian Uprising of 1874*, 44, 47, 54–55.

74. Haley, *The Buffalo War*, 128, 134.

75. Nye, *Carbine and Lance*, 206–10, 209n29; Haley, *The Buffalo War*, 119–20; Smith, *The Caddos, the Wichitas, and the United States*, 111–12; Hagan, *United States–Comanche Relations*, 111; Interview with F. F. Ross, IPH 59:160.

76. Hagan, *United States–Comanche Relations*, 112–19; Kavanagh, *Comanche Political History*, 452; Interview with Mary Inkanish, FF23, Box 2A, CRHC; Interview with Kiowa, IPH 109:17.

CHAPTER 7

1. Journal of the Sixth Annual Session of the General Council of Indian Territory, Composed of Delegates Duly Elected from the Indian Tribes Legally Rresident Therein, from the 3d to the 15th (inclusive) of May, 1875, IC.

2. Ibid.

3. Ibid.

4. Warloope, Caddo, et al., no date, Roll 48, no. 20, KA.

5. Journal of the Adjourned Session of the Sixth Annual General Council of the Indian Territory, Composed of Delegates Duly Elected from the Indian Tribes Legally Resident Therein, 1st to 9th (inclusive) of Sept., 1875, IC.

6. Ibid.; Prucha, *The Great Father*, 743.

7. Interview with Lucinda Hickey, IPH 5:54–65.

8. Ella Robinson, "Indian International Fair," *Chronicles of Oklahoma* 17 (December 1839): 413–16.

9. Interview with Joseph Martin, IPH 60:295–300; J. Ross to Ward Coachman, October 5, 1879, Reel 37, no. 30812, CRNR.

10. Weslager, *The Delaware Indians*, 432.

11. Statement by Niastor, Chief of the Tawaconies, May 15, 1883, FF1, Box 4, CRHC; Report of E. B. Townsend, July 26, 1883, FF2, Box 4, CRHC.

12. Elisa Chandler to Indian Agent, May 29, 1883, Roll 39, no number, KA; Commissioners' Press Book from March 11, 1885, to October 25, 1885, August 31, 1885, p. 136, FF11, Box 4, CRHC; Hume to Grant Foreman, January 15, 1944, FF28, Box 4, CRHC.

13. Interview with Jenny and Cecil Horse, Kiowas, pp. 23–24, T-141, vol. 34, fiche 193, DD; Interview with Guy Quetone, Kiowa, pp. 7–8, T-149, vol. 37, fiche 209, DD; Interview with R. B. Thomas, IPH 68:234; G. L. Brewer to Major Rᴧndlett, August 31, 1900, Roll 39, no. 612, KA.

14. Interview with John Buntin, Riverside Teacher, IPH 89:319–53.

15. Interview with Mrs. Mark Penoi, Cherokee, IPH 70:167–70; Interview with Sara Ann Davis Smith, Caddo, IPH 9:531–54.

16. Interview with Mrs. Cragg Goetting, Caddo, IPH 105:405–408.

17. Interview with Martha Holt, Chickasaw, IPH 29:348–50; Interview with Jim Cobb, Chickasaw, IPH 2:136–38.

18. Interview with Sarah Pohoscucut, Comanche, pp. 6–7, T-202-I, vol. 28, fiche 162, DD.

19. Quote in G. W. Grayson, *A Creek Warrior for the Confederacy: The Autobiography of Chief G. W. Grayson*, 149–50; Hagan, *United States–Comanche Relations*, 152, 175.

20. Grayson, *A Creek Warrior*, 151.

21. Ibid., 46, 54.

22. Interview with G. Lee Phelps, White, IPH 8:213–22. While the interview is with Phelps, much of the interview is McIntosh's first-person account of his missionary activities.

23. Ibid.; Interview with John D. "Cap" McIntosh, Creek, IPH 71:177–89; Interview with Jobe McIntosh, Creek, T-548, vol. 29, fiche 167, DD; Interview with Bertha Prevost, Wichita, T-686, vol. 54, fiche 303, DD.

24. Interview with Mrs. J. J. Methvin, White, IPH 71:312–16.

25. Kechie Joe to Col. P. B. Hunt, August 21, 1881, Roll 39, no. 297, KA.

26. Interview with Mary Cole, Choctaw-black, IPH 20:202–208.

27. Quote in Carol K. Rachlin, "The Native American Church in Oklahoma," *Chronicles of Oklahoma*, 42 (Autumn 1964): 262; Interview with Jacob Rolland, Euchee, IPH 9:32–33; Interview with Kelly Yellowhead, Creek, IPH 94:482–83; Interview with Allen Mihecaby, Comanche, IPH 36:259–61; William T. Hagan, *Quanah Parker, Comanche Chief*, 54–57.

28. Interview with Jack Thomas, Delaware, IPH 46:323.

29. William Leads to P. B. Hunt, July 19, 1878, Roll 39, no. 275, KA.

30. Interview with Bertha Prevost, Wichita, pp. 16–17, T-675, vol. 53, fiche 302, DD.

31. Agent to B. F. Overton, June 6, 1881, Roll 39, no. 293, KA.

32. Report of E. B. Townsend, July 26, 1883, pp. 1–2, FF2, Box 4, CRHC.

33. Ibid., pp. 7–8.

34. Smith, *The Caddos, the Wichitas, and the United States*, 144–46.

35. Report of E. B. Townsend, July 26, 1883, pp. 9–10, FF2, Box 4, CRHC.

36. I. B. Smith to W. P. Ross and H. T. Landrum, February 16, 1877, Roll 81, no. 86, CHNR.

37. D. W. Bushyhead to H. M. Teller, June 13, 1883, Roll 81, no. 486; CHNR; L. B. Bell et al. to H. M. Teller, July 8, 1884, Roll 81, no. 551, CHNR.

38. Interview with Cook McCracken, Cherokee, IPH 6:509–30.

39. S. W. Scott to Whom It May Concern, July 28, 1881, Reel 37, no. 30748, CRNR.

40. Section 8, *Constitution and Laws of the Chickasaw Nation*, October 9, 1876, Roll 5, no document number, CKNR.

41. W. M. Guy to Capt. Lee Hall, May 16, 1887, Roll 39, no. 382, KA.

42. Grayson, *A Creek Warrior*, 124, 155–57, 156n13.

43. R. V. Bot [?] to Charles E. Adams, December 2, 1890, Roll 39, no. 411, KA.

44. Samuel Patrick to Kiowa and Comanche Indian Agent, July 10, 1893, Roll 39, no. 431, KA.

45. Interview with Robert Butler, Cherokee, IPH 89:427–29.

46. John Jumper to War Loupe and J. A. Richards, April 30, 1874, Roll 39, no document number, KA.

47. G. W. Ingalls to Major Jona. Richardson, August 31, 1875, Roll 39, no. 251, KA.

48. Statement of Captain J. L. Hall, October 24, 1885, Roll 39, no. 370, KA; John F. Brown to Indian Agent, August 25, 1892, Roll 39, no. 420, KA; Tams Bixby to James F. Randlett, June 24, 1905, Roll 39, no. 751, KA; Affidavit of Mary Inkanish, ca. 1927, FF6, Box 28, CRHC.

49. John F. Brown, Seminole Chief, to John H. Nofe, April 15, 1890, Roll 39, no. 393, KA.

50. Biography of Mrs. J. E. Hinton, Cherokee, IPH 5:115–21.

51. R. W. Belt to W. D. Myers, June 14, 1889, FF11, Box 4, CRHC.

52. Register of Indian Families, Nos. 83, 187, 213, and 277, Kiowa, Comanches, Kiowa-Apache Genealogical Record Book from the Anadarko Agency (Kiowa Agency), Microfilm B-47, Western History Collections, University of Oklahoma, Norman; Interview with Fred Falleaf, Delaware, T-299-B, vol. 31, fiche 175, DD.

53. Prucha, *The Great Father*, 659–66, 739–46.

54. Grey Eyes to Ward Coachman, May 9, 1879, Reel 37, no. 30811, CRNR; Proceedings of the International Conference of the Tribes of Indian Territory, May 27, 1879, Reel 37, no. 30811, CRNR; John Moore et al. to Ward Coachman, October 16, 1879, Reel 37, no. 30813, CRNR.

55. Report of the Proceedings Held at a General Council of Apaches, Kiowas, and Comanches and other Affiliated Tribes, June 10, 1881, Commissioners Press Book, September 1880, FF11, Box 4, CRHC.

56. Excerpts from Report to Commissioner of Indian Affairs, September 1, 1880, Commissioners Press Book, FF11, Box 4, CRHC.

57. Compact between the Several Tribes of Indian Territory, March 15, 1886, Reel 4, vol. 8, pp. 234–37, CKNR.

58. Prucha, *The Great Father*, 666–69.

59. Speech to the President of the U.S. by Whitebread, Chief of the Caddo, February 3, 1888; FF7, Box 2A, CRHC; Memorial of Hotalke Ematha et al., October 21, 1889, Roll 37, no. 30847, CRNR.

60. Prucha, *The Great Father*, 746–47; Hagan, *United States–Comanche Relations*, 203.

61. Talk of Lone Wolf et al., April 1, 1887, Roll 37, no. 30842, CRNR; Hagan, *United States–Comanche Relations*, 204, 209; Smith, *The Caddos, the Wichitas, and the United States*, 147; Berlin B. Chapman, "The Dissolution of the Wichita Reservation," Part I, *Chronicles of Oklahoma* 22 (Summer 1944): 201.

62. Hagan, *United States–Comanche Relations*, 203, 215, 263; Smith, *The Caddos, the Wichitas, and the United States*, 147.

63. Rennard Strickland, *The Indians of Oklahoma*, 48.

64. Prucha, *The Great Father*, 746–54.

65. W. S. Field to Indian Agent, October 11, 1895, Roll 39, no. 491, KA.

66. Jasper Exendine to S. M. Mays, February 1, 1989, Roll 81, no. 951, CHNR; H. Ludor to the Chief Councilor of the Cherokee Nation, September 26, 1898, Roll 81, no. 956, CHNR.

67. Prucha, *The Great Father*, 775–76.

68. Hagan, *United States–Comanche Relations*, 269; Smith, *The Caddos, the Wichitas, and the United States*, 151.

69. Prucha, *The Great Father*, 754.

70. Merrill E. Gates quoted in ibid., 671.

71. A. Sharp to Maj. Frank D. Baldwin, September 4, 1897, Roll 39, no. 557, KA; Interview with Sarah Fife, Creek, IPH 3:471–73.

72. Major C. Woodson to Colonel James F. Randlett, November 18, 1899, Roll 39, no. 584, KA.

73. D. M. Browning to Capt. F. D. Baldwin, June 24, 1895, Roll 39, no. 478, KA; Interview with James Abraham Givens, White, IPH 84:194.

74. Prucha, *The Great Father*, 743–44, 753–57.

75. Hugh D. Corwin, "The Folsom Training School," *Chronicles of Oklahoma* 42 (Spring 1964): 48–49; Interview with Mrs. A. Avery, Choctaw, IPH 13:7–21; Prucha, *The Great Father*, 755.

BIBLIOGRAPHY

ARCHIVAL MATERIAL

Archivo General de Indias, Seville, Spain. Papeles Procedentes de Cuba.

Chickasaw Nation Headquarters, Ada, Oklahoma. Chickasaw National Records (microfilm).

Oklahoma Historical Society, Oklahoma City.

Cherokee National Records, Microfilm, Indian Archives.

Creek National Records, Microfilm, Indian Archives.

Foreman Transcripts, Indian Archives.

Indian-Pioneer Histories, 113 vols.

International Councils, Section X, Federal Relations, Indian Archives.

Kiowa Agency, Microfilm, Indian Archives.

Sterling C. Evans Library, Texas A&M University, College Station, Microtext Department. Béxar Archives (microfilm).

U.S. National Archives, Record Group 75.

Letters Received by the Office of Indian Affairs, 1824–81, Cherokee Agency, 1824–80, Microfilm 234, Rolls 71–118.

Letters Received by the Office of Indian Affairs, 1824–81, Chickasaw Agency, 1824–70, Microfilm 234, Rolls 135–48.

Letters Received by the Office of Indian Affairs, 1824–81, Choctaw Agency, 1824–76, Microfilm 234, Rolls 169–96.

Letters Received by the Office of Indian Affairs, 1824–81, Creek Agency, 1824–76, Microfilm 234, Rolls 219–48.

Letters Received by the Office of Indian Affairs, 1824–81, Seminole Agency, 1824–67, Microfilm 234, Rolls 800–807.

Letters Received by the Office of Indian Affairs, 1824–81, Southern Superintendency, 1851–71, Microfilm M234, Rolls 833–39.

Letters Received by the Office of Indian Affairs, 1824–81, Western Superintendency, 1832–51, Microfilm M234, Rolls 921–24.

Letters Received by the Office of Indian Affairs, Wichita Agency, 1857–78, Microfilm M234, Rolls 928–30.

Records of the Southern Superintendency, 1832–70, and Western Superintendency, 1832–51, Letters Sent, Microfilm M640, Rolls 17–22.

Western History Collections, University of Oklahoma, Norman.

Lewis Cass Collection.

Confederate States of America—Indian Affairs Collection, M-2135, Box C-6B, Location: 1036 (Minor Collections).

Doris Duke American Indian Oral History Collection.

C. Ross Hume Collection.

Kiowa, Comanche, Kiowa-Apache Genealogical Record Book, Anadarko Agency (Kiowa Agency), Microfilm B-47.

Mrs. John B. Lilley Collection (Minor Collections).

Roley McIntosh Collection, M-45 (Minor Collections).

Musha-La-Tubbe Collection, M-46 (Minor Collections).

Thomas Parker Collection, F1, P-10 (1208).

Peter P. Pitchlynn Collection.

James Reagle, Jr., Collection, R-45, 1240.

GOVERNMENT DOCUMENTS

U.S. House

19th Cong., 1st Sess., H. Doc. 102, CSS 135.

20th Cong., 1st Sess., H. Doc. 233, CSS 174.

22d Cong., 2d Sess., H. Rept. 17, vol. I, CSS 236.

23rd Cong., 1st Sess., 1833–34, H. Rept. 474, CSS 263.

25th Cong., 2d Sess., 1837–38, H. Doc. 276, CSS 328.

25th Cong., 2d Sess., 1837–38, H. Doc. 278, CSS 328.

27th Cong., 1st Sess., 1842–43, H. Doc. 99, CSS 420.

29th Cong., 2d Sess., 1846–47, H. Doc. 76, CSS 500.

29th Cong., 2d Sess., 1846–47, H. Doc. 100, CSS 500.

30th Cong., 2d Sess., 1848–49, H. Exec. Doc. 1, CSS 537.

30th Cong., 2d Sess., 1848–49, H. Misc. Doc. 35, CSS 544.

35th Cong., 2d Sess., 1858–59, H. Exec. Doc. 2, vol. I, CSS 997.

35th Cong., 2d Sess., 1858–59, H. Exec. Doc. 2, vol. II, CSS 998.

35th Cong., 2d Sess., 1858–59, H. Exec. Doc. 27, CSS 1004.

36th Cong., 1st Sess., 1859–60, H. Exec. Doc. 42, CSS 1048.

36th Cong., 1st Sess., 1859–60, H. Misc. Doc. 24, CSS 1067.

36th Cong., 1st Sess., 1860, H. Rept. 532, CSS 1070.

38th Cong., 1st Sess., 1863–64, H. Exec. Doc. 73, CSS 1193.

39th Cong., 2d Sess., 1866–67, H. Misc. Doc. 41, CSS 1302.

U.S. Senate

18th Cong., 2d Sess., S. Doc. 21, CSS 109.

23rd Cong., 1st Sess., 1833–34, 4 vols., S. Doc. 512, CSS vols. 244–47.

23rd Cong., 2d Sess., 1834–35, S. Doc. 1, CSS 266.

24th Cong., 1st Sess., S. Doc. 77, vol. II, CSS 280.

24th Cong., 1st Sess., S. Doc. 247, CSS 281.

27th Cong., 3rd Sess., 1842–43, S. Exec. Doc. 1, CSS 413.

28th Cong., 1st Sess., 1843–44, S. Exec. Doc. 2, CSS 431.

29th Cong., 1st Sess., 1845–46, S. Doc. 1, CSS 470.

29th Cong., 1st Sess., 1845–46, S. Doc. 438, CSS 477.

29th Cong., 1st Sess., 1845–46, S. Doc. 461, CSS 478.

29th Cong., 2d Sess., 1846–47, S. Doc. 1, CSS 493.

30th Cong., 1st Sess., 1847–48, S. Doc. 1, CSS 503.

30th Cong., 1st Sess., 1847–48, S. Doc. 171, CSS 512.

31st Cong., 1st Sess., 1849–59, S. Exec. Doc. 64, CSS 562.

31st Cong., 1st Sess., 1849–50, S. Misc. Doc. 70, vol I, CSS 563.

35th Cong., 1st Sess., 1857–58, S. Exec. Doc. 11, CSS 919.

35th Cong., 2d Sess., 1858–59, S. Exec. Doc. 1, CSS 974.

36th Cong., 1st Sess., 1859–60, S. Exec. Doc. 2, CSS 1023.

40th Cong., 2d Sess., 1867–68, S. Exec. Doc. 13, CSS 1380.

40th Cong., 2d Sess., 1867–68, S. Exec. Doc. 60, CSS 1317.

41st Cong., 1st Sess., 1869–70, S. Misc. Doc. 16, CSS 1399.

UNPUBLISHED WORKS

Jones, Onis Gaines. "Chickasaw Governors and Their Administrations, 1856–1895." Master's thesis, University of Oklahoma, Norman, 1935.

BOOKS AND ARTICLES

Abel, Annie Heloise. *The Indian as Participant in the Civil War*. Cleveland: A. H. Clark Co., 1919.

Albers, Patricia C. "Symbiosis, Merger, and War: Contrasting Forms of Intertribal Relationship Among Historic Plains Indians." In *The Political Economy of North American Indians*, 94–132. Ed. John H. Moore. Norman: University of Oklahoma Press, 1993.

Baird, W. David. "Arkansas's Choctaw Boundary: A Study of Justice Denied." *Arkansas Historical Quarterly* 28 (Autumn, 1969): 203–23.

———. *Peter Pitchlynn: Chief of the Choctaws*. Norman: University of Oklahoma Press, 1972.

———. *The Quapaw Indians: A History of the Downstream People*. Norman: University of Oklahoma Press, 1980.

Berkhofer, Robert F., Jr. *The White Man's Indian: Images of the American Indian from Columbus to the Present*. New York: Vintage Books, 1978.

Bjork, David K., trans. and ed. "Documents Regarding Indian Affairs in the Lower Mississippi Valley, 1771–1772." *Mississippi Valley Historical Review* 13 (June 1926–March 1927): 398–410.

Boyd, Maurice. *Kiowa Voices: Myths, Legends and Folktales*. 2 vols. Fort Worth: Texas Christian University Press, 1983.

Carter, Clarence E., ed. *The Territorial Papers of the United States*. 26 vols. Washington: Government Printing Office, 1940.

Catlin, George. *North American Indians*. Ed. Peter Matthiessen. New York: Penguin Books, 1989.

Chalfant, William Y. *Without Quarter: The Wichita Expedition and the Fight on Crooked Creek*. Norman: University of Oklahoma Press, 1991.

Chapman, Berlin B. "The Dissolution of the Wichita Reservation," Part I. *Chronicles of Oklahoma* 22 (Summer 1944): 192–314.

Corwin, Hugh D. "The Folsom Training School" *The Chronicles of Oklahoma* 42 (Spring 1964): 46–52.

Dale, Edward Everett, and Gaston Litton. *Cherokee Cavaliers: Forty Years of Cherokee History as Told in the Correspondence of the Ridge-Watie-Boudinot Family*. Norman: University of Oklahoma Press, 1939.

Dean, Christopher C. *Letters on the Chickasaw and Osage Missions*. Boston: T. R. Marvin, 1831.

Debo, Angie. *The Road to Disappearance: A History of the Creek Indians*. Norman: University of Oklahoma Press, 1941.

DeMorse, Colonel Charles. "Indians for the Confederacy." *Chronicles of Oklahoma* 50 (Winter 1972–73): 474–78.

Estep, Raymond. "Lieutenant Wm. E. Burnett: Notes on Removal of Indians from Texas to Indian Territory." *Chronicles of Oklahoma* 38 (Autumn 1960): 274–309.

Everett, Dianna. *The Texas Cherokees: A People between Two Fires, 1819–1840.* Norman: University of Oklahoma Press, 1990.

Ewers, John C. "The Influence of Epidemics on the Indian Populations and Cultures of Texas." *Plains Anthropologist* 18 (May 1973): 104–15.

Flores, Dan. "Bison Ecology and Bison Diplomacy: The Southern Plains from 1800 to 1850." *Journal of American History* 78 (September 1991): 465–85.

———, ed. *Journal of an Indian Trader: Anthony Glass and the Texas Trading Frontier, 1790–1810.* College Station: Texas A&M University Press, 1985.

Foreman, Carolyn Thomas. "Black Beaver." *Chronicles of Oklahoma* 24 (Autumn 1946): 269–92.

Foreman, Grant. *Advancing the Frontier: 1830–1860.* Norman: University of Oklahoma Press, 1933.

———. *The Five Civilized Tribes: Cherokee, Chickasaw, Choctaw, Creek, Seminole.* Norman: University of Oklahoma Press, 1934.

———. *Indian Removal: The Emigration of the Five Civilized Tribes of Indians.* Norman: University of Oklahoma Press, 1932.

———, ed. *Adventure on Red River: Report on the Exploration of the Headwaters of the Red River by Captain Randolph B. Marcy and Captain G. B. McClellan.* Norman: University of Oklahoma Press, 1937.

———, ed. "A Journal Kept by Douglas Cooper of an Expedition by a Company of Chickasaws in Quest of Comanche Indians." *Chronicles of Oklahoma* 5 (December 1927): 381–90.

———, ed. "The Journal of Elijah Hicks." *Chronicles of Oklahoma* 13 (March 1935): 68–99.

———. ed. "The Journal of the Proceedings of Our First Treaty with the Wild Indians, 1835." *Chronicles of Oklahoma* 14 (December 1936): 393–418.

———, ed. *A Pathfinder in the Southwest: The Itinerary of Lieutenant A. W. Whipple during His Explorations for a Railway Route from Fort Smith to Los Angeles in the Years 1853 & 1854.* Norman: University of Oklahoma Press, 1941.

Foster, Morris W. *Being Comanche: A Social History of an American Indian Community.* Tucson: University of Arizona Press, 1991.

Gibson, A. M. "An Indian Territory United Nations: The Creek Council of 1845." *Chronicles of Oklahoma* 39 (Winter 1961–62): 398–413.

Grayson, G. W. *A Creek Warrior for the Confederacy: The Autobiography of Chief G. W. Grayson.* Ed. W. David Baird. Norman and London: University of Oklahoma Press, 1988.

Green, Michael D. *The Politics of Indian Removal: Creek Government and Society in Crisis.* Lincoln: University of Nebraska Press, 1982.

Haley, James L. *The Buffalo War: The History of the Red River Indian Uprising of 1874.* Norman: University of Oklahoma Press, 1876.

Hagan, William T. *Quanah Parker, Comanche Chief.* Norman and London: University of Oklahoma Press, 1993.

————. *The Sac and Fox Indians.* Norman: University of Oklahoma Press, 1958.

————. *United States–Comanche Relations: The Reservation Years.* Norman: University of Oklahoma Press, 1990.

Harris, Marvin. *Cultural Materialism: The Struggle for a Science of Culture.* New York: Vintage, 1979.

Harrison, Jeanne V. "Matthew Leeper, Confederate Agent at the Wichita Agency, Indian Territory." *Chronicles of Oklahoma* 47 (Autumn 1969): 242–57.

Hitchcock, Ethan Allen. *A Traveler in Indian Territory: The Journal of Ethan Allen Hitchcock, Late Major-General in the United States Army.* Ed. Grant Foreman. Cedar Rapids, Iowa: The Torch Press, 1930.

Hoig, Stan. "Jesse Chisholm: Peace-maker, Trader, Forgotten Frontiersman." *Chronicles of Oklahoma* 66 (Winter 1988–89): 350–73.

Holder, Preston. *The Hoe and the Horse on the Plains.* Lincoln: University of Nebraska Press, 1970.

Howard, James H. *Shawnee! The Ceremonialism of a Native Indian Tribe and Its Cultural Background.* Athens: Ohio University Press, 1981.

Hudson, Charles. *The Southeastern Indians.* Knoxville: University of Tennessee Press, 1976.

Hume, C. Ross. "Historic Sites around Anadarko." *Chronicles of Oklahoma* 16 (December 1938): 410–24.

James, Gen. Thomas. *Three Years among the Indians and Mexicans.* Ed. Milo Milton Quaife. New York: The Citadel Press, 1966.

Jennings, Francis. "American Frontiers." *America in 1492: The World of the Indian Peoples before the Arrival of Columbus,* 339–67. Ed. Alvin M. Josephy, Jr. New York: Vintage Books, 1993.

John, Elizabeth A. H. *Storms Brewed in Other Men's Worlds: The Confrontation of Indians, Spanish, and French in the Southwest, 1540–1795.* College Station: Texas A&M University Press, 1975.

"Journal of the Adjourned Session of First General Council of Indian Territory," *Chronicles of Oklahoma* 3 (April 1924): 120–40.

Joutel, Henri. "Joutel's Historical Journal of Monsieur de la Salle's Last Voyage to Discover the River Mississippi." *Historical Collections of Louisiana, Embracing Many Rare and Valuable Documents Relating to the Natural, Civil and Political History of that State*. Vol. 1. Ed. B. F. French. New York: Wiley and Putnam, 1846; New York: AMS Press, 1976.

Kappler, Charles J., ed. *Indian Affairs: Laws and Treaties*. 7 vols. Washington: Government Printing Office, 1904.

———. *Indian Treaties, 1778–1883*. New York: Interland Publishing, 1972.

Kavanagh, Thomas W. *Comanche Political History: An Ethnohistorical Perspective, 1708–1875*. Lincoln and London: University of Nebraska Press, 1996.

Kinnaird, Lawrence, ed. *Spain in the Mississippi Valley, 1765-1794: Post War Decade, 1782–1792*. Annual Report of the American Historical Association for the Year 1945. Washington: Government Printing Office, 1946.

Klein, Alan M., "Political Economy of the Buffalo Hide Trade: Race and Class on the Plains." In *The Political Economy of North American Indians*, 133–60. Ed. John H. Moore. Norman: University of Oklahoma Press, 1993.

Kniffen, Fred B.; Hiram F. Gregory; and George A. Stokes, *The Historic Indians Tribes of Louisiana: From 1542 to the Present*. Baton Rouge: Louisiana State University Press, 1987.

La Harpe, Jean-Baptiste Bénard de. *The Historical Journal of the Establishment of the French in Louisiana*. Trans. Joan Cain and Virginia Koenig. Ed. Glenn R. Conrad. Lafayette: University of Southwestern Louisiana, 1971.

Lankford, George E. "The Cherokee Sojourn in North Arkansas." *The Independence County [Arkansas] Chronicle* 18 (January 1977): 2–19.

La Vere, David. *The Caddo Chiefdoms: Caddo Economics and Politics, 700 A.D. to 1835*. Lincoln: University of Nebraska Press, 1998.

Lawson, John. *A New Voyage to Carolina*. Ed. Hugh Talmage Lefler. 1709; Chapel Hill: University of North Carolina Press, 1967.

Lewis, Anna. "Camp Napoleon." *Chronicles of Oklahoma* 9 (December 1931): 359–64.

Littlefield, Daniel F. Jr., and Lonnie E. Underhill. "The Cherokee Agency Reserve, 1828–1886." *Arkansas Historical Quarterly* 36 (Summer, 1972): 166–180.

Lowe, Percival G. *Five Years a Dragoon ('49 to '54): And Other Adventures on the Great Plains*. Norman: University of Oklahoma Press, 1965.

Marquis, Thomas B. *Keep the Last Bullet for Yourself: The True Story of Custer's Last Stand*. New York: Two Continents Publishing Group, 1976.

Martin, Joel W. *Sacred Revolt: The Muskogees' Struggle for a New World.* Boston: Beacon Press, 1991.

Mauss, Marcel. *The Gift: Forms and Functions of Exchange in Archaic Societies.* Trans. Ian Cunnison. London: Cohen & West, 1969.

Mayall, Mildred P. *The Kiowas.* Norman: University of Oklahoma Press, 1962, 1971.

McAlister, Lyle N. *Spain & Portugal in the New World, 1492–1700.* Minneapolis: University of Minnesota Press, 1984.

McWilliams, Richebourge Gaillaird, trans. and ed. *Fleur de Lys and Calumet: Being the Pénicaut Narrative of French Adventure in Louisiana.* Baton Rouge: Louisiana State University Press, 1941.

Mollhausen, Baldwin. *Diary of a Journey from the Mississippi to the Coasts of the Pacific with a Unites States Government Expedition.* Trans. Mrs. Percy Sinnet. 2 vols. London: Longman, Brown, Green, Longmans, & Roberts, 1858.

Morris, John W.; Charles R. Goins; and Edwin C. McReynolds, eds. *Historical Atlas of Oklahoma.* Norman and London: University of Oklahoma Press, 1965, 1986.

Morrison, W. B. "Fort Arbuckle." *Chronicles of Oklahoma* 6 (March 1928): 26–34.

Moulton, Gary E. *The Papers of Chief John Ross.* 2 vols. Norman: University of Oklahoma Press, 1985.

Newcomb, W. W. Jr. *The Indians of Texas.* Austin: University of Texas Press, 1961.

Noyes, Stanley. *Los Comanches: The Horse People, 1751–1845.* Albuquerque: University of New Mexico Press, 1993.

Nye, W. S. *Carbine and Lance: The Story of Old Fort Sill.* Norman: University of Oklahoma Press, 1937.

O'Callaghan, Mary A. "An Indian Removal Policy in Spanish Louisiana," In *Greater America: Essays in Honor of Eugene Herbert Bolton,* 281–94. Berkeley and Los Angeles: University of California Press, 1945.

Parsons, Elsie Clews. *Notes on the Caddo.* Memoirs of the American Anthropological Association, No. 57. Menasha, Wis.: American Anthropological Association, 1941; New York: Kraus Reprint Co., 1969.

Perdue, Theda. *Slavery and the Evolution of Cherokee Society, 1540–1886.* Knoxville: University of Tennessee Press, 1979.

Perdue, Theda, and Michael D. Green. *The Cherokee Removal: A Brief History with Documents.* Boston and New York: Bedford Books of St. Martin's Press, 1995.

Plummer, Rachel. "Narrative of the Capture and Subsequent Sufferings of Mrs. Rachel Plummer." *The Rachel Plummer Narrative*. 89–118. Ed. Rachel Lofton, Susie Hendrix, and Jane Kennedy. 1839; reprinted, n.p., 1926.

Porter, Kenneth W. "Wild Cat's Death and Burial" *Chronicles of Oklahoma* 21 (March 1943): 41–43.

Portre-Bobinski, Germaine, ed. *Natchitoches: Translation of Old French and Spanish Documents*. Natchitoches, La.: privately published, 1928.

Prucha, Francis Paul. *The Great Father: The United States Government and the American Indians*. Lincoln: University of Nebraska Press, 1984.

Rachlin, Carol K. "The Native American Church in Oklahoma." *Chronicles of Oklahoma* 42 (Autumn 1964): 262–72.

Ream, Robert L. "A Nearly Forgotton Fragment of Local History." *Chronicles of Oklahoma* 4 (March 1926): 34–44.

Richter, Daniel K. *The Ordeal of the Longhouse: The Peoples of the Iroquois League in the Era of European Colonization*. Chapel Hill: University of North Carolina Press, 1992.

Rister, C. C. "A Federal Experiment in Southern Plains Indian Relations, 1835–1845." *Chronicles of Oklahoma* 14 (December 1956): 434–55.

Roberts, David. *Once They Moved Like the Wind: Cochise, Geronimo, and the Apache Wars*. New York: Touchstone, 1993.

Robinson, Ella. "Indian International Fair." *Chronicles of Oklahoma* 17 (December 1839): 413–16.

Rollings, Willard H. *The Osage: An Ethnohistorical Study of Hegemony on the Prairie-Plains*. Columbia and London: University of Missouri Press, 1992.

Rowland, Dunbar, and A. G. Sanders, eds. and trans. *Mississippi Provincial Archives: French Dominion*. Vols. 4 and 5. Rev. and ed. Patricia Kay Galloway. Baton Rouge: Louisiana State Univesity Press, 1984.

Sahlins, Marshall. *Stone Age Economics*. Chicago and New York: Aldine-Atherton, 1972.

Secoy, Frank Raymond. *Changing Military Patterns of the Great Plains Indians*. 1953; Norman: University of Nebraska Press, 1992.

Sheehan, Bernard W., *Seeds of Extinction: Jeffersonian Philanthropy and the American Indian*. New York: W. W. Norton & Company, 1973.

Shirk, George H. "Peace on the Plains." *Chronicles of Oklahoma* 28 (Spring 1950): 2–41.

Sibley, John Sibley. "A Report from Natchitoches in 1807." Ed. Annie Heloise Abel. 1807; reprinted, Ville Platte, La.: Evangeline Genealogical and Historical Society, 1987.

Smith, F. Todd. *The Caddo Indians: Tribes at the Convergence of Empires, 1542–1854*. College Station: Texas A&M University Press, 1995.

————. *The Caddos, the Wichitas, and the United States, 1846–1901*. College Station: Texas A&M University Press, 1996.

Smith, Ralph A., ed. and trans. "Account of the Journey of Bénard de la Harpe: Discovery Made by Him of Several Nations Situated in the West." *Southwestern Historical Quarterly* 62 (July 1958): 75–86; (October 1958): 246–59; (January 1959): 371–85; (April 1959): 525–41.

Starr, Emmet, ed. and publ. *Cherokees "West": 1794–1839*. Claremore, Okla., 1910.

Strickland, Rennard. *The Indians of Oklahoma*. Norman and London: University of Oklahoma Press, 1980.

Taylor, Alfred A. "The Medicine Lodge Peace Council." *Chronicles of Oklahoma* 2 (June 1924): 89–118

Thompson, E. P. *The Making of the English Working Class*. 1963; New York: Vintage Books, 1966.

Turner, Clarence W. "Events among the Muskogees." *Chronciles of Oklahoma* 10 (March 1932): 21–34.

Unrau, William E. "Investigations or Probity? Investigations into the Affairs of the Kiowa-Comanche Indian Agency, 1867." *Chronicles of Oklahoma* 42 (Autumn 1964): 300–19.

Utley, Robert M. *The Indian Frontier of the American West, 1846–1890*. Albuquerque: University of New Mexico Press, 1984.

————. *The Lance and the Shield: The Life and Times of Sitting Bull*. New York: Henry Holt and Company, 1993.

Waldman, Carl. *Atlas of the North American Indian*. New York: Facts on File Publications, 1985.

Wallace, Ernest, and E. Adamson Hoebel. *The Comanches: Lords of the Southern Plains*. 1952; Norman: University of Oklahoma Press, 1986.

Wells, H. G. *The Outline of History: Being a Plain History of Life and Mankind*. 2 vols. New York: The Macmillan Company, 1921.

Weslager, C. A. *The Delaware Indians: A History*. New Brunswick, N.J.: Rutgers University Press, 1972.

White, Richard. "The Winning of the West: The Expansion of the Western Sioux in the Eighteenth and Nineteenth Centuries." *Journal of American History* 65 (September 1978): 319–43.

White, Richard. *The Roots of Dependency: Subsistence, Environment, and Social Change among the Choctaws, Pawnees, and Navajos*. Lincoln: University of Nebraska Press, 1983.

Wilkins, Thurman. *Cherokee Tragedy: The Ridge Family and the Decimation of a People.* 1970; Norman: University of Oklahoma Press, 1983.

Woodruff, W. E. *With the Light Guns in '61–'65: Reminiscences of Eleven Arkansas, Missouri, and Texas Light Batteries in the Civil War.* Little Rock, Ark.: Central Printing Company, 1930.

Wright, J. Leitch. *The Only Land They Knew: The Tragic Story of the American Indians in the Old South.* New York: The Free Press, 1981.

NEWSPAPERS

Arkansas Gazette, Little Rock, Arkansas Territory.

Arkansas Intelligencer, Van Buren, Arkansas Territory.

Cherokee Advocate, Tahlequah, Cherokee Nation, Indian Territory.

Cherokee Phoenix, New Echota, Georgia.

Fort Smith Herald, Fort Smith, Arkansas.

INDEX